COLLEGE TEACHING TIPS

Third Edition

Fred W. Whitford
Montana State University

PEARSON

Boston Columbus Indianapolis New York San Francisco Upper Saddle River
Amsterdam Cape Town Dubai London Madrid Milan Munich Paris Montreal Toronto
Delhi Mexico City Sao Paulo Sydney Hong Kong Seoul Singapore Taipei Tokyo

PEARSON

10 9 8 7 6 5 4 3 2 1

ISBN 10: 0205940218
ISBN 13: 9780205940219

To My Mother, Hazel

Contents

Appendices

Preface

This book was originally conceived as a guide that would allow the new instructor or graduate teaching assistant to manage the myriad of complex tasks required to teach a course effectively. Additionally, many seasoned instructors will find this material interesting and useful in updating their courses. The book was not intended to be a heavily referenced work, but rather to contain appendices on teaching. I have used my own teaching experiences in various Psychology Departments for the last thirty years to help illustrate some of the types of problems that you can expect to face. I have attempted to write a lighthearted book that will be fun to read and assist your journey into academia. I, on occasion, stereotyped students, graduate students, faculty and staff; this was, of course, done with the intent of giving you, the instructor, an idea of what to expect in your new environment. I did not intend to be overly critical of these individuals, but rather, honest, about the interactions I have had in the departments that I have been associated with during my career. Having an idea of what to expect in a new environment can be an indispensable tool.

New to this edition:

Chapter 1: A look at the new funding model for higher education.
Chapter 2: New material on retirement considerations, the affects of the Great Recession, and a discussion of test item file validation.
Chapter 3: Developing on-line classes and for profit colleges and universities.
Chapter 8: Added more undergraduate student stereotypes.
Chapter 9: Added more faculty stereotypes.
Chapter 12: A continued expansion of new e-media in teaching.
Appendix B: Updated references.

Teaching at the college level can, and probably will be, one of the most frustrating, and rewarding, tasks that you will be asked to perform in your academic career. I hope this book will help smooth the rough spots and give you a preview of what to expect in this maze called academia.

Acknowledgments

During the preparation of this book, I have had the pleasure of working with several individuals. Of these people, the ones who stand out the most are Dr. Colleen Moore, Chair, Psychology Department, Montana State University, for her unceasing support; Jessica Mosher, Executive Psychology Editor at Pearson for her encouragement in all phases of this book; Nicole Kunzmann, Senior Marketing Manager and Jennifer Nolan, Editorial Assistant for their help with the details of this project, and Betsy Anderson, Administrator, at Montana State University; without their help, this project could not have been completed. And finally, Pat, Jessica, Alex and Nick for their support during the preparation of this book.

Fred W. Whitford
Psychology Department
Montana State University
whitford@montana.edu
http://www.montana.edu/wwwpy/

Chapter 1

Introduction to College Teaching

Finally, I made it! I cannot believe that I was hired to teach college classes; this is the best day of my life!

Every New Instructor

After the initial euphoria dissipates, then what? How do you attempt to teach a college level course at your school? What are the techniques that you should and should not use? How do instructors ever find enough time to prepare lectures? Will I be good enough to be a college instructor? Will my students respect and like me? These and other thoughts go through every new instructor's mind.

This book is directed towards the new instructor or the graduate teaching assistant who has little or no experience teaching. Additionally, the seasoned instructor will also find much of the material in this text useful. I will present this book from the perspective of the new instructor teaching an introductory level class; this material is also relevant to other upper-division courses in your department. I will share some of my time-worn secrets so you can become a great instructor. Throughout this book, I will use the experiences that I have gained in my thirty-eight years of teaching at the university level, as well as the many years of teaching experience of my colleagues in the in my department. I will help you develop a general plan that you can use to start the formidable task of becoming the best instructor in your department and, maybe, even your school.

This book is intended to be a starting place with suggestions on how to proceed. My suggestions are just that—suggestions; I would not presume to have the best teaching style, but offer these recommendations as a starting point for your teaching career. One of the most important aspects of becoming a great instructor is to develop your own personal style; this component of your overall presentation is extremely important and will be discussed later. This book is not intended to cover the vast research area of college teaching; instead I have included appendices to help with your decisions about teaching and to help cover the research on college teaching.

The Great Recession (Current)

The great recession has decimated higher education funding in the last five years. All but two states have deficits in their budgets. The easy way to save money is to lower state funding for higher education and increase tuition. This in effect, shifts the burden more to the student. To cope with this increase in the cost of education, students are turning more and more to student loans. It is common for students to amass student loan debt of $40,000 for a four year degree. Along with this increased debt, graduates are entering very soft job markets. A recent estimate is that student loan debit is now more than a TRILLION dollars! This is more than all of the credit card debit in the United States! This student debt is forever—even bankruptcy will not discharge it.

These trends are the new reality—less state funding, more shifted to the student. An additional disturbing trend is in the area of faculty hiring. Many schools have effectively ended tenure by hiring mostly contract adjuncts instead of tenure track full-time faculty. An argument can be made that full-time faculty are better instructors than part-time adjuncts. With the recession, many full-time tenured faculty are working past the traditional retirement age. They simply cannot afford to retire after losing much of the value of their homes and retirement accounts.

What, in the past, have been considered to be stable private schools, are also feeling the recession. Their endowments are, in many cases, shrinking very rapidly. Their answer is to raise tuition. Some schools are in the $40,000-$50,000 dollars per year range. The real question is, how long this can be sustained?

Loss of benefits and tenure are another recent disturbing trend in higher education. Schools can contribute less to your retirement, pay less into your medical insurance, and have fewer sabbaticals and few opportunities for travel, in order to cut expenses. Some systems are toying with the idea of no longer providing tenure as an option for new hires.

The New Reality Early Century

Funding higher education at both public and private schools has decreased radically during the recent economic collapse. State schools have seen losses of tenured faculty and deep cuts in services and personnel across the board. Private schools, who in the past have enjoyed a relatively high level of funding, have seen their endowments shrink. Even major Ivy League schools are seeing major cuts in faculty and services.

You are very lucky to have a job in this environment and the school administration will remind you of this often. You will be expected to do more with less; student credit hour production will be an important new metric on which you will be compared.

The good old days are gone for the foreseeable future; keep your head down work hard and do not complain about the new funding model. Upper administration really is in a bind. If they do not fill vacant tenureable faculty positions the total student credit hour production will drop. Their short term fix is to hire adjuncts to teach the larger sections. This erosion of tenureable faculty is an ongoing problem and one that will continue into the future.

The Goal

The goal of this book is to make your journey from new instructor to the best instructor in your department a little easier. Many times when you are new to your department, finding someone willing to help answer the simplest questions might be challenging. I hope to offer answers to many of these questions. College teaching can, for many of you, be the best experience you will have in your academic career; getting a good start can be very important. A few tricks and some of my experiences will surely help you through your first college courses.

The Task

Teaching college courses is both a rewarding and a cumbersome assignment. Knowing that you are the first instructor to teach these new students in your department, several of whom may become renowned individuals is exciting. The new eager freshperson, wanting to understand everything, is refreshing. I look forward to the fall semester and the chance to see these excited new students. Additionally, teaching an evening class at least once a year can expose you to the nontraditional age student who can only take an evening course. These nontraditional students bring a perspective from the real world that is often lost in the academic environment. The chance to really make a difference in the way students view the discipline is always exciting. On the other hand, the sheer volume of students in large courses can be a tremendous strain on your energy. Depending on your school, your class size may range from 25 to 350 students. You may or may not have additional support from teaching assistants, graduate/undergraduate students or other faculty to deal with the mass of students. In the past as compensation for these large classes, some schools granted release time from other teaching, committee or service responsibilities. With the new reality of lower funding this is done less and less.

I often spend a great deal of my time handling the mechanics of the registration for the course: determining times and rooms, assigning teaching assistants' duties, writing examinations, writing make-up examinations, grading examinations, making exceptions for due dates for papers and examinations for special students (handicapped, learning disabled, and athletic students), signing add/drop slips, and just attempting to survive the mass of paperwork associated with large sections. Typically, just when you think the extra workload of a class of 250 students is too much, a student will say you are the best teacher he or she has had in college. This type of interaction with students and encouragement from your peers can help you bear up under the relentless pressure to develop your teaching, conduct your research, and present the best course possible.

Class Size

In many institutions the size of the average college class has risen dramatically in recent years. Many introductory classes were once under 100 students and now are well beyond that number, with some over 500 students. Classes between 100 and 500 are really the same class with more seats in the room—see the later discussion of large classes. The factors that contribute to this dramatic rise in students numbers are many, the most salient being funding issues. At many large public institutions government funding has decreased. One method of balancing the budget is to raise the enrollment caps on introductory classes. Introductory courses are typically the best attended classes, and thus are a logical target for balancing the college budget through increased enrollment. Since new instructors probably do not remember class sizes under 50 in introductory courses, you probably will be less frustrated by the changes than more seasoned colleagues. "More for less" is the mantra of many campus administrators. You will have to teach larger sections than in the past and will have to base your decisions on *what* and *how* to teach with this increasing enrollment.

Changes of How College Courses are Taught

From innovations in multimedia presentation software (PowerPoint, as an example), to interfacing the Internet in the classroom, the information age has arrived. I will have a detailed discussion of the impact of the information age on the classroom in chapter 12.

The standard stand-up lecture with students passively taking notes and not asking many questions is also being challenged. Smaller recitation and lab sections are being implemented in some schools. Critical thinking and diversity issues are being incorporated into the classroom. The notion that the instructor is no longer the "Sage on the Stage" but rather the "Guide on the Side," has had an interesting impact on how you will teach.

Much of the material in this book will deal with the how and what you teach in your classes. You are on the edge of some very interesting changes in the field of college teaching. Enjoy the ride.

Find a Mentor

Before you arrive, research the faculty either during your interview or via the Internet to try to discover who would be a good candidate for a teaching mentor. Having a person with experience at your new school can be very important. Look for awards for teaching, publications in the area of teaching, and talk to undergraduates and graduate students for their input.

Compensation

First Contract—Full-Time Tenure Track

Your first contract is your most important contract. If you are being hired full-time, subsequent raises will be based on your original contract. Negotiate to get the highest salary you can in your first contract. You can check other recent hires at your school; usually these salaries are public record. Be sure that you are at least in the median range for similar faculty. If not, negotiate for a higher initial salary. You can also check regional peer institutions for salary by rank and years of service. Ask the school reference librarian or use the Internet for regional salary reports. In a strange twist you may be starting at a higher salary than some faculty who have been at your school for years. The logic is that we can not get anybody good to come to our department without offering a good salary, but many of the older faculty came in at lower initial salaries and with small or no pay raises for many years, are making less than you are being offered. Realize that many of these individuals realize that you should maximize your initial offer, but they still do not like the *new guy* getting either more, or similar, pay.

If you are full-time, you may be offered a start-up package. The package can include moving expenses, funds for office furniture, computer(s), other equipment for starting your research program, class buy-outs from teaching for several semesters, and possibly summer salary for several summers. Depending on your department these packages, especially for research start up, can be substantial. As part of your negations ask for release from departmental and university committee assignments; they may say yes now, but might not later.

This is also the time to negotiate for office and research space. Go for the best space available. Take as much space as you can get, you can always trade it to someone later for something else. Request Graduate Teaching Assistants (GTAs) to help with teaching and Graduate Research Assistants (GRAs) to help with research. These individuals should be negotiated NOW—you may never get another chance. At hire, you are in a power position; the minute you sign the contract you are the *new guy* with the least status in the department. Get all of the negotiations in writing. Administrators will want to say we will work on that or we can negotiate later. My advice is get it in writing or agree to nothing!

First Contract—Part-Time or Adjunct Faculty

If you are being hired as an adjunct or part-time instructor, your contract possibilities are bleak. You will probably be offered classes on a dollars per class basis, the more you teach the more money you make. Your office will not be the best in the building. There will possibly be other part-time adjuncts sharing your office. If you get a computer, it will be the worst in the department, the one no one else wants. Many graduate students will have more status in the department. Faculty may view you as expendable and temporary.

You may possibly have to teach several classes from different areas of your discipline; often your classes are buy outs from teaching by other instructors. The mix of your classes can be very diverse. The downside is that you may be teaching classes you have never even taken as a student, completely out of your area. The upside is that you will be getting valuable teaching experience in areas that you would not normally be teaching. This experience will make you more marketable in the future. Never refuse a teaching assignment, no matter how hard the preparation will be. It will help you in the eyes of the department, and helping is viewed as very important in many departments. Have the attitude, "Sure, I can teach just about any introductory or upper-division classes." This attitude will have long-term benefits.

Benefits

Health Insurance

With the double digit inflation in health insurance, this benefit is more important than ever. Many schools are shifting the major burden to the individual and in some cases have dropped this as a benefit. Hopefully, the health care reform efforts will modify this dysfunctional system.

Paying for health insurance? In the past your parents or your school always took care of this annoying aspect of adulthood. You might be surprised at how much money is deducted from your salary to cover this *benefit.* You don't want the coverage? Too bad. In many schools you have to accept and pay for it. You may see no benefit in health insurance, after all, you are young, healthy, and still indestructible. But the system needs young, healthy individuals to pay for the older, less healthy individuals who have been in the system for many years. You will need it for emergencies and unforeseen major health problems; be glad that it is offered. Many part-time individuals will not be offered health insurance. At my school you have to be at least half-time for six months to be eligible for health insurance benefits; not always easy for a part-timer.

Vacation

This benefit varies widely between schools. Many schools will not provide vacation if you are on a nine or ten month or academic-year contract, but usually will provide this benefit with a twelve-month contract. In many cases the lowest paid staff member giving parking tickets in the parking lot will earn vacation, but not you. If you have this benefit, be thankful. You will be working too hard and too many hours to go on a vacation anyway, so save the hours and cash them in when you leave or retire.

Sick Leave

Most new instructors will receive and accumulate sick leave compensation. You may not need/use these sick hours. If you use these hours you might be viewed as not working hard, so come to work with the head cold just like everyone else. An important use for sick leave is a prolonged illness. In many cases workman's compensation may be applicable in prolonged illnesses. You can accumulate thousands of sick hours over a 40-year career. When you retire some institutions will pay you a percentage lump sum for unused sick leave.

Retirement

If you are eligible at your school, you will be offered a retirement package. With the disintegration of the stock market and related 401K retirements of most faculty, this benefit has lost some of its appeal. Many new instructors do not see the need to invest, their parents just lost most of their retirement so why should they? What am I going to be doing in 40 years? Who cares? Well, those 40 years will pass quickly, so pay attention to the options offered. Many schools will match your retirement contribution, say 7% of what you deposit. That is like 7% of your salary for free. Take advantage of this by maximizing the option. You should maximize this investment even if it means sacrificing now. Invest the money in a stock index fund and forget it for 35 years.

If you have a choice between a defined benefits (traditional retirement after 20 to 30 years) or a matching program, take the matching program. Chances are you could leave this school, and the money in the defined benefit plan has a vesting period (five years is common) and pays lower yields than matching investments.

Arriving on Campus

Becoming Familiar with the Campus

When you first arrive at your institution, what should you do to prepare for your teaching assignment? First, I would recommend becoming familiar with the campus. I would suggest finding a location where you can have solitude from the department and students. This could be in the faculty reading room, in the library, the empty football stadium, or simply an empty bench in an isolated area of campus. There will be times when you need to be alone. Acquaint yourself with the campus layout and define solutions to simple tasks such as finding a parking place (does your school have a faculty parking lot?) or having lunch (which are the best restaurants or does your school have a faculty club?). Arriving during a break in classes can make this task much easier. An additional consideration is what types of services might you want to take advantage of? Your campus may offer options to the faculty which can include (often at a cost) faculty parking lots, athletic facilities, faculty clubs, special seating at sporting events, or a great museum or library. Find out what your school offers and what you think you will use and enjoy.

Arrival at the Department

Mid-morning is the best time to arrive at your department. Monday is not the best day to show up because of the normal confusion associated with Mondays. Try to time your initial arrival during class periods. Between class sessions, many students visit the department office and the congestion will hinder your initial visit. You may have been interviewed on campus for your position so the department may be familiar. But if not and this is your first day on campus, arrive early in order to find parking and your department's building. Ask to see the chairman in an informal department, or contact in advance in a formal department, for an appointment. Upon your arrival, you will probably have been assigned an office and will have to obtain keys for the building and your office (the campus police often performs this function). Now that you have arrived in your office, sit and enjoy the quiet of your new surroundings and read the rest of this book.

"The" Book

If there is not a copy of the faculty handbook waiting for you in your office, ask that a copy be sent to you as soon as possible, or check online, since many schools have made the faculty handbook available on the Internet. This is "the" book and contains everything needed to survive in your new position, i.e., everything from tenure and promotion, to how to deal with student grievances, etc. Read "the" book after you finish this book. If you have any questions about the materials in the faculty handbook, ask for clarification from your department chair.

Meeting the Faculty

Walk around the building to see who is in their office or laboratory. A rule of thumb is that if your arrival occurs during mid-summer, the most productive members will be working and the rest will be on vacation. Introduce yourself to each faculty, graduate student or staff member that you encounter; most of whom will be eager to meet the newest faculty member. During these interactions remember that first impressions are lasting impressions.

Getting a Feel

Hang out for the rest of the day in the department and explore your new environment. Find out how things work. Where is the bathroom? How do you dial off campus? How do you set up voice-mail and e-mail? Where is the water fountain? How about the exits? What is your view like? Determine whether the sun shines into your office in the morning or afternoon, which will determine where you will put your computer. Check on your computer capabilities if a computer is being provided. What operating systems and software have been loaded; is the computer networked to a printer? You should apply for a campus e-mail address as soon as possible. These types of questions can be answered by simply spending time in the department. This is your new place of employment and you will spend a large number of your days in this environment. Do you like it? If not, what do you control that you can change for the better? These suggestions will not only acquaint you with your new environment, but will also allow you some time to relax.

How to Begin to Fit In

I will present a relatively small list of things to consider as you beginning the process of fitting in.

Talk to Students (Undergraduates)

Walk around campus and ask students some general question about your new school. Ask them about their opinions of the institution. Do they like their teachers? Are faculty members accessible to students? Do professors maintain regular office hours and otherwise make themselves available to those seeking help and mentoring? Does the school have a winning sports team? How hard are tickets to obtain? What are the students' favorite aspects of the school? What do these students like least about the school?

Talk to Students (Graduates)

Talking to graduate students is always a valuable source of information in the department and campus in general. Since you probably have recently been a graduate student you can also interact with the graduate students at a different level than you can with faculty. Ask them how they like the department. Is it a good place for them to study? Are they generally happy with the way they are treated? What are the expectations for research and teaching for both graduate students and new faculty? Would they recommend your new department to other students?

Take an Informal Campus Tour

I have been at my school for thirty-five years and have still not been to every building on campus, too busy. Take the time to just look around. How are the grounds maintained? Are the areas clean and the lawns mowed? What about the maintenance of the buildings, are the buildings in good order? You can tell a lot about an institution by looking at how well it is maintained.

Visit the Campus Bookstore

Look through the lists of textbooks required for courses in your department. How is space within the bookstore utilized? Many bookstores make a good portion of their money selling beer mugs and sweat shirts so sometimes the texts books take a more back room position in the layout of the bookstore. How does this bookstore compare to your previous bookstore? Ask to talk to the manager of the text book section; this should not be a problem a month before school starts. Ask the manager his/her philosophy on new/used books. Ask for any college requirements on ordering books. Meeting the textbook manger is an important step.

Search Out Newer Faculty Members

Ask them about the state of campus and departmental morale. Find out what they like and dislike about their jobs. Ask about the quality of students in their classes. Try to draw them out about faculty-administration relations and the general "climate" of the institution.

Announcement Posting Boards

In the department and other buildings, pay attention to announcements posted on bulletin boards. Flyers reveal a great deal about what is going on around campus and the town. Additionally, the types of activities in which students are engaged and attracted to can easily be seen. The cultural life of the institution and the local community can be easily discovered on these boards.

Using the Internet Search for Demographic Information

Every school has most of their demographic data posted and it is easily accessible. What is the total number of undergraduate and graduate students? How many students are campus residents, how many commuters? Do most students work full-time and attend school part-time? How much diversity is there within the student population? What special provision, if any, does the college make for nontraditional students?

(Influenced by Lucas and Murry 2002)

The Rest of Your Life

Become acquainted with the community. This is an ongoing process and can take years, but the following are suggestions about how to begin: Where is a good place to grocery shop? Where will you buy a beverage of your choice after a hard day at work? Where will you do your laundry? What are the recreational opportunities in the community? Some questions are more obvious than others; however, depending on your personal preferences, most college communities can satisfy most of these needs. Where will you live? What neighborhood meets your requirements? I would ask two sources. The first is obvious, as faculty and staff will be very helpful in describing different options and could know of some vacancies available. The second suggestion is to ask students; there may only be graduate students available when you arrive but these individuals will often know the best deals, especially in the housing market. Where do faculty go to relax? This depends on the faculty members.

Many will go straight home after work to a family environment, while others will prefer to stop by a local establishment for happy hour. Some of your first impressions of the different faculty may be formed during these informal get-togethers during the social hour. A point to remember is that even in social situations you are being evaluated just as you are evaluating other faculty members, so act appropriately. Where do students go to relax? Are you going to want to be in the same social environment as the students or would you prefer to socialize only with faculty and staff? How do you get from campus to your home? What are the safest and fastest routes? Getting to know your new environment can begin by subscribing to the local newspaper help answer some of the questions you might have about the local environment. I would also find the latest copy of the student newspaper; this will help define the interests, attitudes, and expectations of the students at your school. Try to get a feel for the town and the campus by either walking or driving around. Take the time to see what the area has to offer. I would schedule at least a Saturday or Sunday exclusively for this activity. The campus and local community are often two distinct communities with minimal overlapping. Try to define both communities in terms of your needs and goals. Consider joining a local community or campus organization as a method of getting to know your new home.

Things You Need to Know to Flourish

The following table contains several topics that you will need to address in you early academic career. This information is intended as a starting point for discussions on the topics. All of these topics will be discussed in depth later in this book, but please take time to consider these topics now.

Performance Expectations

What will be required for professional success? What does the institution value most and reward: teaching or service? Do you need an external grant to prosper? Do you need three publications a year? Are there a required number of hours of community involvement? How do institutional needs and priorities affect you as a faculty member? Many of these questions are answered in "The" book. See above.

Institutional Culture

What is the climate or work environment of the institution? Specific levels of administration have different expectations, what does the school (university), college, department, expect? Does your department suffer from a culture of low expectations about the future, or are they optimistic? The job culture can differ in terms of collaboration, cooperation, and competition. Is collegiality valued or not and if it is how do you achieve it? What is the state of faculty morale and how do you fit into the schema? Is there a rift or tension between academics and administrators, (it seems that this is usually the case.) Are decision-making processes top-down or bottom-up at the departmental, college and upper administration level? Does the faculty feel included in governance and decision making?

Institutional Politics

Who wields power at your institution: President, Provost or Board of Regents? Who is in charge and makes the day-today decisions—department head, Dean or Provost? How do decisions get made—through committees from the faculty and staff or by upper administrators? Is change facilitated or hindered by those who exercise authority? Is "stay the course" the mantra or is "change is good" the key phrase?

Faculty Evaluation

How is faculty performance assessed: written student evaluations, peer evaluations, committee evaluations? Is there general satisfaction or dissatisfaction in the faculty of your department with the evaluation procedures employed? Is the system fair and equitable and if not what can you do about it? What purposes are served through faculty assessments? Will they make you a better researcher, teacher?

Time Management.

Are there any proven techniques colleagues find helpful in reconciling the many disparate demands placed on a faculty member's time and energy? Check with your mentor for ideas and suggestions regarding time management. How do you get all the things you have to do done and still have a family, life and some fun? Please see Chapter 13 for more suggestions on time management.

Institutional and Professional Service

Is it possible to avoid feeling overcome by multiple, often time-consuming service responsibilities? How do you learn to say no? Again, your mentor is invaluable with advice in this area. Does your department try to protect new hires from college and other committee responsibilities? Under what conditions is it advisable to take on burdensome service assignments? How important is service as a component element in an individual's total work profile? Some schools have little or no emphasis in this area; others stress this area. See Chapter 13 for some suggestions.

Teaching and Curriculum Development

Is teaching valued or is it tolerated? The answer is negatively correlated with the emphasis on research and grant writing; the more important grant and research activities are, the less important teaching is. Do faculty peers and/or administrators review teaching performance in any substantive, meaningful way? This again is related to how important teaching is in your department, whether it is emphasized. How important are student evaluations of a faculty member's classroom instruction? This topic is discussed at length in later Chapter 10.

Research and Scholarship

Is published research considered important by the institution? To what extent is it valued, compared with other faculty activities like undergraduate teaching and service? What specific forms or expressions of faculty scholarship are prized most? What is the minimum level of research activity that is considered reasonable and necessary for tenure?

Grant writing

Does the institution value or even require efforts aimed at securing external grants and contracts? What types of support at your school are available to assist faculty in responding to grant opportunities? How are grants administered and what is the administration's fee/cut of the grant?

(Influenced by Lucas and Murry 2002)

The Changing Focus of Institutions

More for Less

Many schools are demanding more teaching or research from fewer individuals. This can be accomplished by making classes much larger and teaching fewer sections. At many larger schools there has been a decreased emphasis on undergraduate teaching. This allows the school to decrease the number of faculty, benefits, and physical plant requirements.

Many schools have placed research funding at the top of the priority list of school functions. With the increased emphasis on external funding and indirect costs, schools have restructured how they are being funded. The new funding formula depends more on these research dollars and less on traditional sources of support which can include state tax money and foundations. This reorganization of funding sources can impact the new instructor and you should be aware that your new school is very different than it has been in the recent past.

Many schools have devoted a large portion of their resources to raising money through private individuals and institutional donors. This new money chase can be productive in the short term, but many institutions develop a chronic institutional appetite for the money.

The Loss of the Dream

The major economic meltdown of the global financial institutions has had a profound influence of the expectation of students, colleges and universities. Tuition has been rising very rapidly, forcing many students to not attend their first choice schools for financial reasons. Institutions are losing their ability to deliver a quality undergraduate education due to funding cuts. Student financial aid is in jeopardy of not being available to all students who qualify. Student loans will be more difficult to obtain, carry higher interest rates, and are very difficult to repay.

Will the system ever recover? Probably not to the level we all enjoyed in the past.

Chapter 2

A Philosophy of Teaching

What are the steps necessary to preparing to teach a college course? It is best if you have several months to prepare and have a specific plan. I suggest the following outline as the basis of a course preparation plan. This plan assumes a three-month window. If you have less time, compress as much as possible into your time frame.

Three Months Prior to Class

Deciding What to Teach

Although not everyone has three months prior to class to prepare, the majority of new instructors will have about three months to consider teaching decisions. After you receive your teaching assignments, I would first turn my attention to identifying the course objectives. Is this class a broad overview covering virtually all of the sub-fields in a discipline, or will it be a concentrated in-depth survey of only a few of the specific sub-fields that you or your department teaches? In most academic systems, quarters or semesters, there is not enough time to cover all the material you would like to cover. Academic quarters have about 40 instructional days, and academic semesters about 45 instructional days to cover, in some cases, an entire text. The question now becomes what to delete from the overall coverage in the course? If you have no departmental restraints, you can delete the areas you believe to be least important in the material covered. Check with your course supervisor or department chair to see if such restrictions exist; be careful not to violate department guidelines because you decided that certain course information was not important. Throughout your preparation and teaching of this course, you can consult with your department head or course supervisor for guidance about departmental policies and procedures. A little common sense requires that you consider the biases of the other more established members of the department when considering what is important to teach in a course. This can be accomplished in several ways. The first is simply to ask them either formally or informally. A second method is to ask the students, both graduates (a great source of both real information and gossip) and undergraduates. Finally, review the other faculty members' books and publications for a hint of what the emphasis in the field is as defined by your department. Ask for syllabi from previously taught courses.

Departmental Focus

When first deciding your teaching objectives, it is very important to examine the role of your department. Is this department an undergraduate service department teaching classes for many other disciplines, or a scientific training department with both undergraduate and graduate students, or a department requiring both teaching and research? What level of preparation do other instructors expect from your students when they enter upper division courses in any department? Do other instructors expect specific tools (e.g., research methods, statistics, or a specific theoretical viewpoint) from your students? Who are your students and what are their expectations of the course? Of course this question of students' expectations is very difficult to answer because many students, particularly undergraduates, do not know what they expect. What are the students' academic goals and how does your course meet these goals? Again, this is a difficult question, but by asking advanced undergraduates and graduate students, you should be able to answer this question for your specific school. Is the department skewed toward a specific end of the academic vs. applied spectrum? If so, skew your course in that direction. These are the types of questions you must answer in order to define your course objectives. If your course objectives are poorly defined, then the rest of the course preparation will be more difficult than necessary. What are the major research emphases of the department? This will affect who teaches which classes and determine the areas that need new instructors.

Many departments will keep examples of syllabi from previous semesters and these can be reviewed to help understand the level and mission and goals of the department. If your department has a formalized Mission and Goals statement, ask for a copy to review in terms of your courses.

School Requirements

Many departments teach a core curriculum course and, thus if you teach this course, you will have school requirements for its content. These requirements may limit your choices of how and what you teach or add requirements to your course content. At my school, Introductory Psychology is a university social science core class and there is a communications component requirement, which requires students to use communications skills, both oral and written. In very large classes, this can be a difficult requirement to fulfill, particularly if you have little or no additional support from teaching assistants. Check to see if there are any school restrictions prior to planning your course. Often someone in the administration will check that these requirements are actually fulfilled. For example, check to see if there are specific school regulations on makeup examinations and if there are, state them in your syllabus.

Preliminary Course Objectives

After determining the restrictions on your course, it is time to write down your preliminary course objectives. These objectives should include the maximum amount of coverage that you will try to complete in your course. This list should encompass more material than can be taught in your school term. As the course takes shape, you will have to limit coverage, but if you have a diagram of the course, it should be easier to see where to cut. The use of computer flow charting can be helpful in this stage of planning. At this point, your list is a rough reminder of the overall plan for your course. It is important to develop your set of objectives because other planning components of the course will depend on these objectives. Several other components, such as the text (how long and how difficult), ancillary readings (how many and what sources), and types of tests (essay, multiple choice, true/false or a combination), will be dependent on the course objectives.

A major consideration when detailing your objectives is to consider what level of knowledge you will expect the students to master in this course. The following are examples of six levels of mastery. These can be a starting point for determining the level and objectives of your course.

Recognition

The student should be able to recognize the correct answer to a problem from a group of answers. This is the simplest level and multiple choice examinations can be used in very large courses.

Recall

This is a more difficult level and can be evaluated with fill-in-the-blank, short answer, and essay questions.

Comprehension

The student should be able to define a principle in his or her own words at a level that fellow students can understand. This level can be used in small group discussions and oral presentations.

Application

The student should be able to take a principle and use it in an applied situation and give several examples of applied situations. Often, this level is examined with essay type questions or short papers.

Analysis

The student will be able to identify the pattern and principles of a given topic. Additionally, the student will also be able to summarize the main points and comment on the pattern. Usually, examinations are in the form of very long essays or long term papers.

Evaluation

The student will be able to compare and contrast methods and principles and make evaluative judgments about the effectiveness of both. Examination is in the form of term papers.

Synthesis

The student will be able to take divergent principles, master the concepts of these principles, and then generate original principles or concepts from these earlier principles. This level is usually required only of graduate students and requires extensive papers, theses, or dissertations.

For the introductory level course, the first three levels of understanding are probably appropriate at most four-year universities. In addition, the next two levels may be appropriate for the honor section of an introductory course or for very exclusive four-year universities. The last level is usually reserved for the graduate level. You are the one who must decide the level of student performance. Do not be too optimistic about your students' abilities, but do not compromise your principles concerning class coverage and level either. Consult the faculty, undergraduate, and graduate students to help determine the level of the students and your class materials.

At this point, take into account how the average student has changed in recent years at your institution. Ask a seasoned teacher in the program for advice on who is taking the course, the best and the brightest or the bottom 25%. If the individual indicates more business majors, then slightly slant toward some business applications. More nurses, more of a slant to applications in the medical profession. This emphasis is minor in relationship to the major content of the course, but necessary based on the changing needs of the students.

First Rough Draft: Course Objectives

Complete a first rough draft of the learning objectives for the class; allow these objectives to "sit" for a week or two. Many textbooks have developed learning objectives which can be a helpful guide. Your accrediting agency may have specific learning objectives that are expected. Good sources for this process are textbooks and instructor's manuals. When requesting desk copies of texts I always ask for the instructor's manual. Many instructor's manuals are now on line making them more available and easier to obtain. Many times the instructor's resource manual or student study guide will contain learning objectives emphasized in the text.

First Rough Draft: Teaching Schedule

The next phase of planning your course is to draft a teaching schedule for the course; this draft will force you to consider which objectives must be trimmed. This draft of a realistic time schedule should help reduce your learning objectives to a more realistic, teachable list. I prefer to use a desktop organizer/calendar that is about 16" x 22" to condense the teaching schedule materials. I like to see the overall fit of these different sections of the course and compare time spent on different areas. This method allows you to get an initial sense of what the course will look like within the time constraints of the academic term. This large format calendar allows about 3" x 3" of working space per day. This space is very useful in getting a feel for the flow of the course and for writing detailed instructions about specific lectures or activities. Use a pencil for this preliminary round of scheduling; there will always be many changes both prior to and after each lecture. An additional small pocket reminder or computer generated calendar is also useful for specific appointments and things to do for each day, but the larger format calendar is a must. For these applications I do not like to use my computer daily schedule. I like to erase and change exam days, chapters assigned, video presentations; this first rough draft is too fluid and changes too often to use a computer schedule. After I have finalized the schedule, I add the material to my daily computer schedule. This schedule is in my computer start-up menu and the first thing that I read every morning.

Textbooks

Now that you have a general sense of what the course is going to look like, it is time to consider the text(s) for the course. Currently there are a large number of texts in most disciplines to choose from in the market. With the consolidation of publishers, this number has been reduced somewhat, but a reasonable number of diverse texts still exists. Many of the textbooks have changed in recent years; some have been dropped, some have been shortened, some even combined. Many of the textbooks that have survived the publishing mergers are the strongest texts in the field. I always want to look at the "package" of ancillary material before I select a textbook. Ask for, and you usually will receive, the test item file, instructor's manual, student study guide, CD-ROM and Internet site password. The ancillaries will help give you a feel not only for the text, but also what the students will find useful.

Escalating costs of textbooks are a major source of concern and scorn for the students. The notion that books are of a lesser value than in years past can be seen in the used book market. Students will sell their books back to the book store for a small fraction of the original cost. The work put into the understanding of the material is irrelevant. A new even more shocking trend is to "just rent the book." Send it back at the end of the semester just like last night's DVD.

Choosing the Best Text

Ask other faculty members in your department for their input; they will all have their favorite texts. Your department may have a standard text for all the sections of a class. If this is the case, ask the course coordinator for the text currently being used in your department. There is always a tremendous variability in what you and your colleagues will consider the best text. Remember it is the best text for your needs for your course so pick the one you want.

The Level of the Text

A very important consideration when choosing a text is matching the level of the text to that of the students. Many of the publisher's representatives that you will see in your first year of teaching will target you for a sales campaign because you may not understand the best methods for selecting the best text for your class. Following are some considerations when beginning the process of text selection: first, when will the text really be available to the class? A firm date, not a date like, "by the fall term." Then when will the ancillary package be available? I ask for the test item file, instructor's manual, student study guide, CD-ROM and Internet site password for each text that I am considering for adoption. Much of these materials can be accessed directly at the publisher's web site. Promises about dates and availability of ancillary materials are easily made, but often not kept.

By the time you are ready to select your text, you should have an idea of the level of your students. This level can be divided roughly into high, medium, and lower levels. Ask your publisher's representative for a text appropriate for your level. On occasion, publisher's representatives will have a text that is not appropriate for your level, but they will try to convince you to either adopt a text with a level is too high or too low. Resist these sales pressures; they are more interested in the sale than how well the text meets your needs. There are always several texts for each level available to choose from during each term.

Traditional or Essentials Text?

Recently, many publishers have developed a second smaller version of the text. These are usually called "fundamentals" or "essentials" versions. They typically are standalone texts and have individual editions. These "essentials" versions can range from a simple combination or deletion of chapters in order to reduce length or a completely new edition written to a lower-level audience. Many times the "essentials" editions are paperbound in order to save money on productions costs and thus have a lower cost for the students. When considering an "essentials" text, I usually ask for the differences between the editions, which your sales representative can help define.

Is an "essentials" text right for you? If you are looking for price, these texts usually are less expensive than the traditional text. The "essentials" version might have a smaller ancillary package. Do most of your students sell their texts back to the book store at the end of the term? If they do not you may want them to have a nice hardbound reference to use in other classes. The most important question, is the "essentials edition" too low of a level for my students?

Custom Chapters Only Texts

A recent development is the concept that you pick only the chapters you are going to use and the publisher will make up a text that contain only those chapters. There are advantages to this approach. First, the student gets a text that is less expensive than the traditional text. Second, if you are going to use this text the next term, your local bookstore will have an exclusive text in the used book market and the bookstore manager will like this. Third, the publishers will not have to worry that the texts will end up on the used book market. Lastly, production costs are lowered for the publishers and fewer materials are consumed making the text.

The major disadvantage is that students cannot sell the text back at the end of the term.

These types of texts are worth considering and the publisher's representative will be pleased that you are using a unique text.

e-Textbooks

E-textbooks are an attempt by publishers to develop a new format for their texts. The typical e-text is a stand alone copy of the text that is only available in an electronic format. Many students are now using Kindle, Nook, i-Pad, Smartphone or other electronic devices for a majority of their personal reading. The move to electronic texts has been picking up momentum.

The advantages are that students will have all the texts in one place—their e-reader. They do not weigh anything and they are always available—you can't misplace them. Publishers like e-texts because there is no used book market. Typically the book expires after some preset date, usually 6 months. No shipping and handling costs to the bookstore, you typically order and download online.

Some of the disadvantages are, the students have no book in the future since many of us still like a "real" book we can use as a reference. It is more difficult to annotate an e-book than a traditional text. Finally, no used book for the students to sell back at the end of the term.

Obtaining Examination Copies of Possible Texts

Now that you have achieved the status of faculty member, you can request that publishers send you examination copies of their texts (see the individual publisher Web sites, also easily found with a Google search). Check http://www.facultyonline.com/ for an excellent Internet source for selecting and ordering textbooks. As a final source, the departmental administrator will have a list of publishers for requesting examination copies. When you send for an examination copy, your local publisher's representative will be alerted that you have been hired to teach and are interested in adopting their text.

Meeting the Publisher's Representative

You can expect to meet regional or local publishers' representatives from the major publishing houses either in person or on the telephone. Meetings usually occur in the beginning of a new term. I find that with the mergers in publishing there are fewer publishers' representatives and they visit campus more often. Seems odd, but expect visits in the summer. Yes, the late summer, when the spring semester starts (January or February), and of course the week prior to the bookstore's ordering deadline. The publishers' representatives will be happy to assist you in selecting a text, particularly one from their company, on the recently published list. The publisher's representatives typically work on a combination of salary/commission, and the adoption of a course text is lucrative due to the typically large enrollment in many undergraduate classes. Once you have met your first publisher's representative, expect others from different publishers; they seem to travel in groups and stop by in the same week. The first several representatives will be interesting to talk to, but after the tenth in a one-week period, you will probably tire of the constant "sell," which will vary from almost no pressure to a very hard sell. Depending on your personal response to sales pressure, time spent with these individuals may range from interesting and enlightening to boring and obnoxious. Realize that these representatives work very hard and are on the road away from family and friends much of the academic year. Be courteous, take a serious interest in their books, and take the time to remember their names, faces, and publishers. Many representatives will help with this memory process because they will give you a business card with their phone number, address, and other company information. I write the month and year on the front of the card as a record of the visit. I then store all the cards together with a binder clip in my desk drawer. This record keeping is important due to the large turnover of publishers' representatives. Outdated cards should be removed as new representatives emerge in the late summer or early fall. I also like to get the e-mail and telephone numbers of the regional sales director, in case there are problems your local representative can not handle. This is handy when your representative is unavailable, does not make deadlines, or does not perform as you would prefer. A call to the boss usually produces fast results.

Most of the representatives are very cordial, interesting individuals and a kind word or sincerity from you can make their work experience less tedious. If you have ever lived out of a suitcase and traveled on the road for an extended period of time, you can appreciate how hard they work.

During the Publisher Representative's Visit

Ask when the current edition of the text you are interested in will be available to your bookstore and try to get a firm date. Many times publishers are somewhat overly optimistic about these delivery dates. Then ask what ancillaries are included with the text and when they will all be available; be specific, as ancillaries are notoriously late. This availability date is important because you want all the materials at the start of the class, not just the textbook. Not having an instructor's manual or test bank at the beginning of your first term can be a disaster.

Textbooks in college courses are often revised on a three-year cycle. Since the original publication of the textbook, many major publishers have started offering an essential, fundamentals or other short version of the normal major text, (see discussion above) often in paperback. These shorter versions can be useful if they fit the level of your students and they are often less expensive for the students. With consolidations and mergers, publisher's representatives will have a new (though usually only revised edition) text for you each year to consider for adoption. Many publishers would like you to change to a new text as often as possible, due largely to the used book market. If you find a text that you like, stick with it, and with any luck, the future editions will also be to your liking.

Factors in Text Selection

I always look first at the overall coverage of the text. Are all the appropriate chapters listed in the table of contents? Then I read some of the passages that are very hard for the students to understand. Review the chapters that relate to your research emphasis to see how the material you know the best is covered. I then look at the layout. Are margins used for definitions? Are the tables and figures well done and useful to the students? Is color effectively used? How does the text "feel" in terms of a fit? Will the students like the text? I can remember my first psychology text; I still have it. It was a book that consisted of only text; no pedagogy helped keep me awake. Today's students expect an attractive, interesting layout. All good texts strive for a comprehensive overall fit of color, artwork, and pedagogy. Always factor the publisher's representative into the equation when selecting a text. Is the representative going to get you a new computer disk for the test item file in two days when yours crashes? Are you going to be glad to see your representative when he/she comes to visit? Does the representative seem like the kind of person you can work with? These are important considerations. Remember, it is your choice; pick the text you want, and do not submit to sales pressure.

The Ancillary Package

In recent years the emphasis on the "package" has increased as publishers strive for the best package; some of the items are of little use, but most can be very helpful in your course. The following is a brief description of the items that you can expect to find in the text package.

Test Item File

At a minimum, a test item file should have 100 multiple choice items per chapter. Nice touches in the test item file are more items or additional editions. I just received a test item file that has over 1000 pages of mostly class tested items; this is a very impressive test item file. A mark of a publisher that really is at the cutting edge is a class-tested test item file. These are often complete with summary statistics. Essay questions, fill-in-the-blank, true/false, and matching items also should be included. Test item files become obsolete very quickly; exams and copies are stolen and become part of the campus culture. I give all my students their examinations and use entirely different items for each semester. I believe this levels the playing field for all students.

I ask for a demonstration disk or Internet access code, and make sure the programs run on our equipment and that the software is designed to be used by secretaries, not computer science graduates. In the not-too-distant past, this compatibility issue was a serious consideration. I have found recently that some testing software is simply too complicated. The programs do much more than I would ever want or need. With the demo disk or download I can see if I want to spend days trying to learn how to run a program.

Many instructors, including myself, write and collect their own test items. I have developed a significant number of lecture-related questions and use them to examine the student knowledge of my lectures. I use the publisher-supplied test item file to evaluate the student knowledge of the text material. These text based items have been used by many other instructors and errors have been corrected by the publishers.

Instructor's Resource Manual (Paper)

Instructor's resource manuals are a tremendous source of valuable information on how to teach your course; you will use a good manual a lot and throw away a bad one. Ask the representative to send you a copy of the instructor's resource manual prior to adoption so you can preview this important item. The manuals are a valuable source for helping develop your teaching plan, learning objectives, and your course lectures. For the seasoned instructor there are still many useful additions to class materials to be found in an instructor's resource manual. Since the paper version is all but extinct, most are available online.

Student Study Guide (Paper)

Student study guides are an important resource for the students. They will lower their anxiety level about testing and are a good method of studying for examinations. Here again, the quality of student study guides vary, so ask for a preview copy. The study guide should be coordinated with the test item file and the instructor's resource manual. If ancillaries are not coordinated, the students can be studying a specific emphasis while the instructor's resource manual and test item file are emphasizing something different. These ancillaries are always authored by different individuals; you can telephone or e-mail the authors with specific questions concerning this part of the package. Much of the material in paper study guides can be found on more interactive Internet sites as paper study guides become obsolete. These paper versions are going the way of the dinosaurs and are now available online.

Practice Test Questions for the Students

Recently, publishers have supplied sample test questions for the students. These are either integrated into the text or as a standalone ancillary item. I like the standalone type; the students use them often and it helps lower test anxiety. These materials are also being replaced by comprehensive Internet sites.

Overhead/Slides

Historically, overhead/slide packages were a must for large classes. They are useless in this century.

The Twenty-First Century

How times have changed! I threw out all my slides and overheads. I have upgraded all my lectures to a multimedia format (PowerPoint).

The chalkboard (whiteboard) is dead. Some of the really "old" timers still use the chalkboard (whiteboard), but fewer and fewer are using this method.

Multimedia is the best method for the new instructor to use. You are usually familiar with computer applications. If your school has multimedia capable classrooms, explore what is available. If your school does not have the capability, see if you can write a grant or otherwise obtain funds to start a multimedia classroom. I have found that there is usually money for innovative teaching methods; you just have to look for it.

PowerPoint

PowerPoint, or some similar multimedia presentation software, is essential to your teaching. Why would you take the time to develop written lecture notes that you would copy onto a chalkboard or overhead transparency every time you give the lecture? Fast forward to the 21st century! Students love this type of multimedia lecture format. You will love it too! I find myself constantly updating my presentations; it is easy and fun to improve your lectures. Add a photograph from the Internet, switch the order of a concept, add more information, or delete confusing material. It is so easy! Save to a disk or upload to the server and your *new* lecture is complete.

Almost all textbooks published today have a set of PowerPoint slides for the text material. The quality and depth of the presentations will vary greatly among publishers and even individual texts. Ask for a sample of the presentations; these will indicate the level you can expect. Use these publisher-supplied presentations as a starting point and customize them with your unique lecture material.

CD-ROM

In the past most textbooks came with a CD-ROM. It could be used either as a student study guide, or for images and text you can download to your presentation software, or prepared with PowerPoint lectures, video clips, and much more.

Videos

Forget 16mm films--wrong century again—and have anything you really need transferred to a more modern format. Videos are a superior addition to your classroom presentation. Many ancillary packages include video materials. This can range from old standards to more contemporary videos produced by the publisher.

DVD

Most publishers now offer DVD versions of all video presentations. These are superior in many ways, including the ability to move quickly to different areas of the presentation.

Both DVD and video presentations can be obtained from a publisher's representative for free if you have a large adoption or adopt with a specific publishing house on a regular basis.

The Web in the Classroom

Currently in many ancillary packages, publishers are allowing direct Internet access by the instructor to the publisher's Internet materials. If you have a multimedia classroom, it should have an Internet connection and thus access. You can use many of the sites to demonstrate principles and examples. Realize that the Internet might not always work when you want it to, so have an alternative.

Downloadable Material

Much of the material mentioned above is downloadable from a published Internet site. Ask your publisher's representative for an access code after you have adopted the text.

Student Interactivity and the Internet

Many publishers are combining much of the material from the student study guide in a new and exciting format on an Internet site. This site is usually an attempt to combine all the needs of the students' testing and content needs with the instructors needs such as tracking home work assignments, examinations scores and grading papers. This is a new expanding and exciting area that will help with your integration of your course. Ask your sales representative for details.

One of the best examples is MyPsychLab, one of the Pearson publishing's MyLab series: a totally interactive student study guide with an e-book, labs, videos, study tools and interesting materials for the curious student. There are many features including practice tests, detailed individual study plans for the student trying to not only maximize learning, but maximize their grade. See http://www.mypsychlab.com/whatis.html for an interesting demonstration. Check with your publisher for access to this new and exciting format.

These items are what constitute a good ancillary package. There will always be extras, many of which I find to be of little use, but investigate them. The "package" should be a major consideration in your text adoption process. As a new instructor, you will use the package more than experienced instructors.

Ask your publisher's representative for a detailed written estimate of the delivery/completion date for ancillaries. I have started classes before receiving ancillaries. Late test item files are the worst, but missing any item is not acceptable. If you know ahead that any of these items will be late, you can plan your course accordingly or adopt a different text. Emphasize to the representative that you expect to have the materials when promised; be firm and demand realistic delivery dates. A recent development is to publish textbooks in the summer just prior to the fall term. This is fine when it works, but can leave the instructor without critical items, including the text, when classes start.

Custom Publishing

In the last few years there has been a large push to "custom publish" existing textbooks. This custom material is usually provided by the instructor and makes the text suitable for your class only. The push will include a description of how you can receive a royalty for providing as little information as your syllabus to be appended to the text, or you can even select the chapters you will teach in your class. Why would a publisher be so interested in a custom text? With a custom text there is no text buy-back value except for your class. The used book market is a major problem for publishers and this is a method to deal with this problem. Advantages to the student are often a lower initial price for the text and only the chapters they "need" for the course. Advantages to the instructor are that you can add any materials you would like to enhance your course. You must make the decision if the custom materials are worth the cost of not allowing the student to sell their books on the used book market.

Shrink Wrap

Another change in the textbook market in recent years is the movement to shrink wrap additional materials with a new textbook. For example, the student on-line study guide access code may be offered as a free shrink wrap item to be included with each new text purchased. Other popular items are readers, case books, Internet site codes, and CD-ROMs. All of these options allow the instructor to have the material he or she would like the students exposed to during the course. Advantages to the student are the material is with the text and not an option for the course, the text can still be sold on the used book market, and many of these free items have a real value to the students. You must weigh the cost of a new book versus the package item's worth.

Ordering the Text through the Campus Book Store

After you decide on the text, ask your departmental administrator to order the text through your campus bookstore. Be sure to include all the materials that you want ordered, such as student study guides and additional readings, CD-ROM or additional texts. Bookstores usually have a deadline for ordering texts. Many times this ordering deadline is flexible to order books for the next term, so ask your departmental administrator for the real deadline. If you can meet this bookstore deadline, do so, but do not be pressured into making a poor choice because of an arbitrary deadline. Remember, you will be using this text for at least one year. Be sure to have the correct ISBN if you are ordering a package, the one for the text is different than the package.

Get to know the bookstore manager and the textbook supervisor; these individuals can help you out in an emergency. You might increase the enrollment in your course, be short textbooks, and need a favor to have the additional text rushed through the system. Stop by and introduce yourself the first week that you are on campus.

Ordering the Text through the Internet

This fall term I have seen an increased activity by Internet sources in the new and used book market. For an example see http://www.textbooksource.net/. The flyers around campus promising large savings on Internet textbook ordering are also increasing. You might consider if this is a viable alternative to the campus bookstore. If you think you can save the students money by using the Internet, do the following first: Tell the bookstore your Internet quoted price and see if they will match it; they will try. Next, think of the problems of mis-shipments, short orders, and returns. Are a few dollars saved worth the effort? And of course, do not forget the shipping charges. As the Internet matures this alternative may become more attractive, but currently I do not find either the real or imagined savings worth the effort. Many schools have alternative book stores very close to campus and these bookstores will compete directly with the campus bookstore. Finally, there are the mega book chains in many towns and of course on the Internet to check for price considerations.

Two Months Prior to Class

Begin to Develop Your Course Syllabus

Two instructors with the same text are likely to emphasize different aspects of the text, and you should start to think about the contents of your syllabus. Ask other instructors, your departmental mentor, or your departmental administrator for examples of past syllabi. These syllabi will give you a good format as well as the depth of presentation expected. See Appendix A for an example of my introductory course syllabus.

Number of Instructional Days in the Term

Consult your schedule of classes to determine the number of actual teaching days; there are holidays and special events when students will be excused from class. Do not forget that you will be giving examinations; at many schools these occur during regular class time. It is important to avoid scheduling examinations either before or after important events or holidays. Students always want an early start for the holiday and study very little during holidays or special events like homecoming weekends. Try not to penalize students for enjoying college life; remember how much you enjoyed taking examinations. Write down the total number of teaching days; you will need this number later.

Defining Lecture Length

One difficult aspect of developing a syllabus is to calculate the length of your lectures. Most schools utilize a 50-60 minute schedule for Monday, Wednesday, and Friday classes, and schedule 75-90 minute classes for Tuesdays and Thursdays. Also, do not forget the possibility of night classes which typically meet in a long block, such as 180 minutes per week on one week night. Calculate the number of lectures per topic in terms of the class length, and remember that you will likely teach both in the 50-60 minute and 75-90 minute time frames during your first few years in academia. Will you be very good at these calculated class period estimates? No! Invariably you have too much material to cover in the class period. Try to schedule at least half a class period every two weeks to either catch up or lose time in the schedule. A lecture that is too short before a test is much better than cramming two lectures into a single period. You can always have a review session if you are short of coverage.

Defining Examinations

In a typical semester-long course, I would recommend at least three, possibly four, examinations of the course materials, excluding midterms (which are losing favor in many institutions) and finals. Students prefer smaller examinations of less material, because if they receive a poor examination grade they are not doomed to failure in the class. Midterms and finals are usually set by the school; therefore, you must restrict your schedule to conform to these requirements. Consider giving examinations online. Several advantages include reduced use of class time, students get immediate feedback about their scores, and the students can take the examination on their schedule. Talk to your publisher's representative to see if they have an online testing program. Most publishers do.

Defining the Schedule

Should you be worried that you are not finished with your teaching schedule? No. Several factors demand that you keep an open schedule as long as possible. First, the emphasis of the text material that you have chosen could change, according to your own wishes or due to outside constraints. You should attempt to stay as flexible with this syllabus as you can. I like to type a preliminary syllabus and hang it on my wall; as time passes, I usually will see improvements or changes to my original thoughts and can mark them in pencil on the original. I have very rarely used the first draft of a course syllabus. I have, on the other hand, printed hundreds of copies of the syllabus only to find errors or changes that I must make. Check with the departmental administrator to see the time line needed to produce this syllabus and allow three extra days. In my upper division courses, I survey the class the first meeting day and modify my class schedule and syllabus according to the student population in the class and their needs. I will add a lecture or two or introduce a topic the class has indicated they desire. If your class is small enough and your department allows for this flexibility, I would recommend this option of tailoring the content of the course to the needs and needs of the students. The students will see this as your attempt at allowing student input into their education. You can still teach the course the way you want, but this student input makes for a better class. Of course, if you have a class of 100 or more students, you really cannot use this option.

First Draft of the Syllabus

Produce a first rough draft of the syllabus and be as detailed as possible using your desk top organizer. I pencil in exams, holidays and other important information to see how everything fits. I count the number of lecture days between examinations to try and keep the intervals equal. Be specific about dates, times, and locations of all examinations. If recitation sections are held, be specific about locations and times. Leave as little to the students' imagination as possible. I usually do not like to add the times of films and videos to the syllabus because of the slippage factor (being too long or too short with your lecture material) in the lectures. Surprise students with films or videos; if you let them know you are showing one, many students might skip class that day, but of course, the best students will attend. Guest lectures can be added to the syllabus, particularly from outside the school community. When I have a guest lecture, I ask students to invite other students or faculty. I usually put a copy of all materials for the course on reserve in the library; note this in the syllabus. Add any special circumstances, either yours or the school's. For example, is attendance required in your course, by you, or the school? Where will grades be posted? Note building and room or area of the hall where this material can be viewed.

Many schools now require that your syllabus be posted on the Internet for easy access by students and other interested parties. I would like to encourage you to post your syllabus even if not required to do so. Students have a habit of losing things, and a syllabus is usually the first item that disappears.

Syllabus Considerations

The following material should be considered before you complete the first draft of the syllabus. You can use this as beginning check list of required material. Add any specific departmental or school requirements as needed. There are two perspectives in the following material, first from the instructor's perspective and secondly, from the student's. My syllabus has grown from a single page to 6-8 pages depending on the course. The amount of very detailed material has grown and specific departmental and school information must be added.

From the Instructor's Perspective

Basic Course Data

Course number and title; core class designation, the academic term for which the course is taught; class times, days, course website address, and building/room where lectures will take place.

Instructor Information

Instructor's name, title, office location, regular office hours, phone number, e-mail address, emergency outside-of-class contact procedures.

Course Description

Catalogue or other official course description; information about what curricular requirements the course satisfies; elective credit, core course requirement, required of academic majors. List the prerequisites for the course, enrollment eligibility requirements, such as upper-division standing or a specific major.

Course Objectives

Statement of general instructional goals; what you expect to give the students. Specific learning objectives for the course; many texts have outlines of course objective in the instructor's ancillary package. With accreditation taking a major place in the new academic landscape of the 21st century, your school may have specific learning objectives. Check to see if these exist and if they do, use them. Many publicly funded schools' survival depends on meeting the learning objectives. Many academic disciplines have their own learning objectives. For example, the American Psychological Association has specific learning objective/outcomes for psychology curriculum. Recently, publishers have been using these types of learning objectives in the construction of texts and have methods of documentation that the objectives have been met. If these accreditation issues are relevant to you, check with your publisher's representative to see if they have this type of material available.

Internet Sites and e-Media

Both your own site and the publisher's should be included. Any additional e-media discussed in chapter 12 should also have the URL or address included in the syllabus.

Reciprocal Expectations

What you as the instructor expect from students; regular or required attendance, classroom attentiveness, compliance with assignment deadlines, and your policy on tardiness or absences from class. Specific behavioral considerations like talking during lecture, cell phones, reading a newspaper, which you would like to curtail. Your school will probably have a set of expectations, check the Web site and include them if they exist.

Student Expectations from You as the Instructor

Preparedness, accessibility, responsiveness to questions; course evaluation criteria, usually set by your department or the school; recommendations for achieving success in the course; teaching methods to be employed and how class time will be utilized; lectures, discussions, and student presentations. There should be no secrets about how to succeed in your class.

Policies and Procedures

Requirements governing excused and unexcused absences, tardiness and class attendance; penalties for plagiarism, cheating, and emergency procedures and policies.

Grading

Explanation of grading criteria and procedures; types of tests or quizzes; length and types of questions: essay, short-answer, true/false, multiple choice; your relative weighting of homework, projects, special assignments, class participation; extra credit; availability of make-up exams; penalties for late submission of assignments; detailed instructions for submission of papers or other written assignments.

Student Study Aids

Sample test questions or study guides for examinations; you will provide. Address of your course Internet site. Sample test questions or study guides for examinations. Address of the publisher's Internet site (the Pearson MyLab series is exactly what students need as a study aid). Are there review sessions conducted by yourself or a TA? Will you supply lecture outlines or presentation slides (PowerPoint) handouts?

Texts and Supplementary Materials

Title and author of the texts. ISBN for the text and other materials for the course. Is the book optional or required for the course? Are the laboratory materials, or fees? Are there recitation/lab materials that are required for the course such as journal materials?

Course Schedule

Weekly or class-by-class schedule is very difficult to create. I prefer a more general approach for all events except course examinations, these are set in stone. Submission deadlines for assignments, papers, presentations should all be given. I am constantly either long or short with my lecture material for a specific text. I prefer to have this freedom to modify my presentation. I know many instructors generate very detailed, inflexible schedules, but I really would rather have the freedom to explore interesting topics suggested by student questions.

Special Needs Considerations

How will you, as an instructor help students with special needs attend and succeed in the course. Your school has a policy for helping these students and you may be required to post the material on your syllabus. Check with your course supervisor or mentor for these requirements.

From the Student's Perspective

Where and When Does the Course Meet?

Are there any planned changes to the regular schedule; extra sessions, field trips, special assignments? Are there recitation or laboratory sections? What is the schedule and where are the meeting rooms?

Why is the Course Important or Significant?

What is its focus? For whom is it intended, majors or the general student population? What are the prerequisites and are there any other restrictions on enrollment?

What Books Will I Need for the Course?

Are the books required for the course? Which are merely recommended or optional? Are course materials available online?

What Supplies are Needed for the Course?

What materials are required for laboratory or recitation sections? Which are merely recommended or optional? Are course materials available online? Are there lab fees? Material fees, user fees, super tuition for the course or laboratory or recitations?

Who is the Instructor?

What are his or her qualifications and background? Where is his or her office? What are the teacher's office hours? If I need help, can I just drop by or will I need to make an appointment in advance? Can I communicate via e-mail? I review this important material the first day of class.

What are the Basic Goals or Objectives of the Course?

What will we be doing to meet those goals? What is the grade distribution and what is it based on? What do I have to do to get a specific grade in this class? What kind of grading will be used? Will the grades be based on examinations, papers, or laboratory reports?

What is the Attendance Policy?

If I have to miss a class or a test, what is the make-up policy? Do I need to notify someone in advance if I am going to be absent?

Will the Instructor Offer "Extra Credit" Assignments?

Does class participation count? Will I have to talk in class? What kind of extra credit can I expect and how many course points will be available?

(Adapted from Lucas and Murry 2002)

The first syllabus is always the most difficult. After you have developed the first syllabus you can use it as a template for other classes and sections. Cut and paste changes to the template for easily updated syllabus.

Types of Teaching Methods

Planning for class depends on the type of teaching method you are going to adopt. There are several different approaches; one possible choice is the "straight" stand-up lecture with no student input or interaction. This method is largely out of favor with both students and faculty, although some faculty insist on this method. A second choice is a more modern approach that encourages student questions and input, but this method can be restricted by the number of students in your class. I use as many demonstrations and examples of the principles under study as I can, since the greater the exposure to a principle the more likely the students will understand it. If possible, stay flexible and vary your presentation from day to day; lecture one day, conduct demonstrations or activities the next, and lead discussions the following day.

To Post or Not to Post Presentation Slides?

A question has arisen with the advent of the use of presentation software: should the instructor post the presentation slides to the Internet so each student can have access to the presentation slides?

Advantages: students could download and print the slide before the lecture and simply augment the slides. Students could get the slide and the bare minimum for your lectures if they miss a class. Some international students can use downloaded slides to help with their translation from their native language. Students will not waste time copying material from a screen.

Disadvantages: students will not attend class because they already have the notes. Keeping the material on the slide to a minimum can help keep students attending class. This is not really the best way to approach education, but many students really do not think your lectures add that much. Other disadvantages are that you will not be able to change/update your slide without posting the new version to the Internet. Some students will have the wrong version (the one posted yesterday) and complain that the examination was unfair because you changed the material in your presentation slides. I personally do not think it is worth the effort to post. Students do gain something from sitting and listening to lecture even if it is a minimal socialization with you and the other students in the course. The major reason students come to class is for YOU. They have textbooks, publisher Internet sites, a CD-ROM, the student study guide, and many other helpful materials, but the reason they should come to class is YOU.

If you decide to post, you can use Blackboard, D2L, WebCT or your publisher's Web site as the vehicle for these postings.

Much to my dismay, I have found that a significant number (ranging up to 50% of my students) do not bother to print the presentation slides. They continue to sit and copy that material from the screen, which holds up the class. Strongly encourage your students to print the slides.

Other Course Requirements

Are there any required recitation sections, discussion sections, study sections, laboratory meetings or small group meetings? If there are, be sure to discuss with your course supervisor or chair how these sections are to be staffed and how to fulfill the requirements. If these are not required by your department, you may want to integrate some of these alternatives into your teaching approach. Students often find alternatives to the straight lecture formats very interesting. The size of your section can be a limiting factor in the types and varieties of the alternative methods that you try, but give them serious consideration. See Chapter 7 for some suggestions.

Lesson Plan Pros and Cons

During your career as a student, you have undoubtedly interacted with other students in the education department of your school. It may seem that these students and their instructors are obsessed with the lesson plan. You probably laughed at the prospect of assigning every minute of the class period to a specific topic or activity. The current question is whether you should use the dreaded lesson plan. I would say no. A college-level course should be flexible enough to explore interesting topics and tangents introduced by students and not be constrained by an artificial system designed to engineer students through their education. Some of the best interactions and thinking the students will have and do is during tangential discussions. These tangents are a good place for students to get a glimpse of your personality and explore the field. Besides, how boring to do the same lecture every term.

Begin to Write Your Lectures

History of Lecturing

Prior to the invention of the printing press, lectures were the main method of passing on knowledge. Professors or masters would read their hand-written lectures to students; these lectures were then passed from professor to students, and when the student eventually became the professor, some current knowledge was added to the lectures and this information was passed on to the next generation of students. This method was far superior to the earlier word-of-mouth method. In the word-of-mouth method, stories were told from generation to generation with no control over the original content. This method could explain some of the miracles of earlier times, owing to the simple conscious or unconscious elaboration of common events.

With the advent of printing and books, the lecture method has survived. Why? There are four primary reasons:

A Lecture Is a Contemporary Event

Since a lecture is a contemporary event, it can update the text materials in a course. Most texts in will have a three-year cycle between editions. Add this to the lag time for journal publications and other texts and the most current the material in your text can be is three to five years old.

I often present materials that I have just read in the newspaper, a journal or on the Internet minutes prior to class. The ability to stay current is an important aspect of the lecturing system and keeping the discipline current.

Although we would like to think that all lectures are updated each term, the sad fact is that many are not. I am sure in your undergraduate career you had a professor who read old, stale notes that were so out of date they were of little use. Do not let this happen to you; remain current and update each lecture every term. I make a promise to the students and myself to update each major lecture section every time I give the lecture.

A Lecture Has In-Depth Coverage

The lecture format allows not only for the transfer of information from one person to another, it also allows the demonstration of little-known relationships that may not be in the printed materials. Many texts do not have the time or space to discuss specific topics at length and in depth, ranging from the introductory to advanced levels. Additionally, the lecture allows conventional wisdom to be challenged, the classic theories with up-to-date research to be evaluated, and a new and different perspective on old problems.

A Great Lecture Is a Great Lecture

If you have ever attended a great lecture, you will never forget it. I attended a lecture by Buckminster Fuller that was so inspiring I still remember it thirty-five years later. Great individuals are sometimes great lecturers; if this is the case, attend as many as you can. Many schools conduct an invited lecture series; ask for a schedule of speakers. Great lecturers are so enthused with their subject matter that they convey this feeling to the audience. When this happens, it is a great experience. Even beginning instructors can strive to inspire the same passion in their students. When one good student decides to change majors and become a psychologist, it makes the effort worthwhile to me. You may develop into a good lecturer and even deliver a few great lectures; it is the passion for the subject matter that makes this difference.

A Lecture is Interactive

A lecture can and should be interactive. Encourage student questions and input. This is not your Nobel acceptance speech. Allow the student to help drive the direction of the lecture.

Lectures Define a Commitment to Scholarship

Lectures can serve as a method of instilling commitment to a life of scholarship. Act as an example of this scholarly goal for the student who aspires to the academic profession by being a mentor to the student and instilling principles that have been passed down through the generations: honesty, ethics, and love for the discipline.

(Adapted from Allen and Rueter 1990)

Writing Your First Lecture

First Rough Draft

I start by using the rough teaching outline from the desktop organizer/calendar as described earlier. In terms of this time line, start writing your first lectures. Hand writing or word process the first lecture draft is a personal choice. Realize that many of these first lectures will be changed as you see what works and what does not in the classroom. I like to use pencil for hand written first drafts. It is really a bit scary to think you are the one who must choose what materials will be included in your class. I use other texts, graduate and undergraduate class notes, journals, the Internet and my research interests to develop these lectures. An additional source of inspiration for beginning lectures can be found in the instructor's resource manual. Many will have short mini-lectures already prepared. You can use these mini-lectures as a starting point and add your material to them. Remember, lectures are a reflection of your personality. Do not be afraid to show the students who you are; some will like you, others won't. You will remember the ones who like you and hopefully in time forget the rest. Every section of every term is different; there will be sections you cannot wait to begin, while others are like going to the dentist's office every Monday, Wednesday, and Friday. Every instructor has his or her set of biases that makes teaching unique. In an undergraduate class, everyone teaches the same basic material from different perspectives. The students will soon learn the instructor's teaching perspective and you will develop a following of students who both agree with and like your teaching perspective. Do not try to copy someone's style or approach; be yourself because it is much easier. This is a great place to discuss teaching and lecture writing with your mentor in the department. Start to select the presentation slides provided by the publisher that you will integrate into your lectures and use these as the basic element from which your lectures are developed. A two month head start on the lectures will give you time to refine each lecture and still stay ahead of other course commitments. Realize that you do not want to write all your lectures now, but rather identify the strengths and weaknesses of your style and lectures, modifying your later lectures to enhance your strengths. As a minimum I like to stay 2-3 weeks ahead of the class with my lecture preparations.

Structure of the Lecture

Make a skeletal structure or outline of the materials that you want to cover in your lecture. I usually try to outline the main points to be covered in the lecture. These main points should cover all the materials necessary to complete the lecture. Try to find an appropriate presentation slide for each major topic and major sub-point. This may not always be possible, but as the years pass, you can add to your collection through other publishers' materials and the Internet. Each main point can usually be subdivided into in-depth sub-points; it is your decision how many of the sub-points are to be covered in each lecture. At the undergraduate level, cover only the items necessary to complete a general understanding of the main point. Leave the subtle differences and depth of coverage for the advances upper division and graduate courses. If you do not adopt this strategy, you could be lost in an endless lecture on very minor points. Students will lose interest in the material during a very in-depth lecture at this level. These very in-depth points are the content of the upper-division course. The students take these upper-division courses for the details and techniques they provide.

Learning Points

You can decide if you want to use the learning points concept. The introduction of the lecture's main topics in outline form is presented at the beginning of the class as a presentation slide or handout. Many students prefer the handout method because they can then fill in the material during the lecture and they will not miss any of the points that you wish to emphasize. A disadvantage to this method is that you must stay reasonably on track in your lecture and this gives you little room for student interaction. A possible compromise is to begin your teaching career with specific learning points and then make them more general as your lectures develop over time. You can also evaluate how well the students have assimilated the material by assessing the learning points at the end of the lecture. See Chapter 10 for more information about the evaluation of the learning points.

Fleshing Out Your Lecture

Now that you have an outline of the lecture, use your training and experience to flesh it out. I had to sit at my computer and transfer my old handwritten lectures notes to presentation slides. I would still suggest developing a fleshed-out lecture prior to making your slides. You do not have to have these fleshed-out lectures in any finished form. Get the material on paper to see the overall lecture, then make presentation slides.

Decide how much of the lecture to use in your presentations: every word you are going to say, brief phrases, or a single word to jog the memory of an important point. I usually suggest incorporating many details in the early draft form of the outlines of the important points. As you repeatedly present this lecture, you can add or delete information in each section. I do this during the lecture when a new point or way of analyzing something comes up, typically through student input, when a funny saying works or when a student's question logically leads to the next section. During the lecture I update my printed presentation notes with a colored pen, because it stands out from the pencil notes. All of these live events should be recorded as they add new and interesting information that works. I also write comments like "fix this section," insert a big question mark, or simply cross out a section and write "skip" across it. I like to evaluate the flow of the lectures from the heat of the moment; this lets you know what really works in the classroom. When you learn what level works for you, the more you use and update your presentations, the shorter the length of the original structure of the lecture notes will be; a single word may become a 15-minute section of the lecture. These lectures will evolve into something much improved. My presentations notes are a mess to the average student. Some pages are so annotated that only I can understand them. I find it reasonably humorous when a student asks to photocopy my presentation notes. I usually suggest they try another student's notes instead.

Use elaboration in your presentations, which can consist of statistics, making comparisons between different principles, offering contrast between different principles, using quotations as sources, or providing examples and illustrations of the principle under discussion. These are the details and the evidence for a lecture; these are the materials that students expect to learn in the class. If you use all the source materials mentioned above for these details, you will be amazed at how much you will learn from this course.

I use the Internet as a resource for many of my figures and tables. In addition your text's ancillary package will probably provide presentation slides.

Using Audio/Visual Materials

These materials can include graphs, videos, audio tapes, models, brain sections, photographs, maps, and any other materials you can bring to class that will help illustrate your main topics. There are many classroom demonstrations that can be found in you text ancillary package that could be used to enhance your lectures. I like to write in the margins of my presentation notes when one of these items should be presented in the lecture. Using a colored pen will help direct your attention to this note.

A Newer Method of Developing Lecture

Many publishers now offer course development software for the new instructor. Pearson has a very good example of this software, which includes everything a new instructor needs to get started: PowerPoint slides, usually a different level of complexity, selections of multi-media materials that can be dragged and dropped into a lecture, pop-quiz materials, *clicker* questions and other very valuable material for development of your lectures. It is almost too easy now to develop new lectures with these packages.

Lecture Strategies

My Method of Lecturing

A good way to plan your lectures is to tell the students what you are going to teach them, teach it, and then summarize what you have lectured. If you use this format, the students will come to expect it and will be able to follow your lectures more easily.

Tell Them What You Are Going to Teach Them

You can provide an overview of the main structure of your lecture, either using a handout or a presentation slide at the beginning of the class. This material can be in the form of learning points, which often are now available in you text or instructors manual. Students like this method, especially if you always follow the plan. If there are detailed materials that must be copied from the presentation slide make a photocopy and distribute the material to the class, which will save time in class and allow students to have the correct material as an outline for notes on the lecture material. I try to use some of the presentation slides provided by the publisher which are in the text; this allows the students to have access to the original material.

Teach Them What You Are Going to Teach

Spend the necessary time to make certain that the main points are covered and understood by the students. This may take the form of asking students questions, giving quizzes at the end of the class, or assigning short papers on topics covered in the lecture. You can also assume the students understand the materials, which they often do not, and have questions on the examination from the lectures. Are you satisfied the students understand the material? I usually pick several of the best students ask them questions and use them as indicators of the level of understanding of the rest of the class. If the best students look confused about a section of the lecture, I will repeat that section with different examples. If they look pleased, I continue.

Summarize What You Have Taught Them

Using a presentation slide, review the main points of the lecture prior to the end of the class period. Encourage individual students to stay after class to discuss any further questions they may have about the lecture. The students that stay are typically the best students and are of interest to the instructor. Use these students as a gauge to the effectiveness of the lecture.

Evaluate what the have learned

Clicker or other brands of student response software will allow you to evaluate if the students have understood the main points of your lecture. If they have, great, if not, then you can review the parts they missed. Easy, simple, and fast—three minutes at the end of the lecture is all you need to gather this valuable data. This data can also be used to validate that the course learning objectives have been met.

Some Final Lecture Tips

With the outline to organize your lectures, start the preparation for the first lecture. Use your own ideas and methods along with these suggestions to form a standardized method of writing lectures or preparing presentation slides. Consult your departmental mentor for help in the areas of the course level and expected or required material. The more standardized your presentation slides are, the more the students will like the lectures. I keep my presentation lecture notes in a file folder, where I number the pages. I dropped my presentation notes on the floor last term and if I had not numbered the pages, I would have been lost trying to sort them out in front of the class. Now I like to close the file folder with a binder clip in case you drop the folder on the way to class. Always strive to keep your lectures organized and update your presentations slides prior to each class.

I have one flash drive that I take to class with a copy of the presentation slides. Being just a little paranoid I still take my original notes, which I refer to during the lectures. Besides I like the cool look of a folder full of old notes. In technical upper-division, it is essential that you have all the critical material for accurate dissemination of the course material. The multimedia equipment may fail on the first day of class or the most important lecture of the term, so have a backup plan for the lecture. Assume that you will have a problem with the multimedia equipment and develop an alternate plan. Cancelling the class will make you popular with the students, but the lecture time is too precious to waste.

Other Course Considerations

Ordering and Planning for Course Materials

Order CD-ROMs, DVDs or videos either through your library, rental outlets or your publisher. Many publishers have all these materials online and all you need is a password to access them. Make preliminary arrangements for any field trips. Contact guest lecturers, typically someone you know who owes you a favor or someone you want to meet from another school or the community. Indicate that you would like him/her for a specific guest lecture and plan for a specific week. Start to look at the logistics of the demonstration that you are planning and make preliminary attempts to secure any necessary equipment. If you must reserve any material, try to keep the time frame as flexible as possible. Check your multimedia presentation equipment to become familiar with it and to make certain it works. Order any material necessary for labs or recitations.

Special Needs Students

Your school will have facilities for students with physical, learning disabilities or other special needs. The staff that works with these students should be contacted and assured that you will cooperate with their specific programs. Depending on your school, these individual students can be a significant percentage of the school population. Take the time to get to know each of the special needs students and offer any additional help. The students are starting at a disadvantage, but often work harder to overcome their problems. You need to access the Americans with Disabilities Act and include the provisions on your syllabus. See http://www.usdoj.gov/crt/ada/adahom1.htm for more information. Do everything you can to help these students in the areas of privacy, confidentiality concerns, note-takers, recording devices, speech conversion software, and other assistive technology they may require. Many of my students are not physically handicapped, but rather educationally or emotionally handicapped. Dyslexia and other forms of learning disorders are being diagnosed more frequently. Often these students will need to have special accommodations such as quiet rooms, more time on examinations, a reader or transcriber. Contact your student services facilities and review your school's policies. These special needs students are usually trying as hard as they can and become frustrated with lack of progress.

Advanced Students

More and more high school students are taking Advanced Placement (AP) courses and testing out of introductory courses. Having earned credit at the college level these students are free to take more advanced courses. This leaves you with a population of less capable students or students who did not have the opportunity to take these AP classes in introductory courses. I find that the cognitive level of my entry-level freshman students is slowly declining. You may have to reconsider your expectations and level of materials for your course based on this decline. At the upper-division level you have students taking your class who have never taken the perquisite classes, but did pass the AP test. This can be difficult for them; testing out of a class is very different that taking the class. Encourage these advanced students and offer any assistance you can.

Student Privacy

Ask your departmental administrator for a copy of the HIPAA regulations, (see http://www.hhs.gov/ocr/hipaa/). Also, your departmental mentor can help with local interpretations of these very important privacy act regulations. Student privacy is now a major concern. Only you, as the instructor, and your department chair, need to have access to student data.

Four Weeks Prior to Class

The Teaching Assistant

By this time in the preparation process, your teaching assistant(s) (TAs) should have been assigned. Depending on your school, you will either have undergraduate or graduate students. Set a formal meeting date to discuss both their and your role in the course structure. TAs are some of the best and some of the worst aspects of your college course. If you do not have TA support, the publisher Internet site can be very helpful in managing your class - the Pearson MyLab series is a very helpful example.

On the plus side, TAs can assume the responsibility for a tremendous amount of the busy work from the class. Examples are checking class rolls, making answer keys, posting scores, proctoring exams, videos, summarizing test results, leading study groups and producing final summaries and graphs for your final grades. They are also, in most instances, very nice individuals and often just a few years away from the position you now have. They will work hard, but often need substantial guidance to understand the tasks that you wish performed. They usually have a very keen interest in learning how to teach at the college level. Take the time to help these individuals learn how to teach; they are your responsibility.

On the negative side, often it seems that performing the TAs job yourself would be easier than trying to explain this activity. Remember that being a TA has two major benefits: the first is that the TA learns from you how to conduct a course and, secondly, in most cases, the TAs are also paid for their duties with a tuition waiver, a stipend or a grade. Take the time to explain what you want to accomplish and then check the work to be sure the TAs have complied with your instructions. I have had very good and very poor TAs. You should be able to discover the type you have very early on in the class. If your TA is the poor type, be very careful to check all assigned tasks. You will be able to identify poor TAs because they miss meetings, come in late and miss deadlines. Help your TAs remember they are the next generation of instructors.

Assign the TAs to read the appropriate sections of the text, study guide, and course syllabus. Impress upon them the importance of being ahead of the students in the readings, assignments, and general understanding of the course materials.

Two Weeks Prior to Class

Set a Formal TA Meeting

Set a formal meeting for two weeks before classes start for any questions about the structure of the course. Clarify all questions at this time and have the TAs post office hours.

Check Text Materials

Check the bookstore to be sure that your text and ancillary materials have arrived and that there are sufficient quantities for your class. Many times bookstores will not have all the materials you ordered on the shelves by the first day of class and you must adjust your schedule. Put necessary materials on reserve at the library or online.

Contact your publisher's representative for any missing or low quantity items. By now you should have your ancillary package or a password for their Internet site. Run the test item file to be sure that it is compatible with your computer and that the disk was not damaged in transit or that the download was successful.

Projected Student Enrollments

Most schools will register students in advance, sometimes months in advance. At my school we register for the fall semester at the end of March. If this procedure is used at your school, ask the registrar for the projected enrollment for your section; they keep historical data on your classes. Or more likely, this information is now posted on the school's Internet site and you will have direct access to it. This will provide an idea of the number of students that you will be able to add to your section. At my university, the add/drop procedures begin the first week of the term, and up to 20 percent of the class may add/drop. If you do not track these add/drops, you can overfill your class and have students sitting on the floor for your first examination. Another possibility is that you will under-enroll your class, in which case the administration might question why your classes are not at capacity.

Visit Your Classroom

Check out the lighting arrangements, and know which switches turn on which lights. There are typically two sets of switches in each room, in the front and back; find both sets. Check the heating/cooling systems, and/or the operation of windows. As you know, a very hot or cold classroom is not conducive to learning. Check the operation of the presentation projection equipment, Classroom Response Systems (Clickers) and video facilities. Investigate whether you will have to show your own videos, CD-ROMs, or DVDs, or if there is a school service. If there is a service, take the time to meet the supervisor. Check the operation of the overhead projector equipment if used (last century stuff), determine the distance the projector needs to be from the screen, learn where the cord plugs in and, most importantly, how to replace the spare bulb in the overhead projector; they can burn out during the term. If you cannot replace the bulb yourself, locate a back-up projector that you can use on short notice (minutes). The department will usually have an old overhead reserved for this purpose. Locate and test the microphone, if applicable. Then sit in the back row of the room and try to visualize what the students will see. Try to prepare your presentations, slides, and visual aids so that these students will be able to see and understand these materials. This will also give you a gauge of the size to write on the chalkboard (if anyone still does this) or the size to project your slides. Try different styles and font sizes in your presentation slides until you find the best for this specific room. I have found that the students who choose to sit in the last rows of the classroom may not be as interested in the course materials as other students, but the first time they cannot see the presentation, they will complain. Know the room and all the operations of the mechanical equipment. The first impression the students receive should be that you have been teaching in this room for years, not that this is your first class. You will be nervous enough without trying to find the plug for the presentation slide projector.

If the presentation equipment is mobile, move it into a position for optimum projection. I mark the floor, if tile or concrete, with a marking pen to locate the wheel positions. If you have carpet, use tape to mark the position. Test the equipment and run through several presentation slides. Have a friend sit in the back of the room to insure that they can hear you and see the presentation slides. Always assume that you will have to take a few minutes to set up the presentation equipment and download your lecture for each class.

One Week Prior to Class

Finalize

Finalize your syllabus, course and presentation outlines. Ask the departmental administrator to produce any student handouts for the first day of class. Make any last minute decisions about the course content. Remember, no matter how hard you try to make your first class perfect, there will be mistakes. Be flexible and correct the errors with minimum effort and lost time. Often a last minute change can be made and shown as a presentation slide the first day of class.

Final Rehearsal

Begin the final rehearsal for your first lecture and use the actual lecture room if possible. Load all presentation materials into the presentation equipment. Check the operation of this equipment and become familiar with usage. Use a friend, colleague, or departmental mentor to practice the timing and delivery of your lecture. This will give you a feel for the acoustics of the room and how the mechanical components of the room operate, or not. It is better to learn that the presentation projector is unsuitable for the screen or that your transfer disk/flash drive is not compatible with the presentation equipment during a rehearsal and not when 350 students are watching.

Relax and enjoy the rest of the week before classes start; your life is about to get even more confusing, very soon.

Chapter 3

Developing a Structure for the Class

By now you should have completed lectures for the first several weeks and be planning and writing subsequent lectures. It is important that you keep at least three weeks ahead of the class in preparing your lectures; there are always unforeseen problems that could disrupt your schedule. An illness, a family emergency, or an accident could compress your time to prepare lectures. I also think that it is important to let these lectures sit for a couple of days before you finalize and proof the content. You may have a better feel for what works in your lectures after you have presented the first few. Be flexible and willing to change in order to maximize your first presentation of each lecture.

General Considerations for the Class

Guest Lecture Confirmations

Re-contact your first guest lecturer and set a specific date, time, and topic or title. Occasionally, a guest lecturer will not be able to honor the commitment made earlier when planning your course. If the inability to honor the invitation is sincere, ask to reschedule for a later date. Often the guest will be happy to do so. This opportunity to reschedule also gives you the chance to judge the motivation of the guest. Guest lecturers offer the opportunity to have an expert in your particular field give a short but interesting presentation. Choose the guest carefully; he or she, for the most part, welcomes the opportunity. One advantage of guest lecturers is the ability to fill a gap in your experience. Select these individuals because they will, first, give the class a new perspective that you might not feel comfortable presenting and, second, they will give the students a break from your lectures and a chance to experience a different lecturer. It is a nice touch to take your guest out to lunch either before or after the lecture.

Managing the Large Class

Classes over 100 Students

One aspect of the large class often overlooked is that students, as a rule, do not like to sit through lectures. A student's interest level is usually the class period minus 10 minutes. This seems to be a universal constant. Try to use guest speakers, films, videos, and demonstrations as much as possible to augment and break up your lectures. Keep student interest high and, thus, attendance at a maximum. This is very important. There are fewer events more disappointing than arriving at a large class to find about 30 percent of the class attending. You should strive to motivate your students so that they want to attend every class period. One of the best reinforcers you can receive is a spontaneous positive comment from a student about your class. These comments motivate you to want to work even harder.

Classroom Response Systems (Clickers)

Using clickers in large classes can have several advantages. First, you can easily obtain class attendance by having the student initialize their clickers by pushing a response key. Taking attendance was almost impossible in a large class in the past. Second, you can give short quizzes at the beginning of the class, which allows students who are attending to get course points. This method also helps encourage students to read the text in advance of the lecture. Third, you can use clickers for exams. Display your exam questions one at a time for 45 seconds using your presentation software, have the students respond with their clickers. This will save lots of paper and money for your department. Students generally like clickers and believe that they enhance the classroom experience.

Demonstrations in the Large Class

Demonstrations are a must because they do not involve direct student participation. Some volunteers from the class may be needed, but the class as a whole does not have to participate. Some demonstrations are very short and can be used as lecture lead-ins, while others will take an entire class period. Use these demonstrations to add flavor to your lectures and break the straight lecture-only format. As you find good demonstrations, add them to your lectures, and continue to try out new demonstrations each term. Demonstrations can be found in the instructor's resource manual of most texts and at the publisher's Internet site.

Activities in the Large Class

Activities, on the other hand, are very hard to manage in a large class. They involve class participation and usually are not appropriate for the large lecture course. Even though activities are hard to accommodate in a large class, try a couple during your first term; this will give you a feel for the type of problems that you are likely to confront in future activities. Activities can be found in the instructor's resource manual of most texts and at the publisher's Internet site.

Alternate Formats for Activities in the Large Class

An alternative format that could be built into courses at your school is the use of recitation or lab sections. Students sign up for a specific time in addition to the lecture time. For my introductory course my department has chosen a weekly format of 3 hours of lecture and 2 hours of lab. This allows us to have a lab section meeting every other week. During the lab sections we do activities, demonstrate principles from lectures, discuss these principles from different perspectives, collect data from class experiments, discuss the examinations, give practice examinations, and answer questions concerning the lecture. The staffing of these sections can be trained, upper division majors, paid teaching assistants or graduate teaching assistants. Lab sections serve several functions for the students. First, it allows the students in the lab section to have a better understanding of the course content because we limit the size of the sections to 25 students. Many of the principles are discussed in the smaller sections and are better understood by individual students. Secondly, the lab section allows students to have direct access to a "teacher" to ask questions and discuss topics in greater depth. Finally, this format allows students to meet other students and have more personal interaction in an otherwise very large lecture class. The undergraduate and graduate instructors receive several benefits from this recitation format. They are allowed to "teach" other students about the topic area, with the department carefully monitoring their teaching and secondly, they experience teaching. This first interaction with students can help them with career choices. Finally, they can list this teaching experience on their vitae when applying for graduate school or employment.

My department has hired paid GTAs to conduct these lab sections in my introductory course. Since these instructors are paid employees of the university, we can allow these GTAs some latitude in what they teach. The benefits to the GTAs are they get to have primary control over their sections and gain valuable teaching experience. In addition, they receive a reasonable salary and they can list this teaching on their vitae when applying for other graduate schools or employment. Either plan could work at your school. Discuss alternatives with your course supervisor or department head.

For upper-division classes, laboratory sections can have similar advantages for the students and the instructors.

Structured Journals in the Large Class

In the past in addition to the recitation sections, I have also instituted a structured journal writing component in my introductory course. This journal writing consists of two types of items. The first are structured items that are keyed to the text materials and coincide with the lectures. The students must read the text and attend the lectures to be able to write these journal entries. The students like these entries because they allow them to study the text materials a little at a time and force them to keep up with the readings. The second type of entry is the personal entry that is not keyed to the text or the lectures, but rather is of a personal exploration nature with each individual thinking how the course material impacts a specific aspect of their lives.

This format gives the large class a more personal touch and is gaining favor around the country. The students like the recitation sections and the journals and so do the recitation leaders. If these types of changes are beyond your control, you might suggest them to your introductory coordinator or department head.

Films in the Large Class

Films were a useful tool in the large class during the last century; they allowed all students in the room to have a good view of the content. Unfortunately, many of the visual aids available today are not in the 16mm film format, but rather in video or DVD. Many of the films available are very old, of 1975 or earlier vintage. Many sources for films can be found in the instructor's resource manual associated with your text. I would preview all films before presenting them to the class. I also discuss the fact that since most of these films are so old, the people dress "funny." I usually tell the students that this is how their parents dressed, especially if there is a very stereotyped "hippie" in the film. I will tell the students this is how their father or mother really looked before the student was born. They always enjoy this disclaimer. I do emphasize that the principles that are discussed in these older films are still relevant today and that many of the individuals and situations in the films are classics in the study of specific disciplines. I tell the students to look past the clothes or hair styles and try to understand the principles that are being discussed. A good option is to have the old fragile 16mm film transferred to video or DVD; this process is relatively inexpensive and assures this classic material can be used for many more years.

Videos and DVDs in the Large Class

Videos and DVDs, on the other hand, can be very up to date, interesting, and contemporary. However, there is a major drawback to videos/DVDs: many schools do not have large format projection video players, but rather TVs and VCR/DVD players. These have limited use because of the size of the screen and thus the number of students who can view the programming. A possibility is to show videos/DVDs outside of the regular class time. Plan to have a smaller room and show the video/DVDs several times each day. If you wish, you could keep class roll or have questions on your examination. These videos/DVDs can also be shown in the recitation or lab sections.

If you are using presentation software for your lectures, your projector should have the ability to present videos/DVDs. There is no set-up time as with films. I can show a short video/DVD at the end of my lectures to reinforce important points.

Handouts in Large Sections

Handouts in large classes can be expensive to produce for the quantity necessary, but are useful. I find handouts worthwhile and the students like them. Handouts, such as outlines or summaries of your lecture or presentation slides are always appreciated by the students. Disadvantages of handouts are the costs of production, your time assembling the information, and the problem of students who miss class and want a copy of the handout from a week ago. You will find yourself either carrying a pile of old handouts or having a line of students trailing you back to your office. A possible solution to the handout problem is to include them in the syllabus or sell the students the handouts at cost through your bookstore. Putting the handouts on reserve in the library is also a relatively easy alternative. Finally, posting on the Internet at your class website will allow students to help absorb the cost by printing their own handouts.

Specific Problems of Large Classes

Classes of over 100 students have the additional problem of the background noise level. Very large classes can drown out your voice in the back of the room. Many students in the back of the room may lose interest because they cannot hear you; use the microphone when available. Students talking in large classes disrupt the class and annoy the instructor. One way I deal with the problem of talking during lectures is to ask the offending students if they would like to come down front and share their conversation with the rest of the class. A second method is to mention that the current section of lecture will be on the test or simply put up a new presentation slide. A final method is to talk to the student offenders privately after class; a little fear goes a long way. Our school newspaper is delivered on Tuesdays and Thursdays. I always know when the student newspaper has been delivered because the students are all trying to read the paper at the start of class. Ask them to put the paper away; be specific and forceful about this the first time it happens. One method that works is to not enter the room until you are ready to lecture and the class period has just begun. Try to enter from the front of the room near the podium, turn on the presentation equipment, open your notes, and start to lecture. If you are consistent with your arrival time students will become accustomed to this method and will settle down more rapidly. Realize that if you lose control (students talking, rustling papers, reading the newspaper) of a very large class, it is hard to regain control in that class period. A final method is to suggest that today's lectures will be emphasized on the examination.

Cell phones/Smartphone: everyone has one now and they have forgotten, or never learned, the rules of not disturbing others with their conversations. I really do not care about your boyfriend, girlfriend or medical problems. I request that they never bring an armed phone to class. A ringing cell phone disrupts the entire class. I than tell a story (urban legend) of a colleague that confiscated a ringing cell phone and then reserved the option to call any one in the world the he wanted. That usually puts a halt to cell phones ringing in class.

Texting is an ongoing problem. At any one time in a class of 100, probably 20 students are texting. I find it disheartening that students would rather waste time texting than listening to the lecture they paid for, but then, I am old-fashioned.

Learning Student Names in the Large Classroom

I find that it is almost impossible to learn the names of students in large classes. I do tell the students, however, that I remember most of their faces. I can make the distinction between students who have been in my class and those who have not. Several years after a student has taken Introductory Psychology, I will see him or her in a grocery store and recognize the face; I always say hello. Not knowing the students' names is advantageous in that you cannot be biased in your grading.

Internet Applications in the Large Class

Because you have Internet connectivity and projection facilities in your classroom, you can choose an Internet site to end each lecture. Set your browser to the site and spend the last several minutes of class exploring the site. You can access the publisher's Internet site to demonstrate student features or use demonstration and activities the published has posted.

Developing an Internet Site for Class

It is expected that you have a dedicated site for your class or use a publisher's course management system. I would include at least the class syllabus, presentation slides if you decide to post these, home-work assignments, and exam grades at this site. You should also develop a home page for your academic materials and link to your department home page. Use software provided by your textbook publisher or commercial products like, Blackboard WebCT or D2L.

Managing the Small Class

Advantages and Disadvantages of the Small Class

Small sections (30 or fewer students) have their own pluses and minuses. The first positive is that you will get to know each student's face and, possibly, name. Students like to have a personal relationship with the professor. Secondly, discussion is possible during the course of your lectures and we all know that many times the most interesting and important principles are developed during these class discussions. Small classes have a different feel than large lecture hall classes. I get the feeling that I am teaching students, not just lecturing to a full auditorium. Several advantages of the small class are that eye contact can be made with individuals, students can't sleep in the back, there is less talking, and the students feel they are active participants, not simply going to the "show." Unfortunately, very few schools have the resources to fund small sections of introductory courses. If you have a small section, you are very lucky.

Learning Students' Names in Small Classes

Learning students' names can best be accomplished by making a name/face association. I pick out some physical characteristic of the individual—style of clothing, hair style, accent, or other physical characteristic of the individual and then I make a short story using the face and characteristic. In small classes with a little practice you can learn most of the students' names when you see their faces.

A second method uses the fact that many students sit in the same area or even the same seat in a room each day of class. This second method of learning names of the students is to devise a seating chart with individual names of each student/seat and to ask questions during your lecture to specific students. This use of a seating chart may seem old-fashioned, but it will have two effects. The first is that the students will have an impression that this is a more personal class and, second, the students will have to keep current with the readings to be able to understand the questions you ask them specifically. You could use a classroom response system as an extra credit point system for correct answers to lecture questions in a small class.

Demonstrations in the Small Class

Demonstrations in small classes are really no different than in those of large classes except that students will have the opportunity for extended in-depth discussion during the demonstration. The logistics are the same for you in a small class.

Activities in the Small Class

Activities are a real possibility in small classes; there are many activities available for small groups. Some short five-or ten-minute activities at the start of the class will involve the students in a concept or demonstrate a point and can be used as a lecture lead-in. Activities in small classes are fun for both the instructor and the students. Take the time to plan your activities and modify each activity after the class. Some will work nicely; others will be total failures. Some can be modified by you to fit your particular situation; try to establish a core list of useful activities. Many very good activities can be found in your instructor's resource manual associated with your text.

Journals in the Small Class

The type of journals mentioned in the large group section above could be instituted in the smaller lecture section. This is especially advantageous because you will get to know the students from a different perspective as you read these journals, rather than having your assistants read the journals. You can have the students use the structured questions or make the journal more personal, even to the point of a daily diary of their thoughts.

Films, Videos, and DVDs in the Small Class

Films have no advantage in a small class, but videos/DVDs do, primarily because some schools do not yet have the large format video projection devices discussed above, but rather TVs and VCRs. In a small class, the students can see the TV.

Handouts in the Small Class

Handouts in small classes can be more extensive, with less cost per section. You can use a variety of handouts to supplement your text, but be careful not to violate copyright laws when preparing them. You can give the students handouts for homework and then go over it the next class period. Many of the most interesting new concepts are not yet in print and can be introduced through handouts. You can discuss rapidly changing events that happened within the last week through the use of handouts. Copies of newspaper articles are especially practical for this rapid turnaround and discussion format. The same distribution solutions can be used as discussed for large classes above.

Visual Aids in the Small Classroom

Visual aids are not as important in a small class. You can use the chalkboard, last century technology, in a small class; the students in the back of the class can see the materials. However at a minimum, overheads, if you insist, are still useful and the students in the back of the room can always see the materials. You can pass around photographs, models and other items and be fairly confident that they will be returned.

I still recommend using presentation software even in the smaller classroom. With the trend to increase the size of classes, you may find your small class has changed to a large class.

Developing an Internet Site for Class

It is expected that you have a dedicated site for your class. I would include at least the class syllabus, presentation slides, home-work assignments, handouts, and exam grades at this site. You should also develop a home page for your academic materials, and link to your department home page. Commercial software is available for this: you can choose Dreamweaver, or Nvu, which is freeware. Most textbook publishers have Internet hosting materials for text users.

Managing the Class—General Comments

When Things Go Wrong

No matter how hard you try to set up your class, there will be occasions when things will go wrong. Stay as flexible as you can and adopt the attitude that this is your first try at teaching and that these mistakes can be turned into a positive means of improving your course. The next time you teach the course, it will be much easier; the major mistakes will have been corrected. Additionally, the second time you teach the course you will be less nervous, although you will always be a little nervous. Adopt the attitude that this is your best first effort and improvements are sure to follow.

Night Classes

I have taught many night sections of introductory classes. I find these classes a nice change from the traditional day sections. You will get a very different mix of students; this is especially true if you are in a large city. The students in night classes are often employed during the day or are students who prefer to have more free time during the day to study, do research, or recreate. I find the typical night students to be very motivated and ready to learn. These students come to class prepared and full of energy. Many of these night students are taking Introductory Psychology as their first class in college; they want to see if they like college and if they can perform at the college level. Most of these students are very capable and enjoy an opportunity to learn. I find that many will become full-time day students in the future. I try to encourage these night students as much as possible; they may not have attended college for any number of reasons, from dropping out of high school, getting married, raising a family, starting a job, or simply lacking interest or motivation. These students are now ready to learn; quite a refreshing change from many of the day students. Help these night students navigate the bureaucracy of your school and encourage them as much as possible.

If you can accommodate a night class schedule, I would recommend doing so. Who knows how much fun you will have? As you mature and build a family, these night classes will become less attractive.

Developing an On-Line Class

There is a growing need for on-line classes. Many colleges and universities are experimenting with this delivery system. One of the primary driving forces for traditional (AKA bricks and mortar) institutions is cost of delivery. There is a perception that on-line class will be less expensive to deliver and will generate large sums of revenue for the school. This assumption maybe a little optimistic but there is a real need for this type of delivery. Many students have other pressing issues in their lives like family, employment or mobility issues. Being able to take classes in non-traditional time slots is a major advantage for many students. Many on-line students are taking class for possible career enhancement, higher pay. This may or may not happen, but the perception is that a college degree or classes will pay off in the long run. Is there really a large untapped pool of potential students just waiting for someone to help them? Commercial for-profit Colleges and Universities are now very common and almost all deliver their material online. See discussion below.

Developing the Online Class (History)

This is a daunting exercise and has been tried since the inception of the internet. At my university there have been several failed attempts. The first was in the mid 1990's when there was a large push to increase student credit hours with little funding support. The proposal was for faculty to develop online classes in their specific disciplines. Individual faculty were to receive a one course release for this effort. Hardly worth the effort but many still considered the challenge. I considered doing this until I ask "The" question: who has the copyright on the work? The university said they would retain the copyright, and that the release from one course was enough compensation. Guess what? Almost no one did the courses. The university would just plug in the course with any instructor, usually a low paid adjunct, and make a profit.

The most recent attempt has been to have faculty develop courses with online software like WebCT, BlackBoard or Desire2learn. With the use of these platforms school can more easily convert to an on-line environment. If you choose to make the effort to develop an on-line course try to retain the copyright. You might leave your current position and having an Internet ready course will make you much more attractive to any potential employers.

Online Course Development Tools

There are several good sites for of information on how to develop a site. I like http://www.onlineteachingtips.org/ the most. Another good source is http://www.facultyfocus.com/, or look for any current on-line classes at your school - no need to reinvent the wheel.

For Profit Online School

The business community has decided that there is a profit to be made with on-line degrees. The same reasons for interest in on-line courses listed above apply here. Students must be very careful that the on-line for-profit schools are properly accredited and are a legitimate school with degree granting power. You can buy a worthless degree, BS, MS, or PhD for very little money if you want something to hang on your wall.

There are many accredited online schools that have respected degree programs. Potential students should do a little research to make sure that the degree and fit with the school are really what you want to pay for. Some places to start your search are: http://www.elearners.com/ and http://www.bestcollegesonline.com/.

Chapter 4

Facilitating the First Class Meeting

Sure, I was excited when I got this job, but now it is 15 minutes until my first class meeting. I wish I hadn't accepted this job. Maybe I should go to my classroom. They are starting to fill the room; guess I will go down in back of the stage. Let's see, I have my notes, class rolls, presentation slides, hair combed. Man, am I nervous. Let's see, what was it that I was going to start with? I think I will sneak a peek in the door. Oh no, I think there must be 300 students in there and they all expect me to teach this class. Too late to call in sick. What will I do? Hey, there is a student standing in the shadows. What is she doing back here? "Miss, are you lost? First day in school and first class for you, huh? You say you are scared? Tell you what, let's both pretend we have been doing this for years and go in there and dazzle them, OK? Time to go; "good luck to both of us." Throughout that term this young woman sat in the front row and we both had a great class.

The Beginning of My Teaching Career

Planning the First Class

Preparing the Foundations for the First Class

How do you prepare for your first class? Realize that this may be one of the most stressful events of your academic life, especially if your section is a very large one. Most graduate schools emphasize research over teaching and now you are about to pay for this skewed emphasis. Any time you are in a new situation, you are a little stressed, but conducting your first class with 300 students is really going to be stressful. Some instructors deal with this stressful anxiety by handing out the syllabus and then leaving the class without any discussion—students like this approach. Sure, this reduces the instructor's anxiety, but it does little in the way of constructive use of time. Since first impressions of you and the course are going to last a long time, take this opportunity to work on reducing your anxiety and improving your first impression. One method to reduce this stressful anxiety is to focus on the fact that you know the material in this course better than any of the students. You are the expert!

Give Them Structure

Students expect some form of structure from you. In introductory classes they are typically new students and do not really know what to expect from college classes. The most important thing you can provide the first day is structure. Let the students know what is expected of them in terms of class content, classroom behavior, and what they can expect from you in terms of teaching style. The students attend class wanting to know what the course is about and what kind of teacher you will be. Remember that the students are from diverse backgrounds throughout the community and country and will have different expectations of you and the course. They are all enrolled in other courses; some will be entering freshmen while others are graduating seniors. One of your tasks is somehow to shift this group of individuals from whatever state they enter the classroom toward wanting to study the course material. This can be harder than you think. There appears to be a lag time before students can begin to concentrate after a previous class; this time seems to be about 15 minutes. Your task is to shorten this lag time and get your lecture underway. I think demonstrations/discussions are a good method of re-energizing students' interest in your subject matter. Sometimes a presentation slide that requires the students to copy a significant amount of material as the first task of the period will facilitate this shift to thinking about the course material. I have found that it is best not to let the students continue to talk while you stand in front of the class. Use whatever technique that works, but gain control of every class and do it as early in the class period as possible.

Reducing Instructor Anxiety

Prior to the start of each class period, I like to take ten minutes to clear my thoughts; I just sit in my office, lights off, telephone off the hook, computer off, with the door closed, and relax. If anyone asks what I am doing, I tell them that I am meditating, which is partially true. I need this relaxing time to lower my anxiety level and prepare for the task ahead. Even after 30 years of teaching I still need this time. Taking a walk, getting a drink of water, staring out the window, or taking a final look at your lecture notes may work for you. Find out what relaxes you and use it just prior to class. I dislike it when a student comes to my office with a problem five minutes before the start of class; this interruption throws off my preparation and timing for the entire class. When I enter the classroom, I head directly for the podium. With a presentation software podium, start to boot the system, which usually takes several minutes. After reaching the podium, I look around the classroom and try to make eye contact with as many students as possible. Strange, yes, but this allows me to do two things. First, no matter how many times you enter a large classroom for the first class period, there is a level of anxiety; I still get nervous after 30 years. This pause to look at the class allows me to see if there are any familiar faces in the class. It could be a person you met in the student union building, at a party, or in the department. One recognizable face will help lower your anxiety or you might see your department chair or Dean, thus raising your anxiety significantly. Don't worry, he/she usually is too busy to attend your first lecture. Second, at this time I begin to pick out the individuals to whom I will direct my lecture. What do I mean by individuals? There are 300 individuals in the room! One of the techniques that I use is to select four or five students in the classroom to direct my lectures to; pick students from different sections, left, right, front, and back. How do you pick them? Your own personal taste dictates this, but I find someone who dresses differently or has a different hair style; this allows me to find this student at the beginning of each lecture. I use these individuals to monitor their note taking and adjust my speed of presentation so that my lectures are not too fast or slow. I can observe perplexing looks in these target individuals and go over difficult sections again. Bored expressions on these target students means speed up this section of lecture. Laughter at some of my attempts at humor are marked down in my notes for use in future classes. It is really weird; what I think is funny often is not, but students will laugh at inane comments for years. These attempts at humor are nice to have as a break during boring sections of your lectures.

Making Personal Contact

After the first class meeting is completed I always like to talk to as many students as I can right before my next lecture starts. This may entail standing by the door just to smile and saying hello to students as they enter. I also like to make a casual acquaintance with the individuals in the first two rows of the classroom. These are usually your best students and are often the nontraditional students. A problem with many classrooms is that they look the same. You will know you are in the right room when you see these front row students. The students like personal contact; they feel more like individuals. If I am early to a class, I do not stand in front of the class waiting for the starting time but rather walk around to different sections and talk to individual students, which reduces my anxiety and lets me meet more students.

Show No Fear

Do not show any fear of teaching the subject matter or the students will quickly learn to disrespect you. Try not to admit that this is your first class on this subject matter. Act like you have been teaching this course for years. If you do not know the answer to a question, tell the students that you will research the best answer and provide information at the next class period. As you gain teaching experience, you will be able to synthesize answers on the spot. Students have an intrinsic respect for professors; do not lose your class's respect the first day. Show no fear!

The Class Icebreaker—What First?

This is it! No more fooling around. What first? Write your name and the course title and course number on the chalkboard or show the first presentation slide with your personal information. Or start your presentation software with an interesting slide or picture; humor is good here. This may seem very simple, but it will relax you and the students will know they are in the right classroom. I always have a few new freshmen who do not know the rooms or numbers and think that they are in a physics class, so announce the title and course number. Additionally, most of the students in the room are seeing you for the first time; they can start to make the name-face associations between you, the course, and the room.

In a Small Class

Go around the room and ask each student his/her name, major, year, where he/she is from and what I like to call a "claim to fame"—bungee jumped last weekend, first hang gliding flight, made the football team, presidential scholar, foreign student, traveled over break—anything they think is special about themselves. This gives you a chance to know the composition of the class by major and year and you can start to learn the names and faces of the students. This also puts the students at ease and allows them to get to know who is in the class and who they might like to meet.

In a Large Class

Ask for a show of hands by year. In introductory classes I find: entering freshmen typically at least half of the class, then sophomores, juniors, seniors, and graduate students. This quick impression of the large class allows you to get a feel for the level of the class. Also ask for a show of hands for major; be general, like "engineering," not "civil engineering." This will give you a rough idea of the types of majors to whom you will be lecturing.

I always welcome the new freshmen and give them a short pep talk on how "these are the good old days." These are the days of great academic and personal discovery and they should be savored. I also make a few remarks about how these new students need to balance their academic work with other social aspects of college.

Hand out the Syllabus

In both small and large sections, hand out the syllabus, see Appendix A. I make a presentation slide and go over each section: grading, when papers are due, examination dates, assigned chapters, makeup examination policy, and extra credit. Answer any questions the students have concerning the general content in the syllabus. Post the syllabus to your course web page or course management software.

Give a Detailed Explanation of the Course

In addition to the syllabus, what exactly is expected from the students and how will they be evaluated? This should take the entire first period. During this time, the students will have their first impression of your teaching style. The students will often evaluate this first encounter in terms of how enthusiastic you appear to be during your first meeting. The students want an objective class; be as fair as possible with the students and treat them as adults. A brief overview of the class will also give the students their first introduction to your lecturing style.

Explaining Grades

Grades are always a major part of the students' concerns. Be as objective and fair as you can with grades. You have been in school for many years, often in a different part of the country, and you may not be familiar with the level of student expectancy concerning grades at your new school. Take the time to ask students, faculty, and your departmental mentor what is an average grade for this class, department, and institution. After you get to know the class better, tell them that it is not the grade that counts, but rather the knowledge they gain from the course. Evidence of this principle can be found in the Graduate Record Examination (GRE) and the career that you are now trying to prepare them for. They will wish they had paid attention in all those undergraduate classes when the real evaluations come in the future, not some letter grade. Structure the course to be as fair as possible. No special favors like extra credit opportunities should be given to any student simply because they came to your office and asked. All students must have the same opportunity.

Care about Your Students

Students also want an instructor who cares about the students as individuals and attempts to understand their problems. I always think of the students as my responsibility and it is my duty to do as much as possible to help them through this first course in the discipline. This may entail conferences in my office, help in finding tutors, calming the students prior to a test, or just understanding the problems of being an entering freshman or returning nontraditional student. I enjoy seeing my students several years later graduate from the university; many become acquaintances during their college days. See Chapter 8 for more details.

Do Not Bore the Students

Finally, students do not want to be bored. Students already have plenty of boring classes in the large lecture situations; let yours be their best experience. You do not have to be a stand-up comic, but try to lighten up the lectures with a little humor. This humor can take many forms, from jokes about college sports teams, politics, and local problems to presentation slides of cartoons from the newspaper or Internet. Have a little fun with the students; it will do both of you some good. When you are done with your lecture for the day, quit. Do not try to pad the last few minutes, let them go a few minutes early. I always tell the students they can take the last four minutes of the class to study for the examination, which they find funny.

Things to Consider When Structuring Your Class

The following are some suggestions about how to maximize the impact of your presentations when designing your class.

Come Prepared

Do not let the class flow without structure. Have a lecture planned and stick to it, detail the schedule in the course syllabus. The use of learning points is a good method to give structure to the class if you choose to use them. Presentation software can add an element of color and motion to your lectures and are expected as a minimum in today's classes.

Always Start the Class on Time

If you are late, the students will realize when class really starts and they will start to come later and later. Make the first several minutes very important. While your computer is booting, talk about the next examination and give specific details about projects. Make the first material of the class relevant to the examinations so that students who are ready and taking notes will be rewarded. Use clickers to encourage the students to arrive on time in order to receive point for clicker participation.

Avoid Philosophical Questions in Large Introductory Classes

The students typically do not care about the meaning of life, philosophical, or ethical applications of academic principles. In smaller upper-division classes these types of questions can be very productive. Ask questions that do not require a large amount of background knowledge. These introductory students will not have the necessary background to answer very complex questions.

Respect Your Students

You have finally achieved some status in your academic area, but do not try to reduce your frustrations by showing disrespect for your students. Remember, you were a student several years ago. New instructors can become obsessed with their new status and power, not treating students with respect—do not be guilty of this.

Establish that You are in Charge of the Class

Do not let students talk or be disruptive in class. Occasionally, there will be a student who asks questions that seem inappropriate to the main theme of the class. If this student persists, ask the student to save the question for after class or during office hours. It is relatively easy for students to get their instructor off track and onto a tangent. Most students can figure out that this tangential material will not be on the examination, and some students will try to direct your attention from the lecture. If students continue to talk during your lectures, use the "evil eye" stare at the offending student and stop lecture until they stop talking. This really works. If necessary pull the students aside after class and ask them not talk.

Use Terminology that is Appropriate for Your Students' Level

Do this both in your lectures and in examinations. When 50 percent of the class asks the meaning of a specific term on an examination, you know that the level is inappropriate. Students have a decreasing vocabulary when entering college or university.

Examinations for Introductory Classes: Be as Specific as Possible

Make the questions easier than you think they need to be. You have just learned the material at a level the instructor must master, not an entering freshman. If you have examination questions specific to your lectures, tell the students the first day of class and just prior to the first examination. I identify my questions as lecture questions and write them so that if a student is in class they will probably get the correct answer; if they are not in class it is very difficult to guess the correct answer.

Do not Write Tricky Questions on Your Examinations

If a student knows the material, he or she wants to receive credit for a correct answer. Do not be obscure in your wording or syntax.

Ensure Material on the Examinations will be Covered in Class

I usually leave about 1/2 of a lecture's materials off the current examination to be sure I cover all the material. As you teach the class, you will learn how much material you can cover in a specific time period. It is always better to be short on the last lecture rather than long to avoid rushing to complete the material. Be sure that you tell the students where the material for the current examination ends in the class notes.

Minimize the Turnaround Time for Examination Grading

If you are giving multiple choice questions, have them scored as soon as possible. With essay tests, I like to schedule the test for a Friday so I can have the tests scored by Monday morning. The use of course management software can minimize this turnaround time issue.

Encourage Students to Challenge Examination Questions

I have the students write their challenges out on paper and then come to my office to discuss their answers. If I agree with the challenge I have a copy of the reason for the change and then file the challenge in my grade change folder. More recently I have allowed students to e-mail challenges.

Encourage Students to Check Answer Keys and Postings

If there are discrepancies, again encourage the students to stop by your office to check their score. I offer to hand score any exams students questioned. I rarely find errors, but it allows the students to feel like they are being treated fairly.

Encourage Nontraditional Students

These can be students over traditional age, international students, English as a second language students, individuals with special needs, and persons with both physical and learning disabilities. I like to take the time to help these students and encourage them as much as possible. In many cases, they are just starting college and have relatively low self-esteem.

Discuss Cell Phones in the Classroom

I tell the students to take out their cell phones and turn them off. When a cell phone finally rings during a subsequent class I have some cutting remark to make to the student; choose this remark in order to maximize the impact on the offender, but not at too high a level. I find the more humorous the remark the more likely students will turn off their cell phones prior to class. Texting is now a major issue in lectures. Students are good at hiding their texting activity. I sometimes ask students to raise their hands if they are texting; the number will be much larger that you might think.

Student Questions for the First Day of Class

It is paramount that the first day of class be conducted in a manner that will excite the students about the class. I have taken classes as an undergraduate where the instructor just wrote his or her name on the board, (yes a chalkboard) handed out the syllabus, (usually only one page) then announced the first assignment, and let the class out early. The class really never got any better than getting out early. You set the tone for the course and have this opportunity only once in the class. The following is a brief list of questions the students probably have but for various reasons will not ask. Try to address these questions in your introductory lecture.

Take the time to try and remember what it was like when you were an undergraduate and the types of questions you had the first day of class.

Who are You and are You Any Good at Teaching?

Are you Dr. Jones, Mr. Jones, Professor Jones or Fred? Let the students know and set the tone for future interactions. You can also mention your academic qualifications and how long you have been teaching the course. Some personal information can also help the students to understand who you are. I always tell something about golf or the old ski bum days. Again, setting the tone for future interactions is important and this is really your only opportunity to create the first impression in the course.

What Academic or Practical Skills Will I Get from this Course?

What are the specific tools and knowledge can I expect to gain in this course and is it worth the effort? If you are not a major and this is an upper-division course that is not required in your major and is intended to be a very rigorous course, perhaps an audit is in order. Having to compete with students for other majors in their required courses can be very difficult.

Who is the Course Designed for?

Is this a core class for the general population of the school or a course for specific majors? Is this an upper-division course for which prerequisites are necessary? Is it not intended for majors but rather to expose non-majors to the area, like a general astronomy course? Knowing if the course is intended for their needs will help them decide if they really want to take this course.

Who are the Students in the Class?

Are all the students of a specific major? Are the students all seniors? Does everyone seem to know each other and you are the odd person out? How comfortable are you going to be with these other students?

What's this Course About?

Your syllabus and course catalogue should answer most of these questions, but it is still a good time to review what you think the course material is to be covered. This will also give the students a hint of the flavor of your teaching style.

Will the Students Enjoy this Class?

Discuss the syllabus and goals for the course. The syllabus will be specific about how you hope to meet the goals but reinforce what you consider to be the most important points. Introduce your teaching assistants and have them indicate office hours and other contact information. Reinforce the use of any course

Web sites or publishers' CD-ROMs or Web sites available for the students. Let the students know why you consider this material so important and interesting

How Do I Get a Good Grade in this Course?

Again refer to the syllabus, see Chapter 3, which should cover all the mechanics involved in grading. The syllabus, if well written, will leave little room for questions concerning your grading policy. I discuss that one of the hardest part of any class is finding the level of the class: how hard is this class academically and how hard to I have to study to achieve a certain grade? Give any hints about this process that you can, and the truth; a drop now is better than a bunch of "F" grades later.

Introducing the Required Materials

The Text and Ancillary Materials

Introducing the text and ancillary materials is best accomplished by simply bringing them to the first class meeting. Hold the text up and explain that this is the only text that will work for this class, not a friend's book from a different class or term. I also have the study guide and any other ancillary materials recommended or required for the course. I have recently also made a presentation slide with a picture of the text and ancillary books covers and leave these on the screen as I discuss each book. If you have these materials on reserve at the library, which I recommend, tell the students their location and how long they may check out the materials. If you want a little humor at this point, say something like, "I put these materials on reserve so that if any of you have a course cancelled and you did not bring your text, you can use the reserve text for a couple of hours of study." Many students will think this is funny; so do I. Discuss your course management software, WebCT, D2L, CourseConnect or Pearson MyLab series and how to use it.

Classroom Interactive Systems (Clickers)

Discuss your expectations of the use of clickers in your class. Let the student know if they need to bring the clicker to every class and how you will be using the clickers.

The Add/Drop Problem

In a typical school you will be flooded with students wanting to add your course. It is important to know if your course is at capacity. Also the capacity of the classroom? You should know this before the first class by checking the computer printouts available from your department administrator or your school's Internet site. Ask your supervisor what the departmental policy is for adding students. Do not look like a "rate buster," adding too many students or an uncaring instructor by not adding enough. Follow and use your departmental procedures as a justification for not adding students. Many students will have desperate stories as to why they must add your class. If you have any discretionary power to add students, think about what is a valid reason to add the class, e.g., seniors needing the class to graduate, working single parent, college sports team members, those needing a prerequisite for upper-division classes, or new majors. Decide the types of justification you will allow and devise a method of selecting students to add to the course. If there are many students wanting to add the class and few seats left in class, conduct a lottery; at least this is a fair method. You will have a number of drops/no-shows for each class. Ask your department chair, supervisor, or departmental mentor what percentage of students may remain of the final class roll and add the approximate number to fill the class to capacity. Be careful not to overfill a class, or you will have students sitting in the aisles at the examinations. Sign all drop slips and note the number for your records, keeping a running total. Be firm with students who have missed the first class and want to add when they stop by your office; tell them the class is full. The add/drop system can be very frustrating and time consuming.

Evaluate Your First Teaching Experience

Return to your office and review your first day's performance. What were the high points? What makes you want to return to the next class? Also, what were the low points? How could you improve these areas? Write these suggestions down and put them in your course folder or add changes to your presentations slides for the next time you teach the class. I use a folder for each section of lecture including the introduction to the class.

Go home and celebrate! But not too much; remember, you have to write next week's lectures tomorrow.

Chapter 5

Considerations in Developing Examinations

Most colleges and universities use traditional systems of evaluating students, commonly called grades. Included in these methods of evaluation is the use of examinations.

Ramblings about the Grading System

For many students the emphasis on receiving a letter grade next to his or her name on a transcript is even more obnoxious today than in previous generations. I find this trend has greatly increased in just the past five years and continues today. Many students believe that the short-term reinforcement of receiving a high grade in a course is the major reason for attending college. To that end, they will go to great lengths to receive a high grade in your course. On the first day of class when I review how grades are earned, while discussing the syllabus, I tell the students that they all have one hundred percent of the course points and thus an "A" in the course. Now all the students have to do is not lose points on the examinations, which I will deduct for the total course points. I like the idea of subtracting points for errors rather than adding points for correct answer. So now to receive the coveted "A" grade all the students have to do is not lose any points on the examinations. I have often thought this minus points system would be a superior method of grading. Too many years as a behavioral psychologist studying reinforcement theory, I guess.

Many, but not all, students are like any other organism in a Skinner Box. They will learn the minimum amount necessary to receive the reinforcement. The method that you use to structure your examinations can modify the students' behavior. If students learn that all they need to do is read the summaries an hour before the test, or if they can get the notes from a friend and receive the grade they want, then that is what they will do. If a student can get the old test and pass the course, then that is what they will do. When writing examinations, you must try to modify these behaviors. A central task of your course is to give the students a general overview of the content area.

Students learn if they must attend class to get a desired grade; many will not attend class because they have more (perceived) important things to do. Several methods can be employed to assure attendance if you consider this an important element of your course. The first method can be course points for attendance; this method may work in high school, but probably not in many colleges. This can take a very large effort on your part in large classes. Attendance has been mitigated recently with the advent of "Clickers," also called Classroom Response Systems. They allow an easy method of keeping track of attendance in the classroom and awarding course points for attendance. Discuss these with your publisher's representative if you are interested. Clicker points can be based specifically on the material from the previous lecture. You can include clicker questions when developing test items for the examinations. I prefer to write items for the examinations that are specific to the lectures. I tell the students that at least one-third of the items on an examination will be specific to the lecture. This reinforces coming to class and note-taking; getting someone else's notes is not enough to understand the nuances of my lectures. I try to write these items so that only the individuals who were in class are likely to get the correct answer, not the students who borrow notes from other students.

If your department or school has a policy of percentages equaling a certain letter grade, (A=90%, B=80%) be sure you are aware of this policy and conform to it. Some schools use the +/- grading system. This method has positives and negatives. A positive is a couple of points does not determine a big grade change, B to A for example. The students get more credit for what they have done in the class. A negative is that the grade intervals are smaller so a couple of points can make a difference more often between a B and a B+ grade. In order to help alleviate tension on the first day of class and to give the students a feel for my teaching philosophy, I tell the students that the grades they receive are not important, but the knowledge gained in the class is important. At this point, they usually laugh or at least want to. I hope eventually many of these students will understand that this short-term reinforcer of a letter grade is not all that a college education encompasses. A very good example is when the students are taking the Graduate Record Examination (GRE). The GRE is a good example of being tested over what you know about a specific subject, not what your grade was in a course. The world of work does not place any importance on the letter grade in a class, but rather how much you learned in the specific course. A new employer will expect you to be competent in your field, and if you are not he/she will simply find a new employee who is. Some students won't listen, but tell them anyway. Many students will say they "need" the grade to get into graduate school, some professional school, or an upper-division course in their undergraduate major. Perhaps we should have fewer professionals who "need" a grade this much.

You have completed several aspects of your education and could have been one of these individuals who was too interested in grades. Let's see how good you are at telling students that grades are not the most important aspect of a college education.

Examinations

Types of Examinations

When considering the type of examination to give in your course, there are several factors that should be taken into account. First, consider the amount of time that you or, in the best case, your teaching assistant will have to spend in the preparation of the examination and then grading the examination. In my experience, I have found that there appears to be a negative correlation between the amount of time spent constructing the examination and the time grading. For example, essay examinations may be one sentence long, but it may take an hour to grade each student's answer, while a multiple choice question may take 10 minutes each to develop, but involve no grading time by you or your assistants if you use computer scoring.

Many times the choice of the type of question on an examination is limited by the class size: large classes (over 50 students), multiple choice; medium classes (30 to 50 students), short answer, matching, fill-in-the-blank, or multiple choice; and for small classes (fewer than 30 students), essay questions are possible and you can also use a combination of the other methods mentioned above. In a large class, multiple choice questions are the only possible choice with the low number of TAs available to many instructors. It should be noted that all practical alternatives should be used to evaluate the students. Evaluating a student's knowledge of as many aspects of content area as possible is the most effective method of gaining a true representation of the actual knowledge achieved by the student. The adoption of journals is an alternative method of evaluation that does have promise, (see chapter 7). I have tried to develop strategies for students to self grade or grade other students' written work, although this can be very difficult to achieve. Finally, an additional consideration when selecting your type of examination is the level of the students (discussed in Chapter 2).

Construction of Examinations

Essay Questions

Essay questions should require students to integrate the class notes and the text materials. Additionally, this type of examination will focus on the analysis of the problems being discussed and, in some cases, the applications of the principles that have been introduced.

Essay questions provide the most information about the depth of knowledge of the subject matter. The main disadvantages of this format are the amount of time needed to grade each student's examination, and the subjective nature of this type of evaluation. I have found that this form of evaluation should be limited to three items per hour. With essay questions, you will know the students' depth of knowledge on a few select topics. This form of evaluation also has a subjective nature; the answers are not correct or incorrect, but are shaded between the two. Students will often challenge points on essay examinations because they believe that there may be several correct answers or lines of reasoning. The students usually feel a perfect score on an essay item is more easily attained than the instructor does. Publisher Test Items Files are a valuable source of essay questions.

Short Answer Questions

Short answer formats, which include short answer questions, fill-in-the-blank, and matching items, are a good method of evaluation because they allow for a wide range of topic coverage; you may have up to 20 short answer formatted questions per hour. This format will give the first-time instructor the opportunity to evaluate how well the class is progressing in terms of the students' understanding of the principles introduced thus far. If possible, this type of format could be developed for computer scoring. Many publishers now include computer scoring programs in their text's test item files.

Multiple Choice Questions

Your text ancillary package will include a test item file keyed to the text. This test item file is very important. During your initial evaluation of the "package" that is included with the text, you should spend time evaluating the test item file. I will not adopt a text until I have the current test item file in hand and I can evaluate how well the questions are written. Many test item files will break down the items in terms of difficulty: easy, medium, and difficult. Additionally, some texts look at the type of information the specific item examines: basic knowledge, application, connections between chapters, or critical thinking. Many test item files are keyed to the text pages. This is helpful if a student challenges an item on the examination. I usually will not adopt a first edition of a text because the test item file is often weak and the coordination between the test item file, student study guide, and instructor resource manual is insufficient. It is your initial task to evaluate this test item file or you may find yourself writing your own items. Writing items is a task you should do for your lecture portion of the text, but it is an extra burden to write text questions for the rest of the examination. Recently, Pearson publishing has developed a method of test item validation. Each item in many of their test item files has accompanying statistics. These statistics include point biserial *r*, a measure of how well the items discriminate between poor students and good students. This is a valuable set of data when developing your exams.

A second source of questions that is often overlooked is the students'. Ask the students to write their own items and submit them to you as part of a homework assignment. You can then choose the items that you like and use them on the examination. I usually like to limit these items to less than 25 percent of the items on the examination. These student-generated items will tend to be very subject matter specific and at a higher level than the items in the publisher's test item file. Usually only the better students will submit questions given the option not to submit items. Use this multiple choice question writing as an option in your course or as an extra credit assignment.

Number of Items for a Multiple Choice Examination

I have found that most of my introductory students can tolerate one item per minute for up to 60 minutes. Anything over this number and they have trouble finishing; anything less is too easy and could limit coverage of the material. I would rather have several smaller multiple choice examinations than a very long examination, and so would most students.

Loading the Computer Software

As soon as I receive my test item file from the publisher I load the software on my computer. This allows me to be assured that the software arrived in good working order, without damaged CDs or missing files from the download. Additionally, I can start to try to unravel the mysteries of how the software works. Each publisher has adopted a different type of testing software and there is a learning curve. Try an example test to get a feel for how this software works. If you have problems most publishers have a help line or contact you publisher's representative directly for assistance.

Publishers' Internet Sites

A recent trend is to eliminate the use of paper test item files and CD-ROMs for text test banks and replace them with publisher's Internet sites which are secure and password protected. Obtain the proper password from your sales representative and log on to the site. I like to make a trial exam in order to figure out the operation of the site. Better to know how it works now than in the last minutes before you are trying to produce an exam. I also like to print a hard copy of the test item files. Ask your publisher's representative if they will do this for you when you adopt their text.

Using the Test Item File (Paper)

The first thing I do when I receive my printed test item file is write or rubber stamp my name on the inside cover and on the outside page edge of the test item file. Next, I decide where I will leave the test item file in my office for the school term. This is important because misplacing a test item file can be very frustrating while trying to construct an unbiased examination. Did you lose the test item file? Did someone steal it? Where is it located now? These are not the questions you want to lose sleep over during the term. A compromised test item file is worthless. I always put the test item file back in its safe place in my locked office!

When I am choosing items for the printed test item file for my examination, I use a colored pen and write the school term, year, and section at the top of the first page of each section in the test item file: F06 (02). Then I mark each item I want to include in the examination in the test item file with the same color pen.

If you have multiple sections, use different colors for each section. This method is easy for the person doing the physical test construction and allows you to have a graphic representation of the items already used in the test item file. After I have the items marked, I count them and write the total with the same pen next to the term, year, and section. I use the same test item file as long as I use the text; this helps reduce using the same items repeatedly and also lets you know when your test item file is depleted. A major reason I change texts is that the test item file is exhausted. For example, at my school, we teach seven large sections of our introductory course a year and most test item files will be used up after one year, assuming no repeated questions.

After I have chosen the items for my examination I use the publisher's software to produce the examination. One recurrent problem with each new examination software is integrating questions you have written yourself. Take the time to understand how this can be accomplished. Most examination software can scramble questions and alternatives which will help with multiple sections.

Computer Test Scoring

A good tip is to go to the test scoring center and meet both the supervisor and the individuals who do the computer scoring. If possible have them show you the facility and explain how the equipment works. You might not really care, but act interested; these people have a stressful job. Since many of these computer centers are located in the basement of the library, it is good to remember life in the basement of the library can get really dull and anyone showing interest in the scoring process will be remembered and appreciated. Someday you may need to have a special run of test scores; hopefully, these staff members will remember your visit favorably. Ask the supervisor if there is a cover sheet for the exam scoring and ask for copies. If you have questions on how to fill out this form ask the supervisor for assistance.

Writing Your Own Multiple Choice Examination Items

For the first-time instructor, writing your own multiple choice items may be very difficult. I would recommend writing these items only for your lecture questions in the beginning. When writing your own items, a good strategy is to limit the number of distracters (incorrect answers) to three. A four-choice item examination is enough to have questions that will probe the student's level of knowledge. I like to limit the use of "all of the above" or "none of the above" as the last alternative to a maximum 15 percent of the items and I try to be careful not to establish a pattern of having these items being either correct or never being correct. When writing your own items, be sure not to develop a pattern in your answers like using the "C" alternative as the correct answer too often. Make the correct alternatives as random as possible. After some practice, try writing a few questions from the text material. This is easily accomplished by modifying current examination questions from the test item file. When you write your own items, be sure that the items covering material questions are a significant part of the materials in the text. Often I find myself being too specific when writing this type of item; the students will often perceive specific items as unfair and not a good sample of their knowledge. Be sure to use language that is appropriate to the area under study and to the level of your students. We all become locked in our research fields and must make an effort to re-learn the vocabulary of the other sub-fields often covered in a specific course. Avoid trick questions; the students will not like them, although the best student will often correctly answer these questions. Don't make the items so difficult that none of the students can answer correctly. Remember that a multiple choice item is designed to separate the students who know the concept from those who do not. If the item is too hard, no student answers correctly except the students who guess; this is the worst case. A difficult aspect of writing good multiple choice questions is writing good distracters, which are the wrong answers. Spend time writing the distracters. Distracters separate the good students from the poor students.

How to Identify a Good Publisher's Test Item File

How can you tell which is a good publisher's test item file? I use several criteria in the evaluation. First, I look at the number of items per chapter. One hundred is the minimum I would accept in a test item file. I then move to a chapter that the students typically have problems with in your specific discipline. I then evaluate some random items. Some of the areas I can assess are the correctness of the grammar and syntax and if the level of the vocabulary is similar to the text. Are the items evaluated in terms of, high, medium, and low levels? Are they evaluated in terms of content, basic knowledge, and applications? Do the items contain many "all of the above" or "none of the above"? Too many of this type of answer may mean the test item file author was running out of distracters or in a hurry to finish. Does this test item file have the same amount of coverage per topic as the text? I also like to evaluate the student study guide and the instructor's resource manual for coordination. A subjective question might be the visual appeal of the test item layout. Are the answers associated with each question located on the same page? Few readers like turning to the back of the test item file to find answers to questions. Finally, how many editions has this test item file been through? The more the better is not always a good indicator. I generally avoid first editions because of poor test item files. Has the publisher developed a method of test item validation such as point biserial *r*—a measure of how well the items discriminates between poor students and good students? If they have not ask them why.

Writing Short Answer Questions: General Case

Writing true/false, matching, fill-in-the-blank, short answer, and oral items can be difficult for the new instructor. I would first try to locate examples in your test item file or student study guide to use as a resource. If the questions are specific to your lecture, try a few on your first examination. As you gain experience writing exam questions, you will be able to expand the quantity and types of questions used. Start off slow and see what works for you and your class.

I suggest that you use the following information about examination questions as a guide in your examination construction.

True/False Items

True/false items are difficult to write because the item must be 100 percent true or false. Any exception to the true or false case negates the answer. Students are very good at finding the one example that will negate your question. I should know; I was doing this all the time as an undergraduate. Try a few true/false questions and be lenient on individual exceptions when grading.

Matching Items

Of the two basic strategies with matching items, one is to provide the same number of matching items as answers; this is the easiest type of item, particularly when a student does not know the last correct answer. The other alternative is to provide more answers than there are matching items. This can become a very difficult type of examination if properly done. Try a brief matching type question on your examination and expand as you become more familiar with the types that work best.

Fill-in-the-Blank

Fill-in-the-blank can be an effective method of testing. This is like a multiple choice item without the choices. These can vary from easy to extremely difficult, depending on your ability to write the items and the level of your students. Look in the student study guide for good examples of fill-in-the-blank items. These items are often used by the students as examples of test questions and should be used more in examinations.

Short Answers

Short answers are just that—short answers. You can limit the amount of space available for the answer on the examination and thus the length of the answer by listing several items per page and leaving the amount of space between each item as the only area for the answer. Short answer format should be used to ask specific questions for which the students need limited time and space to answer.

Oral Examinations

This is the most rigorous type of testing. You will always remember the oral defense of your graduate thesis or dissertation. This type of evaluation can be used for small classes where the instructor wants to know the scope of the students' knowledge. It is very stressful for the students, but this method will let you assess the knowledge the students have acquired in the class.

Many student study guides use the above types of questions, with the exception of oral examinations, to help the student learn the material in the course. Students will be familiar with the formats and should have little trouble with these types of items.

How Many and What Type of Questions

Ask other instructors or your mentor what types and levels of questions they use in their examinations and use their response as a guide for your examinations. A nice mix of the types of questions listed above will test all facets of the students' knowledge, but this method is impractical in most large classes. Experiment with the mix and find the best combination for you and your students. Remember, your first examination does not have to be perfect, so don't worry. When constructing examination items, try to plan ahead for scoring methods. Can you use a template or computer scoring (by far the most common method), or must you use the standard TA working on the weekend method? The more efficient and well thought out you are in the planning stages, the easier the grading.

When to Evaluate

Timing of the Examinations

Students consider examinations a very important aspect of their education, due to their overemphasis on grades. In order to calm examination anxiety, I like to have several examinations each term, up to as many as four. Many of us remember the older method of a midterm and a final as very stressful and not the most productive method of demonstrating knowledge. I will divide the term into thirds or possibly quarters with each section culminating in an examination. This method allows for at least one examination prior to course withdrawal period; if a student fails an examination, he or she can drop the course without penalty, nothing on the transcript. This withdrawal period allows students to have a second chance in their academic career rather than flunking out the first term. This early examination gives the students the opportunity to discover the kind of examinations to expect for the rest of the term and to modify their study habits in order to maximize their examination scores.

After the first examination, I offer students the opportunity to come to my office to receive some special study material I have collected over the years. These materials help students organize their studying and give them tips on how to study. See http://www.mtsu.edu/~studskl/ for more information on these tips. I also can give them advice on tutors and study groups available on campus. These students are typically good students who want to learn, but lack the skill; many improve drastically with the next examination. I track these students by asking them how they did on subsequent examinations. Many of today's students need this guidance on effective study habits because they were not taught these methods in high school.

Our withdrawal period extends past the three-quarter mark of the semester. This allows students to typically take three out of four examinations prior to the drop period. I have heard that this drop late option is very popular in the freshmen dorm crowd. They see it as a way out of a bad grade in a class. Just take the "W" at the end of the semester, looks OK on the transcript and Mom and Dad won't see an "F." The school really likes this because you pay tuition to take the class and when you get the "W" you have to enroll and to pay again. Plus freshmen tend not to flunk out the first year with this method and schools are constantly looking for ways to retain freshmen students for the second year.

Picking the Right Number of Examinations

Frequent short examinations (I prefer three or four per semester) are a better plan for a course as opposed to the older traditional format of a midterm and a final. Several short examinations provide maximum feedback and a chance to change study habits in order to adhere to the requirements you are placing on the students in your courses. They also serve as a barometer by which an instructor can gauge the efficacy of his teaching. Additionally, this gives the instructor time to adjust if necessary.

The Final Examination

Most schools still have some sort of final examination requirement, usually occurring after the conclusion of the regular teaching term. Many schools have dropped the comprehensive final exam, but your school may still require this examination. Check with your supervisor, departmental mentor, or department chair.

I prefer some form of a non-comprehensive examination for a final. I try to allow the students to choose the materials they prefer for their final; of course, this must be thought out in planning the course. One method is to group chapters not assigned during the course and then allow students to pick one group that is of special interest to the student. I like to have at least three groups of two chapters to choose from. An alternate method is to have a group of additional readings the student could select for the final. Allowing the students to choose their final examination material is a nice touch. The students get to study some aspect of the discipline that you did not have time to cover in the regular term. The students like the freedom of selecting a topic of interest for further study. Although the logistics can be a little frightening with a large class, try this system. When using multiple topic finals, I ask the departmental administrator to produce each individual examination on a different color of paper. I arrive at the final ten minutes early and set up chairs in the front of the classroom. The number of chairs is equal to the number of choices for the final. I then tape a color coordinated sign to each chair stating the examination number or chapters covered by each final. I then put the corresponding examinations on the corresponding chairs. Then I hand out the computer scoring sheets (if used) and have each student mark an unused area of the scoring sheet with a special code, in case of a mix-up of the scoring sheets. This code can be anything, but the number of the final examination group (e.g., 1,2,3,4) is the easiest. When the students have completed the computer sheet, I emphasize that the students must pick up the examination of their choice from the specific chair it is located on and (this is the important part) when they have completed the final, they must return the computer scoring sheet to the same chair. I use a little threat and tell them some of the horror stories of students who failed to comply and thus received a grade of "F" instead of an "A" because they put their computer sheet on the wrong chair. Be very careful that you have the correct computer scoring key for the correct pile of computer scoring sheets. I use a binder clip to separate the completed examinations with the answer keys on the top of each pile of computer scoring sheets. If you can, try this system of choice on the final; the students really like it.

Testing in a Large Class

Selecting the Type of Questions

With large classes you will surely use some form of multiple choice or objective computer-scored examinations. I always deliver the computer scoring sheet to the computer scoring center myself. These examinations are sensitive and should not be compromised. Even if you have the best assistant in the world, do not trust him/her to deliver the exams to the computer scoring. If they are lost or comprised it is your fault, not that of your assistant. During the planning phase of your course, ask for the types of statistics available with your examination scores from the computer scoring center. They will vary from school to school, but get as much data as you can with each examination. If your school can produce bi-serial *r* statistics, request the information. They can be useful in evaluating your own test items.

Cheating in the Large Class

Cheating can be a problem in a large class. I simply round up four or five TAs and instruct them to help proctor the examination. I give the TAs detailed instructions of what to do if the suspect someone of cheating, which means come get me and I will handle it. If you are lucky, the proctoring of your examinations will be considered part of the TAs' assignments and you will not have to attend the examinations. I would still attend at least the beginning of the examination period to make sure the examination begins smoothly. At the beginning of the examination I give the students a short "do not cheat" lecture intended to let them know the consequences. I have found that the sheer mass of the TAs' presence will stop most cheating. (See Chapter 6 for more information on cheating).

Testing in a Small Class

Selecting the Type of Questions

In a small class you can use any or all of the types of testing described earlier; the mix is up to you. In these small sections, I would suggest avoiding multiple choice items if possible. The other forms of evaluation give a more complete picture of the students' knowledge of the content. Additionally, I find that the better students like the more subjective forms of evaluation.

Cheating in the Small Class

In a small class you can proctor the examination yourself; I tend to trust students in the smaller classes because they are still individuals, no deindividuation, familiar to you, and you trust them. To cheat in a small section is to lose the professor's trust.

General Considerations

Taking the Heat

After every (yes, every) examination, you are likely to have some sort of hostile behavior directed toward you concerning specific examination items or the examination in general. I have developed a system that works well for deflecting this aggression and turning it into a learning experience. I tell the students with challenges to write their name, student number, and section number on a piece of paper, then the question they want to challenge. Next, I tell the students to look up the answer in the text or lecture notes and write a minimum of a paragraph explaining why their answer should be considered. This response can include page numbers, quotes from the text, or citations from lectures. Finally, I ask them to bring this paper to my office during office hours for discussion. This system has several benefits to both the students and the instructor. First, the students have the incorrect answer at least 95 percent of the time. With this system the students get direct, correct feedback about the concept which allows them to correct their cognition. The students realize they were initially wrong, but now understand the correct concept. The other 5 percent of the students who still do not like your choice of answer will comply and write down the requested paragraph of explanation. About 2 percent of the students will then show up for the discussion phase of this method. Of the students that show up, probably less than half have a valid point and I will award them credit for the specific item on their examination.

But what a great system! I now have a record of why I gave the credit, so I file it in my course grade folder until I calculate final grades at the end of the term. Yes, a great system! The students like it because you are fair, and it shows you care about the students' understanding of the principles of the content area. Instructors like it because it decreases the pressure from students of large classes. The students learn the correct concept and if you decide to give credit, you have a record for your files. Try it! Trust me on this one.

Chapter 6

Grading Considerations and Mechanics

When you were preparing to teach this course, you developed a syllabus that detailed the course requirements. As you developed your syllabus, you took into account the course objectives, school and departmental requirements, and needs of the students. Now that this process has been established, it is time to evaluate the implementation of the course and the students through grading.

Managing the Evaluation System

Developing a Grading System

A grading system must be as fair as possible because students desire and deserve to be evaluated in an equal, unbiased way. Depending on the types of evaluation that you have decided on in the planning stages, the course examinations can range from totally objective multiple choice items to the more subjective essay questions. During any evaluation, the student should always be given the benefit of the doubt. I always err on the side of the student. Each class has its unique needs and you should develop your system accordingly.

The Mechanics of Grading

The File Folder Method

I use the file folder method to keep track of the materials students generate during the course. Examples of each class's specific folder contents are: name lists and summary statistics for each examination), makeup examinations, dean's excuses for missing examinations, extra credit summary sheets, and credit for successful examination question challenges. Make a separate folder for each section of your classes. This folder should be stored in a safe place; loss of these materials would be a disaster. Most of these documents are one of a kind and difficult to replace. Depending on your level of paranoia, you might decide to make a photocopy of the materials. I like to store the individual student computer sheets and/or examinations in my office. The better your system for finding specific student copies of individual examinations, the fewer problems. You will have, on occasion, students who think there is an incorrect score on their individual examination, particularly computer-scored examinations. I have known of two computer scoring errors in the last ten years. However, I have experienced numerous student-generated errors, for example, using a hard lead pencil, not filling in the scoring sheet dark enough, skipping items, and writing in the margins, to name a few. Above all, you must reassure the students that your records are correct. The best method to assure the students of this is to hand-score their examinations while they are present. Compare the student computer score sheet or examination to the posted answer key. All materials are stored in my file folder until the final test is completed and I post the changes to the final computer files. This system can act as a backup for your course management software, which could accidentally be lost or destroyed.

Early Computer Methods (Last Century)

Several of my colleagues use various computer programs to organize their grades. Most major publishers will include a grading program with their texts and more advanced systems like WebCT, Blackboard or Desire2Learn. For a small class, using these programs can be a good method, but posting each entry to the computer program requires a lot of effort. I prefer to have the computer scoring center (Information Technology Center) keep track of my examination scores until after the final and then update and print a summary sheet for all the students. Check with your test scoring service for options. In my department, we can interact with the main frame computer from our office computers. We can download all the student files and annotate the files with extra credit, recitation points, journal points, and any other corrections that are necessary prior to printing the final grade list. Spreadsheets are also useful in managing large amounts of student data. These computer scoring center files are secure and you will need special access passwords to the scores. If possible, use this method to save the time of posting and totaling the scores by hand. Ask your supervisor or department chair for programs currently used by the department.

Computer Methods

I had a programmer in the computer center (Information Technology Center) write a custom program to download and manipulate my grades directly from the test scoring service. This program is secure and does all the calculation, progress reports, D and F reports, final posting for students, and final grade roster. It takes about 2 seconds to calculate all this for over 700 students. I had this program adapted to a more general form, (tests scores, papers, quizzes, labs reports, and extra credit) and disseminated to all members of the department. This method is far superior to the earlier computer methods but can be very expensive and is usually only useful in your course.

Check with someone in the department who teaches the same classes you teach for advice on what they use and how it can be adapted to your classes. Usually these individuals are happy to share grading programs. You can develop your own system with software like Excel if you have the time and want to invest the effort.

Current Computer Methods

Publishers have made large advances in their computer grading programs. Many have made these programs adaptable to your needs, some offer Internet storage and posting. Use these programs if possible; they are usually part of the free ancillary package.

I currently use a commercial course management system, including WebCT, Blackboard and D2L and several other brands. The advantage of using a commercial course management system is that you are not tied to a publisher's system and thus their textbooks.

Examination Item Security

In my large classes, I let the students keep their copy of the examinations. The logic is simple; if someone wants to compromise the questions in the test item file, they will find a way, so I simply give the questions to everyone. If students would work as hard studying the materials as they do trying to scam the testing system, they would be better students. So rather than a few groups having the old examinations, the entire campus has copies. I have the old tests and answers on reserve in the library and post copies of the old test on the class Internet site. Be sure if there are multiple sections with multiple instructors that you inform the other instructors if you are going to allow the students to keep their examinations.

The Demand for Fast Turnaround Time

Many students expect rapid turnaround times for examination scores. In order to accommodate students, I post the answer key immediately after class in the same location where the examination scores will be posted later. The students can then take their examinations and compare their responses to the answer key to find their score on the examination. I find that about 50-60 percent of the class will check the answer key immediately after the test. I also post the answer key to my course management software (D2L).

Use the following to help determine the turnaround time for your examinations.

Multiple Choice and True/False Examinations

With computer-scored multiple choice and true/false tests, the turn around time can be as short as one hour, but overnight is usually a safe upper limit.

Short Answer Format Examinations

With short answers, matching items, fill-in-the-blanks, and essays, the turn-around time is dependent on the number of items and the teaching assistants available. A good tip is to schedule your examination on a Thursday or Friday so you or your assistant will have the weekend to complete the grading. It is important to have as fast a turn around time as possible. When constructing the examination, I like to plan for the scoring of the examination. Part of an examination could be scored by computer. Templates can be constructed for fill-in-the-blank and matching items. Try to make the scoring as easy and efficient as possible.

Essay Examinations

Essay examinations are very time consuming to grade. After your first examination, you will have a better feel for the amount of time required, but I recommend at least 10 minutes for each essay question per student. You can assign your TA to grade these; be sure that there is an established scoring rubric for the TA to follow.

Use of TAs for Grading

Try out your TA by letting them grade a portion of your examinations; be sure to be specific as to what you expect from them in terms of grading. Check all of the TAs' work; most of them will try to do a good job, but often will grade too severely. I give the TA feedback about their performance and suggest changes to make grading more efficient and accurate. After you are confident that the TAs are grading in the manner that you expect, allow them more and more responsibility. I spot check their grading to be sure the quality remains high. If there are any questions concerning grades the TA have produced, I am the final authority. If the students have any questions concerning a grade on an examination and cannot resolve it with the TAs, you must make the decision concerning the grading. I always give the student the benefit of the doubt in such disputed grading situations. I tell my class at the beginning of the term that TA will be grading examinations and that any problems are to be brought to my attention.

Posting Grades

Check with the school regulations and new Federal regulations to see how scores are posted. These rules vary. At my university, student identification numbers were the accepted practice but no longer. Several years ago the accepted method was using social security numbers, but thankfully that method has been abandoned.

Establish a central location to post your examination scores; outside your office door is not the best place since there will be some disgruntled students after each examination. Also, the other faculty in the office hallways will not appreciate 350 students jammed into the hall trying to find their examination scores. Perhaps your department has a specific location for posting scores. Try outside the classroom; if there is an appropriate posting area use it. Realize that if the postings are not secure, they will disappear rather rapidly. I post the key outside of my classroom and all the students gather around after the exam to check their scores. Please be sure you are not disturbing other classes in progress with your posting. Always use the same location after the first examination. I leave the previous examination posting up until the hour before the next examination. I am still amazed that some students will look for their last examination score just prior to the next examination. After posting grades, I put the mean and standard deviation on the summary sheet and then mention the mean and standard deviation in the next class.

The best place to post grades is, of course, the Internet. Use either your own web-site that you have developed for the course or one provided by the publisher. Other options include programs like WebCT, Blackboard or Desire2Learn. These areas are secure and no one can tear down the posted paper printout.

Ask your departmental administrator for a copy of the HIPPA regulations as they apply to posting of grades. Also, your departmental mentor can help with local interpretations of these very important privacy act regulations. Times have changed and student privacy is now a major concern.

Criterion vs. Class Curve Grades

The question often arises, “What does an 87 mean?” Of course, the answer depends on the type of grading plan that you developed in the planning stages of your course. You probably chose either a criterion system or a class curve system.

The Criterion System

The criterion system requires the students to perform at a predetermined level for a specific grade. A typical system uses the following distribution: 90% = A, 80% = B, 70% = C, 60% = D and 59% and lower = F. Or you can use the more complex +/- system with added intervals. Of course, this system has advantages and disadvantages. On the plus side, you can integrate the final grade criteria into your syllabus and the students know exactly what level they must obtain for a specific grade. A disadvantage is that the level of your examination can be either too easy (everyone gets an “A”) or, too hard (everyone gets a “D” or worse). For a new instructor to use this system, he or she must be careful that the level of difficulty of the examination is appropriate to the level of the students and goals for the class.

The Class Curve System

The class curve system allows the instructor to choose the grade cutoffs post hoc. After looking at the distribution of scores, the instructor can either adjust the grade cuts by percentage of grades—15% = "A," 30% = "B," etc.—or make the grade cuts utilizing the naturally occurring trimodal distribution. I plot the data to see the type of distribution for each class. If your class is large enough, the students will typically cluster into three distinct groups (trimodal)—A, B, and C with the D's and F's trailing the distribution. The class curve system is a good method of establishing grades, but it is hard to explain to the students that you just "decide" what the grades are based on the distribution. You will also get more hassle from students who are on the cut line of a grade than if you use the criterion system. I often use the criterion system in introductory classes so the students know the levels of performance required and then reserve the right to lower the cut-off percentages depending on the examination scores. With the curve system, if a student lets another student cheat, he or she is really hurting his or her chance for a good grade.

Other Methods

The use of Z-scores and other normalizing statistics can be used, but you must take the time to explain these methods to the students. These methods may not be appropriate in an introductory level class because the students may not have the knowledge in the area of statistics to understand what their score really means.

Extra Credit

Course Extra Credit

You may decide to allow your students some projects in addition to those you planned for at the beginning of the term; offer these tasks as extra credit. Perhaps students wish to explore topics in greater depth; while earning extra credit. One point—be sure that all the students have equal access to the extra credit points and that these points really are extra credit. Add them to the total points for the class only after the grade cutoffs have been established.

Students often can obtain extra credit by participating in psychology experiments or the experiment alternatives in my department. The following questions should be addressed at the beginning of the term. Where do the students sign up, who keeps track of the extra credit points, what happens if a student or experimenter fails to show up at the appointed time? Many departments will have a formal policy. There are now software companies--SONA is the biggest--that have software designed for online sign up. These programs also track participation and interact with the students on individual scores.

Extra credit in other disciplines can be obtained by writing a formal paper on a topic appropriate or working on a project or conducting an experiment. Be aware that many Internet sites sell course papers. This cottage industry is growing in recent years. How to stop this practice? Have the students turn in their drafts with the final product, since paper mills do not give first, second, or third drafts with the final copy. Assign topics that are not easily obtained, make them specific. For example, do not allow students to write a paper on schizophrenia, but rather on behavioral treatments for catatonic schizophrenia. There are Internet services that will search the paper mills to find matches for any topic. If you are interested see www.Plagiarism.com/ for examples.

Final Grades—Paper to Paper

Processing Final Grades (Then)

At most schools, the administration has not yet developed a system that allows for direct computer input of grades. This often means that you will print out a grade sheet from your computer and then hand copy the grades onto the Registrar's official grade roster and sign each sheet. This task can be time consuming and more efficiently accomplished by two individuals. Be very careful not to make errors; students with lower grades will always be in your office the day after final grades are posted. A worse problem is the student who erroneously receives a higher grade and never reports the unearned higher grade. Many schools allow grade changes only in an upward direction. So the student with the higher incorrect grade unfairly keeps the higher grade. Use your TA to help with the final posting, but be involved in the work yourself; you are the responsible individual. Double check all grades; find and correct missing examination grades, extra credit, and any other problems that arise. Call the Registrar's office for help with any technical problems. You may have grades for students who are not on your roll and students on your roll without grades. Take the time to get this corrected; this is the last chance to correct any errors. Sign all copies and date each page of the roster as requested by the Registrar. If your department does not keep a copy of the grade roster, make a copy for yourself. Be sure to check with the department administrator for deadlines. Do not be late; students may receive late grade reports and the individuals posting the grades at the Registrar's office will be working under time constraints.

Processing Final Grades (Now)

Recently my school has managed to improve this method of submitting grades. We are able to be able to input the grades directly on a secure site and push the "Send to Registrar" button and go home. If you are lucky enough to have online final grade submission, appreciate it.

Processing Final Grades (The Future)

Still after years of using grading software, I cannot directly submit my e-files to the Registrar; I must still input the grades by hand. Sometime soon I will be able to just push a button marked GRADES and they will be submitted. This will eliminate the possible of transcription errors. Can't wait for this to happen!

Dealing With and Eliminating Cheating

Defining the Parameters of Cheating

Cheating is a constant problem; many times new students really do not understand the many ways one can be accused of cheating. To help curtail this problem, my university has an orientation for all incoming students and defines cheating. Additionally, I spend time before the first examination or assignment to reinforce the school's definition of cheating. If you do not do this and the occasion arises when you must confront an individual with cheating, often the cheater will say he or she did not know he or she was cheating. Include specifics on cheating in your syllabi and post the same material on the course's home page.

The most obvious types of cheating include copying another's examination, using crib sheets (many variants), the old write the stuff on the desk trick, write the material on your hat brim, write the material on your arm or other interesting body part, stealing examinations or using a stolen examination from a file system, and/or having another student take his/her examination (a real possibility with a class of 350 students). A myriad of other methods can and will be tried. Laboratory reports are often a source of cheating and can plagiarize work done in groups. A good TA can often spot these attempts at group work. Thoughts can also be plagiarized. Students can use previous writings submitted without references. A final method is paper mill papers. The student calls an 800 number, states the subject and his or her credit card number, and the paper is in the next day's express shipment, or the student can log on to the Internet and download the paper directly.

For examples of materials from paper mills see www.1200papers.com, www.academicresearch.com, www.planetpapers.com. I think a lot is said by these sites about students and how they value their education.

What are the best methods to deal with cheating? The following are a few suggestions you can use to prevent the most common types of cheating. You may discover other types as you continue in your career; be sure to be as fair with the students as possible in resolving these problems.

Copying Other Examinations and Crib Sheets (and Variants)

Instruct your teaching assistants to proctor the examination very closely and warn potential cheaters. Tell them to watch for students using crib sheets or copying from another student's examination. Make cheating as difficult as possible. Ask students to sit in every other seat, if possible. I use parallel forms of the same examination, by randomizing the questions and using two forms of the examination. One of my favorite methods is to print the same examination on different colored paper and tell the students they are different examinations; this only works once, though. If you suspect a student of copying, warn that student. If it persists, confiscate the examination and have the student stay after class. After the examination, explain the consequences of cheating to the student. This might mean an "F" for this examination, for the course, or dismissal from the school. Check your school's regulations or faculty handbook for specific procedures and policies. Be as certain as possible that the student was cheating; it is best to have at least one (two are better) of your TAs witness the incident. Do not let a TA be the primary person reporting the cheating; you should witness the act yourself. Remember, the student may appeal your decision. Be careful.

The Use of Compromised Examinations

The use of compromised examinations to make a "file" of examinations is widespread on most campuses. The solution is to simply change the items for each examination and announce that procedure to the class. Many individuals will not believe you until the first examination. Another solution is to try and control the items on the examination. This can be accomplished by giving a number to all examinations and having the students record this number on their examination; after the student turns in the individual examination, check to see if any of the pages are missing. Maintaining a secure test item file is very difficult. One of the major reasons that I change texts often is because I need a new test item file.

Physical Theft of Examinations

Discovery of the physical theft of examinations prior to the class period can be handled in several ways. Count or number all the examinations and store them in a secure area of the department office along with the computer disks containing test item files and examinations. If the examinations are left in your office, do not leave them in public view and be sure to lock your office when you are not there. The possession of a copy of your final examination prior to the examination time can make a student rich and famous.

Physical Theft and the Internet

If one dishonest person can manage to obtain a copy of the test item file, they can sell or give away the entire test item file over the Internet. With the advent of instant communication many unethical individuals will try to exploit student cheating.

PDAs, Cell Phones, Smartphones, iPads and Other Devices

Ah, technology. Isn't it great? The newest and latest technology can be used in a number of ways to cheat. The best policy I have found is NO electronic devices in the classroom during examinations; also have the students remove their hats. Threaten them with a zero on the examination for cheating, which usually works.

Last semester a student told me that some students were cheating and here is how they did it. They had an individual wait until I posted the answer key usually 30 minutes into the examination, so that when students finished they could have feedback on their scores. This individual would text message the answers for the key; each cheater would just look at the answers on their cell phone and "fill in the dots." The new rule this semester will be an "F" for any electronics, period.

Having another Student Take the Examination

Require student identification cards for admission to the classroom and have each student sign his/her name at the top of the examination. This substitute student can be a larger problem than you might think, especially in classes where the text and the class notes stay relatively constant. Be sure to mention that the identification cards will be required for admission to examinations and include this information on the syllabus. You should be prepared for students who forget their identification cards; one possible strategy is to have the students take the examination and sign the top of the examination and write their identification number. After the examination and before you score the examination, have the student produce his or her identification card and sign a piece of paper in your presence. The student rumor mill will have the news out very quickly that this form of cheating will not work in your class.

Copying Laboratory Reports

The copying of current laboratory reports is very hard to stop. I permit the students to work in groups and then grade the group at a higher level.

Recycled Term Papers

Term papers that are re-printed and re-submitted are hard to spot. This is especially true for papers from other sections or schools. If you have any questions about the authorship of a paper, ask the student to bring in the rough draft and the research materials. Do not allow too much time for the student to produce these materials. Not quoting references is always a problem and falls in the gray area; use your judgment as to what is copied and what is an original idea.

Paper Mill Papers

To stop the use of paper mill papers, assign specific topics that are not likely to be in the paper mill catalog. Assign specific referenced articles or books and instruct students to incorporate these materials in their papers. Paper mill products are easier to spot than you might think; they are usually vague and never address any specific issue.

For examples of materials from paper mills see www.1200papers.com, www.academicresearch.com, www.planetpapers.com. Also see www.plagiarism.com/ for ideas to stop this problem before grading.

After the Cheating Incident

If your school has a written policy for cheating, obtain a copy and read the procedures. This material can either be a separate document, in your faculty handbook, or in electronic form on the school's Web page. You must follow the specific procedures very carefully because students can challenge your decision and it is your responsibility to prove they cheated. Be sure to have at least one other credible witness. Document the incident and report it to the department chair or course supervisor at once.

Accusing a student of cheating can be one of the most disturbing things you can do in your career. You have to PROVE it. Many times the faculty member ends up as the loser in these types of cheating incidents. What to do? Prevention is the best answer. I tell my students that if I catch anyone cheating the cheater will get a zero for the examination and the cheatee (person being cheated from) will also get a zero for the exam. Students are very reluctant to give others a chance to cheat when they know they will be punished. Use as many TAs as you can to proctor the examination. I always state at the first examination that all my TAs are highly trained proctors whether they are or not.

How to Administer Examinations

Instructions to the Students

You should clearly indicate whether or not students should guess on the test items, the time limit for the examination, and any other directions appropriate to your examination. At the beginning of the examination I remind the students where the answer keys and computer sheets will be posted. Finally, I would mention the procedure for challenging examination questions; see Chapter 5. With multiple choice test items, I emphasize that students are to choose the best alternative. I print this statement as a heading on the examination. Many students will try to think of any single specific incident that will make their answer valid. Emphasize that the intent of the examination is not to trick students. I have developed a short lecture on test taking and studying strategies, which I usually give at least two weeks prior to the first examination. Many entering freshmen have poor study skills; this type of lecture can be very helpful in maximizing their performance on examinations. Many schools have instituted student retention programs; this lecture can be part of this retention program. Ask your course supervisor or department chair about this program.

See http://www.mtsu.edu/~studskl/ for examples of how to take tests. I would project and explore this site in class if you have Internet interactivity in the classroom. This type of material can help the students on tests and also calm their fears before the first examination.

Administering the Examination

If the examination requires a computer scoring form, instruct the proctors to simultaneously distribute forms to all students from both the front and back of the class. The students in the back of the class can feel cheated because they did not have the same amount of time for the examination as the front of the class. Emphasize how you want the form completed and the specific areas that need to be filled out. Announce when the examination will conclude and where students can find the answer key and grade posting. Pass the examinations out in the same manner as the computer scoring sheets.

Be as flexible as possible in your testing situations and expect the worst. For example, I have given examinations when I did not have enough copies for the class. What to do? I took several of the examinations, tore off the last half of the pages, and gave them to some of the students with instructions to do the last half first and then raise their hand. By the time the students doing the first half are done, the proctors can switch the halves. Panic yes, but it worked out. I once had my former secretary staple the wrong last page on an examination; use the same type solution as above. Remember that you have to appear to be in charge even though everything is crashing down around you. If a problem arises and cannot be successfully resolved, ask the specific students after the examination if this problem affected their performance grade. Most will say that it did not; if it did, offer a make-up examination or another form of evaluation and remember to err on the side of the student.

Encourage Student Questions

I always encourage students to question any aspect of the grading procedure they do not understand. If a student thinks the computer scoring sheet is incorrect, that student should come to my office and we can check the answer. If the student thinks an essay question was graded inappropriately, he or she should come to my office to discuss the problem, particularly if the TAs did the initial grading. I also tell the students that mistakes are occasionally made and that a grade that should be an “A” can turn out to be an “F” by accident. Students should always question anything they do not understand. They should not be afraid to come and talk about the problem; you cannot overemphasize this point.

How to Avoid Problems with Examinations

The following suggestions can be implemented as a part of your examination routine. If you follow these procedures, you are less likely to have problems with your examinations. Anything that cuts down the confusion during the examination process is helpful. Try the following suggestions and modify or add your own to the list.

Answer Key

Make the answer key early and recheck it prior to the examination. I usually fill out the scoring key from the computer generated test key. I usually do a final check after the examination has started by filling out the examination with the answers from the answer key. A little paranoia is a good thing. If early finishing students find an error on the posted key, check it and make changes to the final scoring key.

Number of Exams

Make more examinations (10 percent) than you think you will need. Often there are blanks, unreadable pages or the administrator has miscounted. It might seem wasteful, but you will end up using most of the copies and you can always recycle the rest.

Computer Scoring Sheets

Bring extra computer scoring sheets to the testing site. Returning to your office to pick up additional computer scoring sheets at the beginning of the examination is one of the worst things that can happen. Also bring a few extra pencils.

Proctors

Make sure your proctors know what you expect from them during the examination. Emphasize that exams are serious; there's no fooling around or loud conservations during the examination.

Corrections

If you have any last-minute corrections or changes (spelling errors or additions/deletions) to the examination, write them on the overhead or chalkboard or on a presentation slide and call the students' attention to the changes. It is much easier to throw out a poor item than to field the complaints.

Exam Turn in Area

Designate a clearly defined area where students must turn in the computer scoring sheets and/or examinations. Tell students ahead of time whether they can keep their individual copies of the current examination, if that is your policy.

Answer Key Check

I re-read the examination during the testing period, answer all the questions, and compare them against the student answer key and computer scoring key. If you find errors in the scoring keys, you should correct them on the spot.

Posting the Answer Key

Post the key after the examination begins; I usually wait 30 minutes. If students learn that you post the answer key on the way to class, they will show up 10 minutes late with the answers memorized. I admit no student to the examination 10 minutes after the exam has started.

Computer Scoring Sheet Security

Personally take the computer scoring sheets directly to the scoring center; losing these sheets is an unbelievable problem. If they are lost make it your problem not an assistant.

Posting Scores

Post the examination computer scores as soon as possible in the predetermined location or on the Internet.

Problems during Examinations

Be flexible. If there is a fire alarm, ask students to leave their examinations on their desks and leave the room. What if the lights go off? Try to have some form of orderly evacuation. If you think the examination has been too disrupted, cancel it and schedule a new examination for the next class period. Re-write the examination and hope the roof does not fall in next time. The roof actually did fall in on one of my classes, almost killing me, but not during an examination. No one was hurt, but it did necessitate the class to move to a different class room.

Make the Examination Fun

Examinations are a necessary part of most college requirements. Rather than dread the examinations, they should consider them a challenge.

Chapter 7

Alternative Methods of Evaluating Students

These alternate forms of evaluation are intended to supplement the traditional examinations. Students often like these types of evaluation; you should try to incorporate as many as possible.

Alternate Forms of Evaluation in the Class

Large Lower Level Classes

In a large class, your options for alternate types of evaluations, other than the examination mentioned in Chapter 5, are limited. This limitation is primarily controlled by the number of students; any number over 100 makes alternate forms of evaluation very difficult. Additionally, the number and experience of your TAs can be another limiting factor. An alternate form of evaluation that we use at my university is an interesting model that is being used more throughout the academic community. It entails the use of a large lecture section with smaller recitation sections. This type of structure permits types of student involvement that do not fit the large course format. At my school, the lecture portion accounts for 50 percent of the course and the labs and online assignment sections are 50 percent of the course. Lab sections allow for the use of the small personal-type group interactions that students like. Following are examples of the types of activities that students can be involved with in the small class section described below.

Small Classes or Advanced Classes

In small classes, recitation sections, or advanced classes, many strategies can be used to involve the students in their learning process. Try to incorporate as many activities as you can in your course; the students like the variety. Use the following types of activities as a starting point for your own ideas.

Alternative Evaluations: Small Classes

These methods are primarily designed for small classes or recitation sections of larger classes.

Case Study

Use case study materials during the class period to evaluate an individual problem. One strategy is to pass out the case study materials at the beginning of the class period and have the large section break down into small five-or six-student groups. Ask each group to discuss the case using the lecture and course materials. The intent is to evaluate the individual case study using the tools obtained from the class. If you wish, you can designate a variety of different case study stations where the case studies are different; then after an appropriate amount of time, rotate the groups to the new stations. Students like to look at individual case studies and try to use the information from the course. To evaluate the students, instruct the groups to prepare a short paper and/or presentation for the next class meeting. Evaluate the presentation and/or paper as a group project.

Debate Teams

Debates are an interesting format which can involve the entire class. Form student teams and choose a side on a current topic in the content area. Use any subject that is current and as local as possible; be creative. These debates should be guided by you, the moderator; be careful not to let the debates turn into a shouting match between rival viewpoints. This format is valuable because the students get a different perspective than they would through the standard lecture format. A nice touch is to let the students evolve into groups and pick their own topics, either the pro or con side of the issue. Then reassign the groups to the opposite viewpoint that they have selected. They will hate it at first, but will gain valuable insights about aspects of the topic that they have not yet explored. This method will also help dissolve false stereotypes and misinformation about the subject area. Evaluate the thoroughness of each group's preparation. Additionally, ask the groups to perform a self-evaluation of their individual members. This self-evaluation can be performed by using a form that allows each student to grade another student's effort, input, and contribution to the group's project. The good students like to have the power to evaluate their group members, while the poorer students do not like this type of evaluation.

Panel Discussions

Panels are an additional form of alternate evaluations. The students can form their own panels or you can suggest several topic areas. The students can prepare and present the panel discussion to the rest of the section. Typically each student becomes an "expert" in a sub-area of the topic. Evaluate the group presentations as a whole. Instruct the groups to use the self-evaluation process described earlier.

Simulate Group Decision-Making Processes

Tell the students to form groups either by themselves or using your direction. Suggestions for decision-making groups are a military unit in a war situation, a large corporate board trying to make product marketing decisions, a group of athletic coaches plotting a strategy for the next game, or any group with a group goal. Each group must try to reach a group decision on the problem. Then, if you have a lecture on the Groupthink process as discussed by Janis (1972), present this lecture. Have the students analyze their group decision in terms of the Janis model and look at the ways their decision went right or wrong. This project could take more than one class period to complete, but it is worth the effort; many of these students will be in similar types of group decision-making situations very early in their careers. Evaluate using a group paper on the decision-making problem encountered by the group. Have each group use the self-evaluation process described earlier.

Small Group Discussions

Pick controversial topics in the content area and then divide the class section into small groups (five or six students) and assign each group to discuss the problem and come up with a group consensus about the topic. Then ask the groups to present their findings on the topic; some debate will surely follow, both between and within the groups. Discuss the advantages of parallel versus independent decision making. Emphasize the point that variant ideas are often the best ideas to come out of these activities. These variant ideas often lead to interesting discoveries; use examples like Watson and Crick's discovery of the DNA structure. Evaluate the groups as a whole and in terms of individual participation. Instruct the groups to use the self-evaluation process described earlier.

Brainstorming

Brainstorming is designed to give the students an opportunity to produce as many ideas as they can in a limited time frame. Brainstorming can either be performed in groups or by individuals. Again, pick topics that are controversial. Explain to the students that they are not to be judgmental of ideas during the first phase of this session. Later the class can evaluate the different approaches to the problem. There will be several ideas that are repeated, but the more interesting ideas are likely to be the novel solutions to the problem. Discuss the latest research on the effectiveness of this method. Evaluate each group as a whole in terms of participation. Groups should use the self-evaluation process described earlier.

Lecture Summaries

Assign specific students to summarize your previous lecture in a 5-minute oral presentation and present it to the class at the start of the period. Use this summary to measure how well your lecture was understood. This process also allows the students to get a different perspective on the materials they encountered in your last lecture. Answer any questions the students have and clear up any misconceptions. Evaluate individuals on oral presentation and depth of understanding of the previous lecture.

Student Oral Reports

Assign students to present oral reports to the class. The topics of the reports should be gently guided. I usually require instructor approval of the topic. Some students will have inappropriate topics and you should guide them into an acceptable area. These reports will give the students valuable experience with oral presentation. The class will receive information on topics that they have had little or no exposure to in the course. Additionally, the level can vary with student reports so the students will receive a very different level of information than they are used to in the lectures. Evaluate individuals on oral presentation and depth of understanding of the material.

Student Individual Oral Examinations

Ask students to present individual oral examinations on specific topics in your office or other appropriate venue. Evaluate the depth and breadth of knowledge of the subject material. This method also allows for immediate feedback.

PsychoJeopardy

You can arrange to play a *Jeopardy*®-like game in these smaller groups. Have the students form teams. Make up questions ahead of time and use the presentation software or an overhead transparency to show the categories and questions. Keep track of correct answers for each team. You could award the winners an extra credit point for the course.

Role Playing

Role playing is a useful strategy for students to gain a feeling for what it must be like to possess behaviors other than their own. Try leading the class in a role-playing exercise; you can be a major player in the exercise. Instruct each student to role play being homeless, a drug addict, a convicted murderer on death row, a person with AIDS, a schizophrenic, or a president of a university that has just received a 25 percent reduction in funding. Use your imagination and situations that are current and relevant to your students. The closer the roles are to real life, the better. Assign a paper and evaluate each student's paper on what was learned from playing a different role. Students will gain useful insights to problems that they otherwise might not be exposed to.

Internet Search

Assign teams of students to do Internet searches on a topic for several minutes during the first part of the class period. You will probably have to move the class to the computer laboratory for this activity, have students use their Smart Phones or other e-capable devices. Have each team designate a spokesperson to discuss the sites they have found. Move the class around the laboratory and have each spokesperson discuss the information they discovered.

(This classification system was influenced by Allen and Rueter, 1990).

These methods are primarily designed for small classes or recitation sections of larger classes. Their use represents a different approach from the traditional testing format usually employed in most courses. The students will like these types of evaluations. You can use these alternate forms of evaluation in a combination with other traditional forms of evaluation to add interesting features to your class.

Alternative Evaluations: Large and Small Classes

Another major group of alternative evaluations suitable for the large class without recitation groups, or the small class, consists of written assignments that students complete on their own time.

The Classic Written Assignment

Assign each student to write an essay, from a short two pages to a maximum of 20 pages. The primary limiting factor in the length of the essay is the amount and quality of TAs you have access to in your department. If you have a small class, you can read all of these essay assignments yourself; in a large class, you must have support. Topics should be open, but must have instructor approval. I help the students with references for materials, where to look for specific articles, journals, books, and suggestions on beginning their essay.

As described in Chapter 6, use the following Internet sites to help stop cheating. For examples of materials from paper mills see www.1200papers.com, www.academicresearch.com, www.planetpapers.com. You can also see www.plagiarism.com for help stopping this problem.

Structured Journals

The use of structured journals keyed to specific materials in the text and lectures is a valuable method of insuring that students keep up with the reading assignments. The students will have to think about the issues you present in order to write their journal entries; evaluate the entries in terms of your lectures and the text materials. The students will like this form of evaluation because it allows them to work at their pace, to think about issues in content area, and to use these journal entries as a method of studying for tests.

Unstructured Journals

Assign the students to write on topics they feel are personally important. Explain that these entries must be focused on the context of the materials encountered in the text and lectures. This type of journal entry allows students to think about personal problems or situations in terms of the content area. This type of journal is best evaluated on a submitted/nonsubmitted basis, since there are no right or wrong answers.

Diaries

Instruct the students to keep unstructured daily diaries of their personal experiences and feelings. This form of exercise encourages students to think about what they have done and how they feel. This type of writing is best evaluated on a submitted/nonsubmitted basis, since there are no right or wrong answers.

Professional Journal Evaluations

Have the students select a topic of interest and locate an article from a scientific journal in the library. The students can summarize the article and include dependent variables, independent variables, statistics used, and summarize the conclusion. They can then argue why this article is either relevant or irrelevant to current trends in the content area.

Popular Press Evaluations

Have the students select a topic of interest and locate an article in the popular press. Many of the publications contain surveys. They can summarize the article and include variables studied and the statistics used to summarize the material. They can then argue why this article is either relevant or irrelevant to current trends in content area.

Internet Evaluation

Have the students search a topic on the Internet and summarize the site explored. What are the common elements and what are the different elements of each site? Are all the sites credible? If not, why?

Online Quizzes

Have online quizzes in your course management system, only available during a time interval you choose. This method can insure that the students are attending class and keeping up with their readings.

(This classification system was influenced by Allen and Rueter, 1990).

Some of the projects mentioned above will fall into the category of collaborative assignments, with groups of individuals working on a common project. Be sure to be very specific as to what you expect from this effort. Give examples and feedback about the projects. How you evaluate this type of written material is up to you; course points, pass/fail, or credit for turning the assignments in are all alternatives.

Many students prefer this type of evaluation over traditional examinations. A mix of both the traditional and the alternative evaluation is probably the best method for most instructors. As you gain experience with your teaching, try alternate forms of evaluations to see which works for you and the students. Do not be afraid to experiment with these alternatives.

Chapter 8

Professional Interactions with Students

Understanding Students

When interacting with students, it is important to know the capabilities of the students you are attempting to communicate with. If you are new to the school, ask other instructors or your departmental mentor for their opinions about the students and their capabilities. Determining the appropriate level to teach the course materials is always a difficult problem. Finding the correct presentation level of the material may be one of the more difficult aspects of adapting to your new teaching position. Teaching at a high level will lose students of modest abilities, but teaching at too low a level will lose students with greater abilities. If you are a former undergraduate at your school, you already will have a good idea as to the level of understanding of the students. I have found that many new instructors tend to teach at levels that are too high in their first classes; they also assume they will be able to cover more material than they possibly can. Knowing the capabilities of the students can be critical to the success of your course. A disturbing new trend in higher education is the area of student retention. Although unwritten, you are expected to pass along every student that you can. You essentially end up teaching to the bottom 25 % of the class. If you grade too hard, expect to have a conference with your department chair. The problem with teaching to the bottom is that you neglect the students you should be teaching to, the top 25%. Never spoken but always in the background: if we lose too many students we will have to lose some faculty positions.

Finding the Level

Visit the Registrar's office and ask to see the summary statistics of the test scores and profiles for the entering freshman class, since these individuals are the majority of the students you will have in your introductory classes. This will be a good opportunity to introduce yourself to the staff in the Registrar's office. This material can also be useful for upper-division classes. Most of this information should be available at your school's homepage. These statistics should include ACT and/or SAT scores along with other forms of high school evaluation, like GPA. Pay particular attention to the ACT and SAT scores; these are national tests and can be used as a rough measure of the incoming freshman class's ability. To see how your college or university is ranked in the national norms, see http://www.collegeboard.org/html/library000.html for further information on these tests. Compare the ranking of your current school with your previous undergraduate and graduate schools. This comparison is a rough measure of the differences in levels at which you were taught as an undergraduate/graduate and the target level of your teaching. Adjust your expectations of your students' academic abilities accordingly.

Another major source of information comes from your TAs, other instructors, your departmental mentor and your course supervisors. Take the time to meet with these individuals and ask specific questions about the abilities of the students and the level of instruction that other instructors have adopted in the past. This level discussion will also help you in your text decisions (see Chapter 2).

Yet another source about students' abilities are the students themselves. If your course starts in the fall term and you are on campus over the summer, go to the freshman orientation meetings and talk to the entering freshman students. Ask specific questions about what they expect from your course, your department, and college in general. These students probably will not have specific answers, but you can gain a feeling for how the students will perform at different levels of expectation. If possible, sit in on a few representative lectures given by other instructors in your department and other departments at your new school during summer classes. These lectures may not be the most interesting ones you have attended while in college, but they are a valuable source of what the students expect from a class in terms of level.

Relating to Students

One of the skills you will have to develop in order to be an effective teacher is the ability to relate to the students, both at the professional level and the social level. With undergraduates, you will interact mostly at the professional level, but with graduate students there can be more social interaction. The following are types of students you are likely to meet in your class. At large state universities like my own, the diversity of students can be tremendous; there will be traditional, shiny-faced freshmen, older vocational rehabilitation students, recently discharged military, displaced homemakers, returning graduates looking for career changes, high school drop-outs, laid-off construction workers, and even former homeless individuals. Overlay this diversity with the ethnic, racial, economic, religious and regional influences, and the mix of students is enormous. I like the diversity of the students in the public university system. These students do not all dress, think or act the same. The mix is always refreshing; when you first walk into the class, you see individuals, not row after row of clones.

The following attempt at a classification system of students is intended to subdivide students into major specific types that one could expect to encounter in a typical classroom. This classification system resembles the trait system of classification of characteristics used by psychologists in the 1950s (Sheldon). Many students will show some of each classification, but few will have only one. Use this stereotyping system to look at the types of students you are likely to meet. I would draw on this information to devise a plan to deal with these "types" of students before you meet them. Knowing how to deal with specific student types prior to encountering them in the classroom is very helpful. You should think of specific responses to the types of problems these students can generate. Additionally, decide how you are going to deal with a room full of a specific "type" student.

The following is an attempt to list the characteristics you are likely to encounter from the instructor's perspective. Although these people exist only in my imagination many of the students you meet will have some of these characteristics. None of the examples listed below are living individuals. This list of stereotypes is not intended to offend any individual student, but rather to give you a sense of the types of students that you may encounter in your classes.

Undergraduate Student Stereotypes

The Self-Motivated Student

Self-motivated learners, found usually among juniors and seniors, are able to formulate their own educational objectives. Most self-motivated students are able to think creatively, participate in class easily, and feel comfortable socially with instructors. Such students prefer independent study, self-paced instruction, problems requiring independent thought, self-designed projects, and student-centered classroom settings. Self-motivated students, while not in need of day-to-day attention, do require an intelligent and caring mentor to ask questions and to provide encouragement. If you can find the time to sponsor a student of this type, the rewards will be great. Often these students are taking introductory classes late in their academic career; they may find the material at too low a level. They also will be taking upper-division courses not because they are required for their major but rather for interest and understanding. These are the "A" students and the ones you will remember the longest.

The Respectful Student

Respectful students enjoy taking college courses and have great respect for their professors. They ask good questions in class and often seek out the professor for additional information. They are innately excited about learning, and they pursue new knowledge with vigor. Respectful learners are a joy for the instructor. They can be counted on to be eager participants in class discussions and to be leaders in small group activities. Frequently, an older, nontraditional, returning student fits this type. These students will often sit in the front rows of the classroom; they do not want to miss anything. These students rarely miss class lectures. Help cultivate these students' interest; they make great majors.

The Perfect Student

This student expects that you will be omnipotent in your knowledge of the subject matter and your presentation. Even though we strive for perfection, few obtain it. This student also expects that they are going to get a perfect point total for the class. If they do not attain their goal it must be your fault. I always prefer to have attainable goals which I can meet. Constantly being frustrated can be a problem.

The Submissive Student

Submissive students expect the instructor to tell them what to do. They expect to come to class, to sit quietly, and to take notes. They neither expect nor desire to interact directly with the instructor. While some professors may welcome a classroom full of submissive students, taken to an extreme, this type of student offers little intellectual or emotional satisfaction for instructors. Whatever the method used, the instructor needs to encourage submissive students to present their own views rather than repeating the ideas presented to them. These students often like to get "lost" in the crowd in the center of the classroom; they feel secure when no one can see them.

The Paranoid Student

Paranoid students are like submissive students in that they want to be spoon-fed. The main difference is that they live in fear that they will miss the feeding. They constantly ask the instructor to repeat definitions and concepts. Paranoid students frequently are competitive and exhibit high levels of ambition, anxiety, and suspicion. These students will often "hang around," either after class or in the hall, or they will walk you back to your office. It is easy for professors to become irritated with paranoid students since they interrupt the instructional flow to request that information be repeated or unnecessarily more fully elaborated. Paranoids intimate that the instructor is out to get them by being vague or intends to be picky by testing for trivial information. These students are frequently the first at your door to challenge examination questions and often the last to admit that they are incorrect. When dealing with paranoid students, the instructor should assure them that tests will involve major concepts and will be fair. Sample questions from previous tests may even be distributed to all class members to assure the paranoid that all is well. You will often find paranoid students wanting to know the correct answer to question #47 from a previous term's test. I assure these students that this item will not be on the current examination, but they insist that this information will give them an advantage. They are likely to increase the frequency of interactions as the examinations or final grades draw near. I have had calls at home at midnight asking for the answer to an examination question I gave 12 months earlier. I usually say the answer is "C" and leave the phone off the hook. Having done as much as possible to calm the paranoid in class, the instructor should ask the persistent paranoid to stop by after class so that his or her questions may be answered without taking up class time. Since the paranoid student thrives on praise, the instructor may wish to provide some when it is deserved. This type of student will fight to get a front row seat in order to attract your attention.

The Silent Student

Many undergraduates are the silent type. Fearful of saying something stupid, they prefer to remain silent. They blend into the background as much as possible during the class period. The instructor should not ignore or give up on silent types, but should attempt to create a friendly and supportive classroom atmosphere that will encourage these students to participate. Instructors may have students discuss questions or issues in small groups so the silent-type will be more likely to participate. In whole-class discussions early in the semester, the instructor may ask such students questions that call for a yes, no, or other limited response. Later in the semester, after the student has acquired confidence, questions calling for an elaborated response may be asked. Be careful not to push too hard with these students; they usually try to escape the situation. Being lost in the crowd is what makes these students feel good; they tend to sit in the middle of the class in order not to be noticed.

The Partying Student

Students who are “party-ers” enjoy the social aspects of class. Party-ers love to talk. Often this student functions in class as the social leader. Additionally, these students view classes as meeting places rather than learning environments. They are attention-seekers (histrionic personality disorder) for whom social concerns are more important than intellectual matters. Party-ers can behave appropriately in class if they are given what they seek: attention. Instructors can let party-ers distribute handouts, organize a schedule for student oral reports, or present a summary of a previous class period. By giving party-ers recognition, instructors can provide the necessary motivation for them to achieve intellectual goals in addition to social ones. These students usually sit toward the back or the side of the class in the company of like-minded students. This position allows them to talk during class and exit rapidly so they can begin the “party” immediately.

The Dangerous Student

This type of student is a bully. He/she will bully not only other students but the instructor. These can include physical and verbal threats made to others in the class and the instructor. It is best to deal with the student early to set the parameter and expectation of behavior in the classroom. If the student does not comply have the Dean of Student intervene. Do not allow this student to control you or the class. This person may have the characteristics of the anti-social personality disorder. If you feel physically threatened call the campus police.

The Unprepared Student

Some students simply lack what it takes to make it in college, often due to a lack of preparation in high school. The unprepared student may lack necessary study skills, career direction, interest in the subject matter, or, possibly, natural intelligence. Some may even be in college at their parents' insistence, rather than their own desire. These students in past decades were often in school to avoid the military draft or the reality of the world of work. The instructor's responsibility is to get unprepared students to counseling services, to remedial services, and to other testing and tutoring services on campus. In many universities, information about such services is included in a handbook of student services. When such information is not freely available, instructors may request it from the Dean of Students office or your departmental administrator. This student will usually sit in the back of the classroom so that you will tend not to ask him or her questions.

The Social Isolate

This student never interacts with any of the other students. He/she comes to class, sits quietly, and takes notes, never offering any input. When the class is over, the student leaves as soon as possible and never socializes with the other students. These students may even dress differently. They are very hard to interact with, since they seem to disappear when given the opportunity. These students will usually sit on the side of the classroom as far away from other students as possible. Dealing with this type of student is difficult, primarily because they are never around. Interact with the student as he or she enters the room; try a comment about the last class or the readings in the text. Any gesture will help break the ice and possibly start to develop an environment more conducive to learning. Many times the student will fade into the class and you will never see him or her again, but an effort should be made to let the student feel at ease.

The Preoccupied Student

Students may be preoccupied with nonacademic pursuits: Greek activities, work, dating, family, drinking, or pumping iron. Second-semester seniors are notorious for "senioritis." This is the feeling that they have had enough of school and that it is time to party before entering the "real world." You may have several in your class. Preoccupied students may come to the instructor with a plethora of excuses for late papers, nonattendance, or shoddy work. One instructor's strategy in dealing with preoccupied students is to let them know that they are not going to get away with this behavior—that their grades will suffer if they do not start attending class regularly and doing the assignments. Once the instructor has established the policy, it must be enforced. However, preoccupied students usually do not care; they only need a "D-" in your class to graduate and either may have already interviewed or obtained a job. They sit anywhere they want and change seats throughout the term in order to maximize their last contacts with other students of like interests.

The Disrespectful Student

The disrespectful student treats college professors with hostility, cynicism, and detachment. They typically are not physically dangerous. Disrespectful students are habitual rebels who sit in the back of the class, make cutting remarks to others of like minds, and generally disrupt class proceedings. Disrespectful students are frequently juniors or seniors who are taking required freshman-level classes and feel that the class is beneath their dignity and ability. I always ask this type of advanced student why they waited to take this "stupid" class until now; they usually do not have a good answer. Instructors who are victims of disrespectful students cannot ignore the situation since disrespectful students can destroy the learning environment for all the students. The most civilized way to deal with a disrespectful student is to arrange a private conference. During the conference, the instructor should openly express how the disrespectful student's actions affect the class. Approaching a disrespectful student on a person-to-person level sometimes causes him or her to behave in a decent manner. This strategy is not, however, universally effective. When a disrespectful student persists in expressing contempt for a course, the student should be told to drop the course. As a last resort, the instructor may ask the course supervisor, the Dean of Students, or the disrespectful student's academic adviser to speak with the student in a firm manner.

The Bad Student Athlete

This student type is often more concerned with staying eligible for the season than learning anything in your class. They rarely attend class; their coaches are constantly concerned with the student's grades and often will send grade progress reports which require your time to respond. It appears the students' coaches are also more concerned about the athletes' eligibility to participate in sports rather than with their education. The "win at any cost" mentality that has been developing in college athletics is growing more prevalent each year. Coaches and programs bring in "Junior College Transfer" students to play the sport for a semester with no intention of the student ever graduating from your school. Ask the athletic department for the graduation rates of these transfer students. You might be amazed at the low number.

The Good Student Athlete

These students are attending school on an athletic scholarship and are making the most of the opportunity. They not only perform well in their athletic area, but are very good students. They have major time commitments to their sport and will strive to be very good students. I will help these students and coaches with scheduling conflicts and work with them to maximize their performance in class. It is nice to watch a sporting event and recognize one of your good student athletes in action. I usually give the praise for both academic and athletic accomplishments.

The Cheating Student

Antisocial is the best description of this student. He/she will lie, cheat, and steal in order to maximize the course grade and minimize their work in the class. These students will do just about anything to obtain a copy of the exam early. See my precaution in Chapter 5 for possible security measures to help you thwart this individual. They will sign your name to documents, intimidate other students into doing their homework assignments, threaten and harass other students. Have the Dean of Students deal with this student after the first offense; avoid this student as much as possible.

The Amorous Student

These students think for whatever reason that you are available for romance. These students must be told very early in their romantic explorations that it is inappropriate for an instructor and student to become involved. There are many cases of romance gone bad at every institution: do not become one of these legends. They will often come to your office hour, stroke your ego, and in general make you feel good. But remember what Nancy Reagan said: "Just say no!"

The Physically Disabled Student

Make all attempts to mitigate any problems for these students, whether it is access to the classroom, or time needed to get from class to class. Call your school's disabled student services office to ask if there are any additional areas that you can help with. You need to access the Americans with Disabilities Act and include the provisions on your syllabus and any other handouts. See http://www.usdoj.gov/crt/ada/adahom1.htm for more information. Do everything you can to help these students in the areas of privacy, confidentiality concerns, note-takers, recording devices, speech conversion software, and other assistive technology they may require.

The Learning Disabled Student

These students have a disability that does not allow them to function well in the academic environment. In many cases these students have to be tested for their disability and will have a card certifying their disability. They may require more time for tests, special quiet testing areas, require readers, or need any number of other services. Contact your disabilities office and ask for the current policies for helping these students. Do as much as you can to help these students; often they will be very motivated. Another disadvantage these students will have is that other mainstream students may resent their perceived advantages in testing and evaluations situations.

The "Special" Student

The entire universe revolves around this student; classes get in the way. They will *need* to take the test early/late because they are in a wedding, going to a wedding, have airline tickets only good on that specific day, have a test that same day, have a real or imagined health problem, a sick or dying relative. Constantly you will accommodate these individual with early/late tests on which they usually earn a "D" or "F." A tremendous amount of time and effort is wasted on these "special" students. Do the extra work and hope that they do not take another class with you. This trend of being "special," or somehow entitled is a very disturbing one. Do students really think they can be "special" in the real world of work?

The "It's Your Fault" Student

This student and often the parents of the student say that they have paid their tuition and thus deserve an "A" grade in your courses. They act as if knowledge can be obtained by simply buying it. The thought of working for knowledge has not occurred to them. The level of expectation is that they paid for the class and came to class so they deserve an "A." I often hear "You gave me a "C" from these students. I suggest that they earned the grade, but they never like that response much.

The Mouth

This student is constantly asking questions in lecture that have no usefulness or are so off topic they really are a waste of lecture time. They constantly want to be the center of attention and love the limelight. Other students typically do not like this person. They see their behavior as a waste of class time and will mention this to you after lecture. All you can do is to avoid long answers to the question. I usually ask the offending student to see me at my office hours to discuss the question; they never show up—no audience.

(These types of students were influenced by Allen and Rueter, 1990)

Use this classification system to understand the motivations of students. Additionally, your understanding of the "types" of students in your class will prepare you to deal more effectively with their behavior and perhaps modify their behavior. Students are your responsibility; you must help all the various types maximize their potential for receiving a college education.

Violence on Campus

An unfortunate trend on the nation's campuses is overt violence. Many campus security offices are developing plans to protect faculty, staff and students in the event of an incident. Make yourself familiar with this emergency plan and the actions you should take to protect yourself and your students. Know the layout of your classrooms and department buildings. Do not be paranoid, but cautious. These emergencies are occurring at an alarming rate.

Graduate Student Stereotypes

The following is an attempt to list the characteristics you are likely to encounter from the instructor's perspective. Although these people exist only in my imagination many of the students you meet will have some of these characteristics. None of the examples listed below are living individuals. This list of stereotypes is not intended to offend any individual student, but rather to give you a sense of the types of students that you may encounter in your graduate classes and as TAs.

The Really Good Student

These dream graduate students are friendly, respectful, and get their work done on time. They will gently remind you of things you have forgotten, like asking if we are having class today when you forget the time. If they were all this good, your graduate program would be a breeze. In classes, research and teaching assignments, they will always shine.

Always Late

This type will always be late. They constantly need more time for the paper that has been scheduled for 3 months; their seminar presentation needs to be scheduled to a later time. These students are lazy and unorganized and will constantly try to take advantage of you. The best advice you can give them is to become organized, use a computer organizer and a large desktop paper calendar to schedule everything due throughout the term. Make them get organized early and it will help you. Do not treat these students any differently; it will only encourage them to continue this behavior.

Can't Decide to Leave or Stay

This student always sees the other side of the fence (different school) as the greener side. They know they could get into other programs either at your school or other schools. Many will apply and be accepted into "better" programs. They will ask for your opinion regarding whether they should leave or stay. Try to give them feedback about potential careers so they can make their own decisions.

Retread

This student went to the "Real World," had a job, and now knows what new career path they would like. They have come back to graduate school with very clear intentions, goals, and methods for obtaining such goals. These students are a delight. They are bright and goal directed and know how to read, understand and follow directions. Help them get though any rough spots; they will be good representatives of your program.

Scammer

Simply, this person cannot be trusted. They are constantly scamming something or someone; you, staff or other graduate students. They are troublemakers and will instigate trouble with other graduate students by starting rumors or presenting disinformation. Stay away from these students; let the senior faculty deal with them.

Disoriented

"Really lost" describes these students. They miss class because they forget and complete assignments randomly, some good, some terrible, but always with duress. With some guidance, these students can become productive. They need to concentrate on their current situation, which is graduate school.

Personality Kid

Everyone's favorite student: smart, attractive and hard working. This is the model graduate student you wish you had been. This person will go far in their career and in life. Try to become associated with this rising star.

Trade for Favors

This student will always be willing to house sit for you, pick you up at the airport, or do other favors, often unethical, to try to influence you for a favorable evaluation. This student is best avoided. They will always call in favors at some point.

Show Me the Money

These students think of graduate school as a way to make money (GTA, GRA, stipends, or lab tech) rather than becoming educated. They will be very happy to do nothing but work, stay enrolled in school, and avoid starting student loan repayments. Advise these students that the object of graduate school is to receive a graduate education, a graduate degree and move on to a career.

Over Stressed!!!!!!

Stressed almost at the level of Panic Disorder, this person tries to run their life (kids, family, or monetary problems) and graduate school, constantly barely making the grade or deadline. They usually are compulsive enough to make it through graduate school, but with tremendous effort. Try to help as much as possible; if things were less complicated for these individuals, they could be very good students.

The Subservient

Allows other graduate student to push him or her around in social and academic situations. This student may have a low self esteem and can easily be influenced by others. Try to give this student some support and help them understand their self worth is higher than they think.

Use this classification system to understand the motivations of the students. Additionally, your understanding of the "types" of students in your class will enable you to deal more effectively with their behavior and perhaps modify their behavior, if necessary. Some of these students may be your TAs, in your graduate classes and understanding their motivation can help you in your mentoring of these students.

Students are your responsibility; you must help everyone maximize their potential in college.

Interactions with Students out of Class

You face an uncharted course when leaving the classroom to enter the undefined area of interacting with students out of the classroom. A general rule is to remember your interactions with faculty members when you were an undergraduate. Now that you are a faculty member and not a graduate student - the social world has changed.

Office Hours

Always be available during your posted office hours. If you cannot keep your office hours (attending a conference is a good example), announce this fact in class. During illness or emergencies, ask the department administrator to post a note on your office door notifying that you will not be in your office.

Conducting Your Office Hours

How you should conduct your office hours is a subject that concerns many new instructors. During posted office hours, you should be in your office—not somewhere else—willing and able to help students. Do not engage in a project that cannot be set aside, like writing a book. Do not talk on the telephone for the entire hour. A former colleague of mine would talk on the telephone for the entire hour, long distance, while several students waited in the hall. When he finally got off the telephone, it would be time for class and he would tell the students to come back later and rush off to class. This is extremely poor form. The students are the reason you are in your office! Read the text or do other light work that can be interrupted. Turn off your computer screen when a student comes into your office to avoid distractions.

Be friendly to the students in your office; ask them to have a chair and show real concern for their problems. On occasion you will have students with personal problems that you cannot or should not handle. Know your departmental and school's referral policy and send these students to the appropriate campus service center.

During your office hours, there is a high probability that you will have publishers' representatives visit. This will happen usually at the beginning of each term and during text ordering for future classes. Give the publishers' representatives the same courtesy that you do to students, but realize that these individuals have second priority. If a student is waiting to see you, excuse the publisher's representative and take care of the student's needs first. The publisher's representative knows that this is your priority and will comply.

During many of your office hours, you will not have visitors. I like to schedule my office hour right before class meets. This allows time to review my lecture notes and catch up on my reading. As examinations near, the frequency of visits will increase, so plan to see more students with specific questions about examinations.

Insist that your TAs post and keep their office hours. Do random checks until you are sure they are available during the office hours. TAs are your representatives and much be available when there office hours indicated they will be.

A Rule You Should Never Break

You must be very careful to properly conduct yourself around students. A sacred rule in academia is to never use your faculty position to gain any favors from students. This includes anything from football tickets to sexual favors. Never put yourself in a position where your integrity can be questioned. The best way to accomplish this is to leave no doubt about your intentions. A good practice, for example, is to always keep your door partially open when a student is in your office. Rumors are a very nasty thing to stop, even when they are unfounded. Be fair; above all, never give any consideration in the area of grades to preferred students. Even a false hint about unethical behavior can mean the end of your teaching career. Obtain a copy of the school's conduct procedures on sexual harassment and instructor's conduct.

Conduct Off Campus

You may meet students off campus or at other functions not associated with the school. You should not shun them, but realize that they are still your students. Do not put yourself in a position you may regret; realize that your new position dictates certain conduct. Do not date your students. Dating your students is considered sexual harassment by many.

The Day of the Examination

It amazes me when I hear of the high number of tragedies that occur on or just before examination day. I can remember going into the department office the morning of my first examination of the fall term and being greeted by the department administrator who said that she wondered what type of tragedy would befall the students today; she was waiting for the phone to ring. There are occasions when real problems and family emergencies will occur; one of the best policies, and probably the most fair, is to have your Dean of Students Services decide if an excuse is proper. Some students will have a valid scheduling conflict with your examination (a student may be on the golf team, for example). That student should make early arrangements with you for a make-up examination. This make-up policy should be clearly stated in the course syllabus. Be as flexible and fair as you can with students when the situation is reasonable.

After the examination, you are likely to get upset students who say they are going to flunk out of college because of your test. Assure them that they probably will not flunk out of college; ask them to see you during your office hours the next day. At this meeting, discuss study strategies and other resources available at your school.

Campus Resources Available to the Student

You will encounter students who will need extra academic help or other types of advice. I encourage students to stop by my office any time to talk about problems concerning school. Most schools offer a variety of services for students with academic or other problems. To find out what is available to students, start with your department's services and others listed in the campus telephone directory or on the school's Internet site.

The following is a common list of services available to students in most universities, colleges and two-year schools.

Entering Student Services

The first resource is likely to be the center or office that supervises freshman students. This office maintains student records and provides orientation programs. At many schools, a majority of the students will enroll in general studies, which performs similar functions. Often services like tutoring programs are coordinated by these offices. Some schools are providing faculty with on-line access to student academic records.

Writing Centers

Sometimes called writing labs, and usually staffed by members of the English Department, the writing center offers assistance with a variety of writing problems. The writing center's staff is often highly qualified. We recommend referring students to this service for any writing problems.

Tutoring Services

On many campuses, the most organized tutoring services are usually those provided to student athletes, Greek organizations, or learning disabled students. But other campus organizations may offer voluntary tutoring programs or serve as agents for more informal peer tutoring arrangements.

Counseling Programs

These programs offer assistance to students with academic or emotional problems severe enough to require such an approach. This program may include a learning resource center or testing program to help students develop better study skills or test-taking behaviors as well as services to help students set educational goals and plan careers. Psychological services are usually available.

Research Services of the Library

It is a good idea to make yourself aware of research services available at the campus library. Depending on the size of its collection and staff, the library may offer individual term paper conferences with the student, presentations about specific resources to classes, and computer-assisted searches. Much of the traditional library servicing is or will be converted to online services. Discuss available services with the appropriate individuals in your library.

Reading Programs

Most schools have a separate reading program or lab to assist students in developing the reading skills crucial to good academic achievement. There may be individual staff or off-campus organizations that specialize in these types of problems.

International Student Programs

With the increasing enrollment by international students many school have developed centers to help these students with language and cultural issues.

Professional Services

In many college towns, students have access to professional editing or research services. Often typing/word processing services will offer editing assistance. You probably want your students to use editing services to facilitate their writing.

Student Health

Most schools have a student health service designed to take care of student health needs. There may be occasions when you will want to refer students to this health service. Health situations addressed at the student health service can range from minor to severe. Be aware of the services available to your students.

Mental Health Center

Many schools have some form of mental health facility often associated with the psychology, counseling, or medical departments on campus. You are likely to encounter students indicating problems in this area. Be aware of these service options and refer students you feel may benefit from this type of service.

Computer Labs

For either class, work, or fun, many schools have computer labs. Take advantage of these labs. They are often equipped with state-of-the-art machines. Surf the Internet, check e-mail, use chat rooms, do homework, search the library.

E-mail Facilities

Many schools have stations available to check your e-mail throughout campus. These centers have become less relevant with the advent of hand held devices that interface with the Internet. Students should make a habit of checking their e-mail at least twice a day.

Sexual Harassment Office

Many campuses have administrative staff dedicated to the problem of sexual harassment in the academic environment. If students ask, be able to direct them to the proper staff.

Wireless Internet Conductivity

As areas of the campus having wireless Internet conductivity installed increase, become aware of these as they are added. Tell your students about this very useful interface. These areas have become less relevant with the advent of hand held devices that interface with the Internet.

(This list was influenced by Seelbinder and Landstrom, 1990)

Your familiarity with the services available will help you to make appropriate suggestions to students who may need help or who may ask you to direct them to other resources. Encouraging students to seek additional help may at times present a problem. Some students may feel you are abandoning them; you will have to reassure them, making clear the limits you face.

Sexually Harassing Environments

It is your moral and legal duty to discourage sexually harassing environments in your workplace. What can you do to reduce any harassing environments? Treat every student the same regardless of their gender. You also have the moral obligation to report any violation in your department. Become familiar with the proper procedures for reporting any harassing situations.

Chapter 9

Interactions with Faculty and Staff

Dealing with Faculty

Your Place in the Big Picture

Being a new faculty member and knowing that you are at the very bottom of the political/power totem pole can foster a healthy attitude. If you are either a new faculty member or GTA, realize that as you interact with the faculty in your department; they are the final authority in judging your performance. Each school has some formal process for student evaluations of your teaching ability and a form of faculty annual review for your performance. However, the most realistic evaluations are often accomplished via informal interactions with other faculty members rather than a formal process. Do not be apprehensive, be cordial, be yourself, while realizing that we are all evaluated during our careers.

Faculty Stereotypes

There are several definitive types of faculty you are likely to meet. The following is an attempt to list the characteristics you are likely to encounter. Although these people exist only in my imagination, many of the faculty you meet will have some of these characteristics. None of the examples listed below are living individuals. Use this information to help direct your interaction with the faculty. Knowing what to expect will allow you to make preliminary decisions about your behavior in certain situations. Besides, some day you will become one of these types.

The Big Gun

This individual is a full professor, with very high status on the campus, who is well known in the research community and may be known nationally or internationally. This is the person you always thought you wanted to be. You will often find that to attain this level of status, these professors have devoted their lives to the study of their content area, often to the exclusion of family, social interactions, friends, and even personal health. They are usually too busy to have much interaction with you as a new instructor. Big guns typically teach very little and usually only at the graduate level. They normally have the maximum political clout in the department and school.

The Small Gun

This individual is probably a full professor approaching the end of his career who never reached the level of achievement that was expected. This person is not renowned for teaching or research, but does an adequate job in both. He/she may have devoted much of his recent energy toward school committee or administration work. This person can be a good ally and will have the time to discuss aspects of your teaching. He/she will usually have moderate political clout in the department and school.

The Non-Tenured

These are the individuals who are trying to do everything all at once. They have good teaching evaluations from students, interact with the senior faculty socially, do as much research as possible, and try to publish enough to be tenured. They usually burn the candle at both ends and have little spare time. They can be a good source of information concerning the power structure of the department. These currently non-tenured faculty usually have little political clout, but have potential for the future.

The Not-Tenured

This person was not tenured in your department. This individual is usually given one academic year to find a new job. Good luck in the current environment with having failed to be tenured in your school. This can happen for many reasons including not producing enough quality research or being a poor instructor. This person is likely very disgruntled and should be avoided. At some time in the future, ask your mentor why this person failed the tenure test.

The Post-Tenured

Many faculty exhibit a post-tenured depression. This may be evident in their teaching and, particularly, in their research. They have finally made it and are taking a breather before continuing the promotion cycle. They are usually good allies and have increasing political clout.

The Post-Tenured (Acute)

This is just a temporary letdown for the acute type, six months and they are back up to speed. Now they have the goal of a sabbatical and need to work hard toward that goal. Could be the kind of faculty member you need to know in the future.

The Post-Tenured (Chronic)

This faculty member is a failure. Thirty years in the department and still an associate professor. This person has always been incompetent in both teaching and research, barely managed to get tenure and now is a permanent fixture in the department. The students do not like this person because they recognize incompetence. Most of the departments can't wait for this individual to retire. Lower political power.

The Promoter

He/she is trying to increase his/her status and rank in the school. The promoter is a good ally and someone you can ask about the dos and don'ts of the department. This individual can often help with questions concerning teaching. Political clout is medium and rising.

The Disgruntled

The disgruntled faculty member hates the department or school. He/she is probably leaving the department very soon, either voluntarily or otherwise. This individual is often the sour grapes type and is best avoided. He/she may have negative political clout.

The Weasel

Outwardly nice, this person is a false front. Always working in the background to maximize their own personal outcomes, whether it be momentary or in political power. This person will change allegiances year after year, with no warning. Thinks nothing of throwing you under the bus if it facilitates self-promotion. Always willing to go over your head, other faculty members' heads or your department chair to get their way. Stay away from this person—he/she can only hurt you in the long run. This individual may have higher aspirations and could become a Dean some day, but never will because of the past misdeeds. Most faculty realize this person's motives, do not like the individual and actively avoid him/her.

The Current Administrator

This is the current department chair. This person is usually promoted from the faculty ranks in your department. If your department is too dysfunctional, the chair may be an outside hire. It is important to realize that the current department chair's political clout is at its highest level and that they are influential at the school, in the department and have considerable power over your life. In many schools, this individual has the final hiring authority, makes GTA assignments, and has major input into the tenure process. This person, in many departments, will also write your annual review. This person can range from great to awful in competence and personality. If swayed by a faction you are not a part of he/she can make your life more frustrating than it needs to be.

The Past Administrator

This faculty member is a former department chair. The past administrator has returned to the ranks of the faculty and may or may not be happy with the situation. As the chair, he/she had a light teaching load, high status in the department and school, but is now required to do more teaching and research. This person can be a valuable resource for understanding the workings of the department and the school. This individual may have higher aspirations and could become a Dean some day. Political clout can vary, but is usually at a high level.

The Absent Member

This individual, for a number of reasons, is not often physically present. He/she is usually tenured. This absence typically has something to do with a consulting business or a clinic he/she is operating. Absent members perform at a minimum level in the department. They often will use the school to legitimize their outside interests. The individuals are usually on the Tuesday and Thursday schedule, thus allowing for minimum time in the department. Clout can vary, but usually is on the low side.

The Dinosaur

This individual is also known as deadwood and is usually older. He/she may have been productive in the past, but is no longer. He/she is tenured and abusing the tenure system. He/she is simply drawing a paycheck. This person performs at or below expected standards for a faculty member in the school, since little can be done about his/her behavior. This person demands the most support, TAs, travel, release time, and is usually undeserving of this special treatment. This person believes that his/her rank permits a special status. In every department I have ever been associated with, there is at least one dinosaur. His/her political clout is usually negative with active members. As in the distant past, it is best to avoid dinosaurs.

The Adjunct

This person is not on a tenure track line in the department. This individual works on term contracts. Trying to hang on by the thinnest of margins, the adjunct must be the best teacher in the department, since there is usually no research commitment. Since this individual is judged on a different scale than the rest of the faculty, he/she tries to be better at teaching than any of the other faculty because the job depends on this. The adjunct's teaching load is always higher, and is paid less than the tenured faculty because he/she is a teaching specialist and typically does not do research. Always the first to go when budgeting is an issue, the adjunct can help tremendously in your teaching. Political clout varies, but is usually low.

The Mole

He/she is there, but he/she is not in sight. This individual comes to work, teaches his/her classes, and disappears. Often he/she comes to their departmental office or does research, but rarely socializes with the faculty or students. This person is often "working from home." This person is best left alone. Political clout on the low side.

Just Leaving

This faculty member is about to retire, usually after a long career at your school. With tight budgets, the norm of the early part of the 21st century dictates that many pre-retirees are given generous inducements to retire early. Some accept the offers and others refuse, wanting to continue in the comfort of high rank and status in the department and school. These interesting individuals will often provide unique and valuable insights into the workings of the department. Political clout is usually on the high side.

Won't Go

This individual has been in the department forever, really forever, the longest survivor of the distant past. Their level of competence can vary. All of their colleagues have retired or died years ago, but this person still gets a check every month, is tenured and there is nothing that can induce the individual to leave. I know of an individual who was over 80 years old when they finally quit. Low political clout.

The Emeritus

In many schools the emeritus faculty holds a very high status. This retired individual often was an internationally known researcher or teacher. This person wants to keep active in academia and usually has an office in the department. If you can approach this individual, you may gain a valuable ally for future interactions with the administration at your school. This individual often knows many of the highest ranking individuals in the administration. A phone call from this person can be valuable. Political clout very high.

The Other New Guy

This person is very much like you: brand new, shiny, fresh out of graduate school or a GTA. Often this person is a candidate to be a good friend. You might share many of the same interests, sports, music, or politics that the rest of the faculty may not. A good friend can help you through the tough times and may some day have high status and political power.

The Bizarre Member

This individual is tenured, and that is good thing for him/her. This person has at least one severe personality/major psychological disorder and related bizarre behaviors and can barely function in real life, let alone teach and do research. The only thing that keeps this person around is tenure. Negative political power.

The Burn Out

Like many stars, they burn brightly for a short time. This person was on the fast track but has fallen off. Now content to teach the minimum and do some research. Losing political power.

The Obsessive

A place for everything and everything in its place is the motto of this member. Office is perfectly arranged, meets class exactly the number of minutes required, is always the first to submit required materials, neat to a fault (Obsessive-Compulsive Personality Disorder). Other than this compulsion to have everything in their life orderly, they can be fun. Often these individuals are very productive in research and grant writing. Why? Because they are so organized.

The Machiavellian Personality

This person has a gift of persuasion though coercion. This type appears very intelligent and always asks the correct questions and has a knack of looking at a problem from a different, more self serving-perspective. They always get their way or will not participate. They are the best at everything; just ask them. They demand a larger share than others of the available resources, like GTAs, GRAs, travel money, office space, or research space. They always use coercion before a important meeting to assure a vote will be in their favor; they do not leave anything to chance. They have been successful in the department because for a while other faculty believed they are as great as they think they are. This delusional behavior is to the extent that the individual really believes the delusion. Fortunately, continued demands for excessive resources and no productivity by the individual eventually leads the majority of the department to understand what a con artist this person really is. These individuals have a habit of moving from institution to institution just before a tenure decision, probably because tenure reviews have exposed the fraud. Stay away from this person, way too much political baggage. Political clout varies depending on how much of the charade still exists.

The Immoral Guy

For some reason this person thinks that is it fine to have sexual relations with students. This person thinks it is fine to have sex even with undergraduates currently in his or her classes. Of course, graduates students are also fair game for this person. This behavior is unethical and illegal in most states. This person's reputation degrades the reputation and status of the department as a whole. Stay away from this person; he or she is just plain trouble. Status low.

The Great Potential Person

Usually a junior faculty member who has recently been recruited to the department with great expectations. Gets all the best, awarded the biggest startup package in the department's history, most research space of any individual, largest office, most graduate students, most travel money, lightest teaching load; with all this support and great potential this person still can not complete and publish any research. All potential, no results. Will probably leave the department soon. Low on the political status index and falling rapidly.

The Grant Guy

This person has a large grant and has had funding for many years. This person can be very well known nationally or internationally. Teaches little, but does excellent research. This person is a lot like the big gun, only with a very large grant. High status.

The Grant Guy, Lost

Same as above, but has just lost the funding which he/she has had for many years. Now he/she faces the unhappy prospect of returning to the teaching faculty.

The Disingenuous

Never to be trusted, this person will look you in the eye and lie to you to better their position. Often teams with the weasel to form a faction. Never trust this person at any level. Political clout varied. Not trusted by most of the faculty

The Mentor

This is the person you may have been searching for to act as your departmental mentor. This person is a very good teacher, is well connected on campus, and conducts a good research program. What makes this individual most important is that he/she is willing to share his/her success with a new instructor like yourself. This person should be courted, and will help you advance your career. Political clout is high.

This is only a partial list of stereotypes. You will find many others in your department. This list is intended as a practical guide to help guide your interactions. Remember, these are the people who will decide your professional fate. There will be departmental factions that may try to recruit you; stay as politically neutral as possible—remain apolitical.

Complete the duties that are required for your position. Volunteer for additional departmental or school duties when appropriate within your teaching and research schedule. Many schools review and consider community and school service as part of tenure and contract negotiations. See Chapter 13 for a more detailed discussion.

Upper Administration Stereotypes

There are several definitive types of administrators you are likely to meet. The following is an attempt to list the characteristics you are likely to encounter. Although these people exist only in my imagination, many of the administrators you meet will have some of these characteristics. None of the examples listed below are living individuals. Use this information to help direct your interaction with the administrators. Knowing what to expect will allow you to make preliminary decisions about your behavior in certain situations. Besides, some day you might become one of these types.

Upper administration is any faculty or administrative position higher than your department at your institution.

Faculty Senate or Faculty Council

This or a similar group represents the faculty as a whole in discussions with the upper administration. Many times this organization's effectiveness depends on the internal leadership. This organization's level of influence can range from very little to a powerful voice of the faculty

Unions

Unions are formed at the request of the faculty and have a formal role in negations with the upper administration. You will pay for this representation and you will be expected to abide by the rules of the union.

Your Dean

One of the most powerful individuals in the upper administration. This person sets the budgets and funding for your department, signs off on tenure documents, signs all renewable contracts, letters of hire and often time can help out with specific needs for funding projects. Usually promoted from department chair either at your school of more likely from another school. This position is many times a stepping stone to higher level administration positions. This can be a very frustrating position for the individual in it. Keep a low profile and make all your interactions professional and cordial. Every Dean has a different personality, some are loved by the faculty, some despised. Some competent, some not. Many times a Dean position is a stepping stone to a better job at another school. Good Dean, bad Dean, you really can not choose, but you will have to deal with the Dean you get.

The Other Dean

This person has the same responsibilities as your Dean but is working in a different college or division at your school. You should have very little contact with this person, but know them by sight and be cordial.

The Vice-Presidents

There are usually several of these positions and might include:, VP for Finance, VP for Student Affairs, VP for Research, VP for Outreach, VP for Distance Learning and Vice President for Graduate Studies. The individuals are the heavy hitters in your school; they control the funding and its distribution. You should have very little interaction with these individuals, but know them by sight and be cordial.

The Provost

The real power behind the throne. This number two makes many of the day to day final decisions, chairs the most important committees on campus and delegates authority to the vice presidents. Can be a very strong personality because he or she must be to manage effectively. Often the next step for these individuals is a President's job at a different school. You should know this individual by sight and be cordial in any interactions.

The President

"The Man or Woman." This individual is the final decision maker, although many of the decisions have already been made by the vice-presidents and Provost. This person is responsible for all the decisions. Many times a major portion of his or her job is fundraising. This person is the "face" of the school and is the recognizable authority off campus.

The Board of Regents, Trustees, Deacons or Similar

These people interface with the State Legislature in terms of funding and policy -making. Private schools may have Directors, or similar boards who interact with foundations and other funding sources. These are the people most removed from the everyday research, teaching and service, but they are the ones who set the policy that will affect your academic life. You will probably never see these individuals except for news conferences and on television.

This is only a partial list of stereotypes. You will find others in your school. This list is intended as a practical resource to help guide your interactions.

Remember, these are the people who will decide your professional fate. They run the school!

Dealing with the Staff

Head Administrator

The head departmental administrator has a tremendous amount of power over your future in the department. In many departments this individual decides what gets done and when. If you are on the wrong side of this individual, your teaching can be adversely affected. Be cordial and professional in your interactions. Turn in required material on time and be cooperative.

The Administrative Assistants (Secretaries)

These are the individuals who do the daily work, copy exams, make handouts, take messages, arrange classroom assignments, order textbooks, and process all the paperwork for the department. Do not make unreasonable demands on these individuals, such as last minute test production or missed deadlines. These administrative assistants may be younger and friendlier than the head administrator, but remember where the power is. Treat these individuals with respect; their job is a hard one with little reward.

The Technicians

They are the individuals who run the laboratories, build the experimental equipment, staff the storerooms and animal care facilities. These are usually interesting individuals with an interesting background. Introduce yourself. You will need their assistance in the future.

Information Technology (IT)

These individuals are critical to your success in teaching. With the advent of the new classroom technologies it is critical that you have a good working relationship with the IT guys. When the computer in the classroom won't boot, a quick call and response for the IT guys can save the day. If the presentation software is corrupted on you machine, again, they can help. The newest technology can be easily evaluated over a cup of coffee with the IT guys. Really get to know these individuals. They are typically very intelligent, quirky people who have a lot of information to offer.

Others You Should Know

The reference librarian is especially useful when dealing with electronic resources. Student services personnel can be helpful in locating a missing student. Contact individuals in the Registrar's office for class time scheduling, room assignment, and grade submission deadlines. Staff in the Research office and the Institutional Research Board help keep you current with any subject (participant) pool requirements. The custodians in your building almost always have an interesting story to tell and can help you with logistical issues.

School Bureaucrats

These individuals are not related to the academic area of the school and are often referred to as the "administration." Depending on their level and function, they either can be very helpful or very obstructive. They are the paper pushers. Lower-level paper pushers are usually more helpful than their supervisors. The best strategy for dealing with this segment of the staff is to make sure you comply with their deadlines and cooperate with them. They will soon associate your name with promptness and a level of cooperation. Their jobs can be very difficult especially concerning grade deadlines, graduation deadlines, and transcript evaluations, so do your best to be on time.

Interacting with School Coaching Staff

At a typical school you will have a number of athletes in your classes. At the end of the term you may receive a telephone call or a drop-in visit from one of the school's athletic coaches. This individual will be very interested in the grades of his/her athletes. I treat these individuals the same as any other staff member. Be careful to resist any influence techniques they might attempt to use on you.

Social Interactions with the Staff

As a new instructor, you may find that you have more in common with the secretaries and technical staff than you do with the faculty members. They are often younger, more personable, less stressed, and more fun to interact with than the faculty. Remember to temper your interactions with these individuals. You are now a faculty member and must act accordingly.

Use these suggestions about these individuals to help guide you in selecting the appropriate behavior for different situations. It never hurts to have an idea of what to expect in your new environment.

Chapter 10

Methods of Evaluating Your Teaching

A major event in your academic career is the continual evaluation of your teaching. Evaluations can come in several forms, from formal to casual. The faculty is, although they may not admit it, evaluating you constantly. Much of what you say and many of the actions you take are being appraised. The faculty may not make a formal evaluation of your classroom behavior and general conduct as a faculty member until it is time for a contract to be renewed or for an annual review. You should not be paranoid about this constant assessment of both your behavior and personality, but rather realize that everyone is evaluated at the beginning of a career in this manner. The faculty wants to see if you "fit in" with the department. On the other hand, you wish to see if this department is where you might want to spend the next 40 years. So be yourself and enjoy your first experience of teaching, while conducting yourself in a professional manner at all times.

Formal Evaluations

Formal evaluations can be in the form of committee reviews or departmental annual reviews. These consist of your submissions of materials about your teaching effectiveness, research, publications, and school and community service. Often committees will visit your class to assess your teaching. A committee or the department head will write a report and forward it to a higher authority. This evaluation process is a traditional method of securing contracts, tenure, promotions, and raises in academia. Be sure to provide an orderly presentation of your materials, be prompt in supplying the requested documentation, and provide everything requested. In a way, this may be the most comfortable method of evaluation. You provide the major portion of the materials and you are judged on your performance, in an objective manner. Personal appraisals by the faculty are factored into the equation at this point, but the major portion of the evaluation should be objective.

Student Evaluations

Formal Student Evaluations

Student evaluations of your overall classroom performance are a major component of an evaluation. Many departments or schools will have standardized evaluation forms which utilize years of normative data on your department. Check with your supervisor for the correct evaluation form and preferred time for administration of the evaluation. The formal evaluations will often compare you with school norms on many factors involved in teaching. In some cases, your evaluations might even be compared to state or national norms.

Informal Student Evaluations

Students are constantly assessing college teaching informally. Casual positive comments like, "Dr. W is the best teacher in the introductory course; be sure to take his section," are common. Negative evaluations are also common. "Dr. B's class is a waste of time; he knows nothing; skip it if you're smart," or "Dr. P doesn't know anything except his research, and all of his classes are the same material despite the course title." These are the types of assessments that are used by many students when selecting a course section. Although these evaluations are informal, they are important and may reach your supervisor. At many schools, student organizations have directories of faculty teaching effectiveness, ease of grading, and how interesting the faculty member has been in the past. These data are usually for sale in a small booklet around campus. This booklet is a good source to explore how your department is perceived by the students, this information can be important as you formulate you teaching strategies, see Chapter 2. After your first year, buy a copy of this booklet to see how you have fared.

Midterm Evaluation

For the new instructor it is a good idea to have a midterm evaluation from the students. These evaluations can be either the formal version used by your department or school or one of your own design. This feedback is critical to mid-course corrections. If students consistently make negative comments on your style, content, delivery, or other issues, use the feedback to modify your course. Failing to use this feedback for course modification can be a critical mistake for the new instructor. You really do not want to be in the Department Chair's office explaining why there are so many student complaints about your teaching; make corrections based on these evaluations.

Stereotypical Teaching Styles

Students can also classify teaching styles into stereotypes; these can be both positive and negative. You should be aware of these different types and strive to be seen as a positive type in the students' eyes.

Negative Teaching Styles

The negative styles involve ineffective teaching methods. First-term instructors are frequently shocked by end-of-course student evaluations. They had assumed that all was well with their teaching and that their students both liked and respected them. Among the styles that students do not like, or respect, are the following. Although these people exist only in my imagination, many of the faculty you meet will have some of these characteristics. None of the examples listed below are living individuals:

The Bore

In the classroom of the boring instructor, the most interested and active person present is the instructor, who talks on and on about the facts, concepts, laws, or precepts. Since the instructor is doing all, or almost all, of the talking, the class period passes rapidly for him. However, the same instructional period may seem endless and boring to the students. Few students have greater than a 50- to 60-minute attention span. Few lecturers are sufficiently dynamic, creative, and entertaining to sustain student attention for such a period of time. What instructors must understand is that most undergraduate students do not share their love for the discipline, yet! The bore merely presents the material to students; no attempt is made to relate the information to student needs and interests. In turn, the students doze, doodle, daydream, read the student paper, talk or do homework for another class. But since the bore is enamored with his/her voice, the bore never notices. If you are this type of instructor, you had better be tenured or teaching required courses.

The Boor

A boor is a person who is lacking in social skills. Instructors who are boors treat their students in a rude, cool, or distant manner. They belittle student questions; they interrupt student responses; they show little respect for student ability; they smirk instead of smile. The most offensive boors are instructors arrogant about their own intellectual achievements. They treat students with great disdain since they consider the undergraduate incapable of the high level of intellectual exchange the instructor values. Not all instructors who are perceived as boors are arrogant. In many cases, instructors who are shy or apprehensive try to conceal their uncertainty by showing little of their personalities to students. In the process they seem overbearing, haughty, and distant. They communicate to students that they do not wish to establish cordial interpersonal relationships.

Students will take the boor's class, but will not recommend it to other students. They will usually take this class because it is the only section offered. See the Machiavellian Personality in Chapter 9 for a further discussion of the boor.

The Flake

The flake suffers from terminal disorganization. He/she is the classic absent-minded professor. Instructors who are flakes have difficulty getting to class on time. Once they get there, it takes them a long time to get everything sorted out. Lecture notes fall to the floor. Tests the students expected returned remain on the instructor's desk. That desk reflects the personality of its user: layers of clutter everywhere, barely a spot available for work. It doesn't take long for students to recognize an instructor as a flake. In addition to looking the part, the flake is intellectually disorganized. Assignments are made in a haphazard fashion. Information is not presented in a clear and straightforward manner. Students will take advantage of this disorganization by turning in assignments late, saying the instructor lost assignments never turned in, and taking advantage of the professor's inability to organize.

The Fake

Instructors are sometimes assigned to teach or assist in courses outside their area of primary expertise. When this happens, it is expected that they will expend considerable energy in mastering the subject matter before attempting to teach it to others. Some instructors, however, decide to take a shortcut through the preparatory process by keeping a few pages ahead of the students and by "winging it." Typically the fake doesn't succeed. When an instructor doesn't know the material, students can tell; factual errors are made, questions are avoided or answered in an evasive manner, information is presented in a hesitant or halting fashion. There is no substitute for knowing the material. To accept a teaching assignment is to take on the obligation of becoming appropriately informed. If you find yourself in this position, take the time to master the material or turn down the assignment. A competent instructor should be able to teach any undergraduate class in his or her discipline with six month's preparation. As you progress in your career, you will be asked to teach classes in which you may not feel totally at ease with the subject matter. Take the challenge to explore new areas that you may have casually explored in your earlier training. Many times this "forced" learning will lead to exciting teaching and research areas.

The Wimp

A wimp is a wimp. Instructors who are wimps are uncertain about matters of pedagogy. They make assignments in a tentative, unsure manner. Assignments often sound more like questions or requests than statements. Wimps refuse to accept responsibility for the courses they teach. When students complain about course content, procedures, or expectations, the wimp is likely to say, "I don't like it either, but that's the way the department wants it done." Undergraduates soon learn that a wimpy instructor is a person to be manipulated rather than respected. Students maneuver the wimp into modifying assignments, changing due dates, and wasting class time by justifying course content and procedures. Do not be a wimp - take a position and defend it. It may not always be the most popular position, but at least have a position.

The Never Changing

This instructor is still teaching the same materials learned in graduate school 25 years ago. For this person, teaching in their content area effectively stopped adding new material on his/her graduation day. The same tattered, outdated notes are used every term. The same false rigor is used to mask incompetence each term. This instructor tends to be very rigid and has a dogmatic lecture style to cover for a lack of current knowledge. Students recognize the incompetence and disrespect the instructor. Students will only take the class if it is required and is the only section available. Tenure is the only thing that keeps this instructor in the classroom and employed by the school.

Positive Teaching Styles

On a more positive note these are some of the types of teaching styles for whom students have respect and are worth emulating. Although these people exist only in my imagination, many of the faculty you meet will have some of these characteristics. None of the examples listed below are living individuals.

The Eccentric

Certain instructors are effective because their exceptional intellect commands the attention and respect of their students. Such instructors have excellent verbal fluency and elaborate ideas expressed by vivid language and imagery. They are often a bit unorthodox in appearance and behavior. Why not? They are college professors. Because of their dedication to the study of their content area, they may give little attention to dress and personal grooming. They develop mannerisms that set them aside from others; they may pace back and forth as they speak to the floor or they may lead a class discussion while sitting cross-legged, guru style, on their desks. But it really doesn't matter. Students like and respect eccentric instructors.

The Entertainer

Some instructors are successful because they are entertaining. They are gifted storytellers and they use language in creative and humorous ways. They dominate the classroom because they like to be the center of attention. But their students don't care. They build illustrative examples from the lives of students. Entertainers take a personal interest in students because they want to adapt their "material" to their audience's interests, needs, and senses of humor. Students will line up to take a class from the entertainer.

The Basic Competent

Some instructors are effective because they have basic teaching competence. They don't display the intelligence of the eccentrics or the humor of the flashy entertainers. Still, they get the job done. The basic competent is the reverse of the flakes; they have clear goals in mind and they communicate their expectations to students in a clear manner. They set and adhere to deadlines. They grade and return work promptly. They are efficient in leading class discussions. When presenting information, they are straightforward. They are never tardy to class. They are always in their offices during announced office hours. They are dependable.

The Super Competent

These are often the best teachers in the department. They know their material so well they often do not need to bring notes to class; they have a very good style and approach to teaching. The students like these individuals because the course content is presented concisely with a little fun along the way. These individuals' classes are always the first to fill.

The Helper

The helper places high time demands on him or herself. Helpers go out of their way to ensure that their students do well. They hold extra office hours before major assignments are due. They hold evening review sessions before tests. They invite students to call them at home with questions. Helpers are basically nice people who treat their students with respect and who are, in turn, liked and respected by their students.

The Mentor

The mentor is a wise and trustworthy person. Mentors teach by example. They have exceptionally high standards of scholarship; they demand a great deal of themselves and, consequently, expect a great deal of their students. Mentors serve as role models of the skills and habits they seek to impart. This is the person you should seek out as your departmental mentor.

Professor Personality

The students love this style; the professor has an outgoing personality, both students and faculty like this person. In and out of the classroom, this individual is always "on," upbeat, and happy. The material in class can vary in quality and quantity, but this person always receives the highest student evaluations.

Cutting Edge Professor

This is a major new type of teacher who has emerged in the last ten years. This person has the best technological toys and knows how to use them. Fancy PowerPoint or other presentation software, Internet activity in the classroom, CD-ROM related homework assignments, course home page on the Internet, uses publisher websites, chat rooms for the class, develops podcasts and uses WebCT, D2L or other brands for class administration and communications. This person always has something new and exciting for the classroom. Students come to class just to see what is new. Often this person is self-motivated; there are usually few external rewards for the tremendous amount of work necessary to present classes in this manner.

The Maximum Content Guy

This instructor really knows his discipline and expects the student to excel in the course even if it is not a required course in the department. Students dislike the instructor while the class is in session, but later realize that he or she is valuable because he or she insists on high standards for the students. Students often will develop an appreciation of this individual after upper-division classes and graduation.

(This classification system was influenced by Allen and Rueter, 1990).

While this system for categorizing instructor styles is stereotypical in some ways, it does represent the range of styles one finds among instructors in a large department. Instructors may, of course, possess characteristics from two or more of these categories. The important point is that instructors need not be locked hopelessly into negative styles. Instructors can change their style as they acquire experience.

Students are very good at picking out the "type" of instructor you are. Strive to be a positive "type"; this can best be accomplished by being honest with yourself and the students. After your first course evaluation, see which of these types you appear to be. Work to change negative attributes and enhance positive styles.

Questions Concerning Student Evaluations

I still feel uneasy after thirty years of teaching when I tell my students that today is evaluation day and pass out the evaluations. I explain to students the importance of this process and that according to the school policy I must leave the room. Trusting 200 freshmen to do a fair and valid assessment of my teaching always produces anxiety.

Questions often arise about formal student evaluations and their effects. Since these evaluations carry tremendous weight in both your department and your school, it is very important to consider the following points. This is particularly true for the new instructor. After thirty years of teaching you learn what to expect on your evaluations and find ways to improve your teaching through your student evaluations.

Are Student Evaluations Valid?

This is the fundamental question. If student evaluations are considered an accurate measure of your effectiveness in the classroom, they should be used as a method of evaluation for retention and promotion. But if they are not a valid measure, what is the purpose of the evaluations? What do they really measure? Student evaluations are weighted heavily in most departments only behind grants and research papers. More research into the validity of different formal evaluation instruments is needed at all schools. Many schools have "standardized" evaluations that are neither standard nor valid. There is little, if any, evidence that a numerical form measures teaching effectiveness, but rather how much the student liked this instructor (personality). Many of these instruments evolved from past failed attempts to evaluate the faculty. Individuals with good evaluations get promoted and gain influence, while those with low ratings may not receive tenure or promotion. It is understandable that the people in power would like the instrument that helped empower them with good ratings.

Another extreme case is the use of national evaluations of teaching effectiveness. In the education department at many schools, students are obsessed with passing the national or regional teacher certification tests. These tests may either guarantee or eliminate them from a job, based on rank order. This is the evaluation process carried to the extreme.

Recently there has been a renewed interest in student evaluations as a method of maximizing the teacher/student interaction. The new direction is to reinforce good teachers with rewards and not the poor ones. It remains to be seen if the resources and willingness of administrators to follow this notion will prevail. The behavior must be reinforced if it is to be strengthen, a simple behavioral principle.

Are Students Qualified to Evaluate?

A common concern of faculty regarding student ratings is if the students are qualified to evaluate. Do they have the proper perspective? Many faculty say that this knowledge and the ability to evaluate can only be gained through experiences outside of the classroom in the real world. Basically, students do not know what they need to know to evaluate their teachers. I tell students to think about ethical issues, but I realize that many will not have the time nor the inclination to do so while in college. I suggest that they might have time to think about such issues later in their careers. I have had former students contact me to discuss issues that I brought up years earlier, after finding themselves in an ethical dilemma. We can all remember the teachers we really disliked while we were undergraduates. In many cases, those teachers were the ones who demanded the most from us at a time when we were not ready to live up to our potential and produce the required results. Now we look back and think that this class was one of the best we had in college. I wish I had taken more classes from that "tough" instructor. So at least in the short term, the instructor who is easy on the students in terms of grades and classroom behavior may receive higher marks on student evaluations. This may be a concern if you are trying to get your contract renewed or receive tenure. Your lenient practices may cheat students in the long run - an uncomfortable dilemma. Maybe an alternate method of asking students for evaluations five years into their careers would be a better method.

Are Students Expert Enough to Evaluate?

Students do not know enough about the material to tell if the instructor is good or not. An important point to remember is that the students come to you with very little knowledge of the content area. You are the expert and choose what is important; you can slant the presentation any way you want and they will not know it. To do a proper evaluation, the students would have to already know the materials, which they do not. Again, the five-year post graduation evaluation may be the answer. Our department chair does peer evaluations of faculty eligible for tenure or promotion. The administration has indicated that student evaluations are not sufficient to support teaching effectiveness for tenure or promotion.

Effects of Personality Factors in Student Evaluations

Another problem often perceived by the faculty is that the students rate instructors on personality factors, not on what they learned in the classroom. I am sure that we can still remember certain professors who had abrasive personalities or were boring, and we probably rated them lower than individuals with friendly, outgoing personalities. One suggestion is to be as interesting in and out of the classroom as you can. Do not be a phony, but realize that personality factors can affect your student evaluations.

Factors Affecting Student Evaluations

Characteristics of the Instructor

Gender of the instructor plays a very small role in the evaluation of the course. Younger instructors are often rated higher than older instructors. This is possibly due to a closer fit in social variables and understanding of the behavior of younger students. Knowledge of subject matter is not sufficient for high evaluations, but you must provide an interesting presentation of the material to enthuse students about the class and the discipline. A boring associate professor in a suit and tie just does not cut it anymore. Remember, you were sitting in the same seats as your students four or five years ago; try to do a better job than some of your professors did.

With the advent of the multimedia classroom even the most boring instructor should be able to have passable evaluations. The presentation mode and attitude can be some of the most important factors in a positive presentation.

Student Expectations of the Class

One of the most important factors is whether the students expect the class to be good or not. If students have heard good things about the class, they are more likely to rate the instructor highly. The class standing of the students also appears to have an effect on the rating of the instructor. Entering freshmen will rate an instructor higher than graduating seniors, probably due to the unfamiliarity of the rating system in the freshman year. Most other demographical variables have little influence.

Maximizing Your Evaluations

In order to maximize your evaluations, several factors should be considered. These suggestions are offered as a method of understanding what the students consider important in the class and in the instructor.

Be Prepared

Be prepared and have a thorough knowledge of your subject matter. Be as prepared as you can for each lecture. This may entail attending other upper-division classes if you are weak in an area. Additional reading in a particular sub-field can also help. Go over your notes and presentation slides before each class. I still can't believe the difference when I do not review prior to the class; the results are below the usual standards.

Be Fair

Be fair to the students in all aspects of the class, from grades to answering questions. Treat the students with the respect they deserve. Err on the side of the students. Do not do anything that will be perceived as favoring one student or group of students over another.

Dress Contemporarily

Do not dress too differently than the other faculty in your department; a suit and tie is usually out of place in many departments, while business, engineering, or education departments might expect a suit and a tie. Similarity in dress with other faculty members in your department will let the students believe that you are approachable. I can remember being intimidated at the prospect of having to talk to a professor in a suit and tie when I was a freshman.

Show Real Concern

Show real concern for the students as individuals and try to understand their problems. Try to remember the types of problems that you had when you were a student. School life is broader than the classroom. Be aware of students' needs and be as flexible as possible.

Stick to Your Schedule

Do what you say you are going to do, when you say you are going to do it. Stick to your schedule. Students like structure. If the only constant in your class is the schedule, then that is a solid foundation.

Follow Your Syllabus

Follow your syllabus to the letter. Do not add any additional requirements. Do not delete any assignments. You may find that some students may already have completed some of the assignments.

Be Friendly

Be friendly and do not abuse the power of your position. Some new instructors may become enchanted with their new status. Be as friendly with students as your personality allows.

Be Fun

This does not mean that you have to be a stand-up comic, but be as light as you can. An introductory class is one of the few occasions the students will have to have any fun in the classroom as a freshman; most classes beyond the introductory level get too serious. Let the students have a feel for the discipline and a look at your personality. Besides, you are going to have to teach this class for many years, would you rather have some fun in the classroom or just read your notes?

Evaluate the Course and Instructor Separately

On evaluation day tell the students to rate you as an instructor, separate from the course content, textbook, or the examinations. I project presentation slides that ask specific questions for this narrative evaluation in my evaluations. For example: did you like the textbook, why or why not? What positive changes to the recitations would you recommend? What positive changes to the journals? This simple strategy will increase your student evaluations in a positive direction. Students can hate the class but like the instructor; this method helps separate the two.

Emphasize the Importance of Evaluations

On evaluation day I tell the students that the evaluations are used for tenure, promotion, and salary increases. Emphasize that the evaluations are very important to the department, school, and you personally. Indicate that you read every comment and modify the course based on the evaluations. They are important!

Taking these factors into account, you will, first, become a better instructor and, second, help maximize your student evaluations.

Other Methods of Evaluation

Student Letters of Recommendation

You may not need them now, but in the future written student evaluations of your performance in the classroom may be necessary for tenure and promotion, contract renewal, or applications for awards. In many instances the students will be asked to submit written evaluations of your classroom performance. This is a nice turnabout to the student letters of recommendation you are asked to write. I try to select several students from each class and ask them if they would consider writing performance evaluations some time. If they agree, keep track of their addresses, telephone numbers, and e-mail addresses for future reference.

Student Oral Evaluations

Oral evaluations can be very informative and yet difficult. If you can accept criticism, invite students to stop by during your office hours to discuss directions that the class could take in the future. Also ask the students for their likes and dislikes regarding your teaching. Ask how to improve your teaching. You will probably only have a few students show up, but they will be your best students. Listen to them; they have good ideas. This is best done after the class grades are turned in.

Anonymous Student Evaluations

Provide a place for students to leave suggestions for your class; this can be accomplished by dropping a sealed letter in your departmental mail box. Most of the comments will be useful in helping with minor adjustments in the class. The constructive suggestions can be incorporated into the next term. Be prepared for the disgruntled student to take the opportunity to take a cheap shot at your class and you; have a thick skin. I can remember reading my first 250 formal class evaluations and finding 95 percent were positive. But there was one very negative evaluation. I can still remember that evaluation from a disrespectful student. I have gotten over the comments but still remember the exact wording.

Faculty Teaching Evaluations

Invite your supervisor and all other interested faculty to attend your lectures. If you want to experience stress, spot your uninvited department chair in the third row when you are really not as prepared as you would like to be for that day's lecture. Remember the problem of not reviewing your notes. When faculty do attend your lectures, they will be valuable in shaping your future teaching. Ask faculty members for evaluations of your teaching and specific suggestions that you can use to improve your teaching. The faculty members who respond most likely are the better teachers in the department.

Self-Evaluation

Evaluating Verbal and Nonverbal Messages

The ability to correctly evaluate verbal and nonverbal messages in the classroom can be a major part of your success and continued improvement of your teaching skills. Students will communicate various messages for different levels of performance in your lectures. If your lecture is very interesting and well presented, the students will smile, laugh at your jokes, ask questions, take notes, and present a general demeanor of having a pleasant experience. This is a positive, rewarding environment for the professor. Professors dream of this kind of response from the class. On the other hand, when a professor is unprepared, the material is not interesting. If the instructor appears not to enjoy the material, he or she may be greeted with sleeping students, yawns (one will start the whole class yawning), frowns, late students entering the room during the lecture, and, my favorite, the blank stare. This is also a type of dream: a nightmare. When you have a lecture like this, upon returning to your office, immediately evaluate what you can do to improve this lecture: more presentation slides, fewer presentation slides, a demonstration or activity, a short video presentation at the beginning or end, or a total re-write of your lecture, with a new emphasis on the materials. It is important to "fix" this lecture immediately, or it will go back into the file and come out next term just as bad.

Student Behavioral Evaluations

As you gain more experience during the term, you should start to look at other subtle nonverbal cues that students will exhibit in the classroom. The ability to attend to these cues and then evaluate and modify your lecture is very important. This can usually be done through classroom experience. The following is an attempt to give you a shortcut on assessing these behavioral cues.

Student Behavior Just Prior to the Beginning of Class

Are they talking to each other and, if so, are they talking about the class or some social interaction? Do the students just sit and wait for class or read the student newspaper? If they just sit and wait, this could be an indication that you are not inspiring the students in this class. Do the students talk to you before or after class? Before the class starts I pick out a "lucky" student of the day and either sit next to the student or stand and talk to this student and any others nearby. I like to spread out this "luck" and see how the students feel about me and the class or life in general. This will give students the feeling that you care about them as individuals.

Student Behavior When the Class Starts

Do the students put away the newspaper, stop talking to each other, and begin to take notes? Do they continue with a negative attitude about the class lecture by not being prepared to take notes and continuing to talk? Do they have questions about previous lectures? Do the students act interested and ready to learn? If not, I turn the light off just like in the theater, until they quiet down.

Student Behavior during the Class Period

Do the students listen intently to your lecture and take notes? Are there questions during the lecture? Are most of the students awake and functioning, or are they simply going through the motions? Are the students fidgeting in their chairs? Are the students eating and drinking during your lecture or doing other class homework? A good class is one that takes notes and asks appropriate questions. Near the end of the class, do the students start to prepare to leave by shuffling their papers and putting on their coats?

Student Behavior after Class

Are students stopping to ask questions about the material in the lecture, or do they just leave by the quickest route available? Do students smile when they see you on campus and stop to talk or just stare straight ahead and not "notice" you? Does anyone stop by during your office hours to discuss the material in class or talk about problems in general? Do the students give you the respect inherent to your position in the school? Do the students use positive terms to describe you and your course to friends?

These are the types of behavioral evaluations that the students give you each day. You should pay attention to these cues and adjust your classroom presentation to the positive side of these cues. If you constantly find negative answers to these behavioral questions, this may be the time for a major modification of your teaching style and content.

Self-Evaluations of the Class and Students

Your attitude toward the students is an important aspect of self-evaluation. Use the following questions to analyze your attitudes toward the students. Be honest with yourself when answering these questions.

Do You Respect the Students?

Do you find yourself thinking of the students as only being there so you can do research or other creative activities? Do you think teaching is the evil you must put up with to have the school resources at your disposal? Do you criticize students for incorrect answers to questions in classroom discussions? Are you very sarcastic about the performance of the students? Do you see them as a necessary means to a paycheck?

Do You Respect the Course and the Discipline?

Are you enthusiastic about the course and does it show in your presentation? Do you criticize the textbook or course director in class? Do your lectures transmit the importance of the subject matter to the students, or is this just another required freshman survey course? How much do you really respect the discipline and how does this show in the course?

How Well Do You Communicate with the Students?

Good communication requires good organization. I always review my lecture notes prior to class; that is why office hours prior to class are handy. I have PowerPoints and can quickly make changes. I can change the order of slides and materials as easily as typing or scanning, adding pictures, video, classroom interactive Internet links, all this with my computer. Transport of the material is very easy; a disk or upload to the main frame computer and then download to the presentation computer in the classroom. I do still take my old notes with me just in case of a technical failure. Back-up saves me once or twice a semester, usually on a Monday!

When lecturing, do you communicate with a clear, interesting, and accurate message to the students? Can they understand what you are trying to say? Do you make eye contact or do you look down at your notes and read? I find myself looking less at the students since I have gone to a presentation format. I look at the computer screen too much and have to make a point to make eye contact with the students. Do you stand in one place all the time? A podium is a nice crutch, but can you leave it? I make myself walk around the room and may even sit down next to a student and continue to lecture from there. This can make class more fun!

Do You Really Care about the Students?

Do you try to learn student names in a small class or at least faces in a large class? Do you project friendliness to indicate that you are approachable? I encourage the students to visit any time they can, not just during office hours but any time my door is open. I like when students approach me off campus and tell me they remember me and they took my class years ago. It is a positive reinforcer to receive unsolicited positive comment. Do you encourage questions during and after lectures? If you discourage questions early on, you will probably not get many for the rest of the term. Is this the kind of class you want? Are you the type of instructor you would have enjoyed as a student? I remember as a student hating lectures presented by boring people who did not care about the students or the discipline. I made a promise that if I was ever in the position to do a better job, I would. Surprise! I finally have the chance and I strive to make my classes the best on campus. You should aspire to the same goal.

If you find yourself answering these questions in a negative manner, it may be time for a major re-evaluation of your aspirations in the teaching area.

Improving Your Teaching

Understanding the Need for Improvement

When I first started teaching I thought my courses were very good. Now many years later, I realize that they were only moderately successful. You will be able to make great improvements in your teaching in the first few years. A first step is that you must recognize that improvement is possible. Realizing the need to improve is half the battle. The other half is constantly striving to improve your presentation, content, and attitude. The advent of presentation software has given many instructors the opportunity for improvement. You must use a critical eye to recognize the weak aspects of your course. If you deliver a weak lecture because you are not an expert in the specific area of the field, read more on the area, attend other classes on the subject, or use the Internet as a source. Improvement is up to you. Identify the areas that you should work on and do the work.

Ask for Help from Your Colleagues or Mentor

Discuss the course with your colleagues, course supervisor, departmental mentor, or department chair requesting suggestions to improve your performance in the classroom. Many of these veterans of the teaching wars will be happy to share some of their secrets. Ask to visit other instructors' classes and observe first-hand the strategies used to teach. Attending other sections can be especially helpful in improving your course. Ask the students who are the best teachers on campus and attend their lecture to observe. If you can, attend local, regional, or national teaching conferences on your content area.

The strategies and habits that you develop in these early courses will set the pattern for the rest of your teaching career. Strive to be the best instructor in your department and, if you fall short, evaluate your weaknesses and then work to improve your shortcomings. Remember, next term you get a fresh start and a new class of students.

Chapter 11

The Role of Computers in College Teaching

In the Beginning

I think back to the Dark Ages when I first started teaching and the PC had not been invented. A lot has changed since that time, particularly with the advent of computer technologies and new methods of communication. The effects of technology in this new century and information age will affect our academic and personal lives significantly. This chapter will outline some of the possibilities that will affect your teaching and professional development. Some of material in this book will be outdated before it is printed, but is offered as an observation of what is currently relevant.

Your Computers

Your Office Computer: How Big and How Bad?

If you are a new hire in a tenure track position you will probably have a start-up package. The amount can vary, but at a minimum you should have enough money for some furniture and a computer. So, what computer to buy? Spend as much money as you can to get the state-of-the-art, everything you always wanted computer. Two reasons: first, you will probably not have a chunk of money this large to spend for a while and, second, no matter how state-of –the-art your computer is when ordered, it is old by delivery time. Live a little - you are going to spend a tremendous amount of time with your computer.

The CD-ROM and Flash Memory

You can use a CD-ROM to take your PowerPoint presentations to the classroom. An even better way to transport material is the flash memory; use this method if your teaching room is equipped with flash memory technology. Flash memory is not as fragile and is compatible with most computers. CD-ROMs are becoming the floppy disk of the past.

iPad, Smart Phones, and Tablets

All relatively new technologies, but with still untapped potential in the area of teaching. These types of hardware will evolve in the future and be integrated into the teaching environment.

The Laptop Option

Consider a laptop computer for home, office, and instructional uses. Laptops used to cost more and had fewer features than many PCs. Recent developments in technology and production techniques have greatly reduced the cost of laptops, while adding most of the features of desk top models. The ability to move your computer is becoming much more important. Many of my colleagues never leave town without their laptop.

With docking station technology there is no reason not to have a laptop. Laptop computers have recently eclipsed desktop computers in total sales. Besides, a nice laptop looks cooler and does not take up most of your desk.

Wireless Connectivity

All schools now have hot zones on campus, such as the library, student union building, various departments and research centers on campus. This new movement to wireless connectivity makes the use of laptops even more appealing. Off-campus installations have also become quite common and include locations like coffee shops, malls, local libraries, and airports. The speed and convenience of these connections are very good and allow for productivity in locations other than your office. Many students will have a wireless router in their housing.

Home Machine

Because you probably own a computer, you might consider using it at home. You will find that you can often get more done at home, with no interruptions from students or other faculty. You probably do not need a powerful machine for your word processing or Internet surfing. The type of IP service is important in considering the amount of time you plan to spend working at home. The more work at home, the faster the service you'll need. Ask if your department will pay for your service.

Satellite providers are now making working from home even more practical from any rural location. No more 2400 baud modem dial-up service. The satellites are compatible to most school connectivity.

Printer

Often the last item you will buy, but, important. Do you need laser quality printing? Yes. Do you need color printing? Possibly. Do you need laser color printing? Only if you have a large start-up package. Make your decision based on what you need and what you can afford. I would ask some of the other faculty what they consider important in their printer. I have two printers in my office and often use them both simultaneously.

Give serious consideration to a wireless printer for your home office or school office. The technology has progressed to the point that they are as good as hard wire printers.

Scanners

These range from a $69 flatbed scanner, which I finally purchased, to multi-function printer fax production scan machines. Spend a little money on one and you will be surprised how often you use it. Much of the technology is being replaced with PDF technology.

Adjuncts

You will probably get nothing in terms of computers. So bring your own or buy one when you get to campus. Often the school's local Information Technology center will have bundle pricing on machines you can take advantage of. You might be able to scrounge an old computer from your department but it will be next to useless and you will probably spend a lot of time trying to make it work.

Computers Are Essential

Keeping track of e-mails from the department and your colleagues is an essential feature. The communication age requires you to be current in technology and software; SPSS, Excel, and Word are minimum requirements. You will spend a portion of every day at Internet sites; much time can be consumed looking up research journals and publishers' sites, adding to your home page, posting grades and homework assignments.

Testing programs provided by publishers are your friends. The computer test item files, ranging from great to barely adequate, are essential in your class testing. I write lecture questions and use these test item files in every class. I do not let anyone write or select items for my examinations. The software for computer test item files can be a challenge to learn, so try them out early. Many publishers are turning to Internet sites to house their testing materials. Good connectivity and a reasonable computer are essential for developing exams.

I find myself using my word processing programs daily. I cannot imagine how we could have survived without modern word processing, but I can remember. Plus, we now have spell check—my personal favorite.

Course management software is essential for you to run your course. Either commercial or publisher-provided software will provide you with the necessary tools to teach in the 21st century.

Computer Viruses

Get a good anti-virus program and update it regularly. Most new computers come with virus protection, but you must keep DAT files current, since there are computer viruses being produced hourly. I run my scanner in the background each day. If you have any concerns with downloading attachments from someone you do not know, delete them. Spyware is a new and continuing problem which will require a program to eliminate it. Your Information Technology center can be very helpful in protecting and fixing virus problems. Buy the best virus protection you can get and keep it current.

The Internet

With the advent of personal computers in the mid 1970's, the potential for tremendous growth in communications began. Local networks had been in place since that time; most of the network research was sponsored by the military. Since 1983, the Internet has developed from a small experimental research project designed for military applications to the largest network of computers in the world. The Internet is, in essence, a collection of networks and routers that function as a single large network.

My First Time

I still remember the day I saw the Internet in action. The department chair called me into his office to show me something. This is never a good sign, but I went in anyway. His computer screen was slowly painting an image (1200 baud modem in those days). He asked me what I thought it was. It looked like a beach ball, but it wasn't. As the image emerged line by slow line, I recognized the Earth. It was the GOES-7 west coast satellite. How cool! I never looked back and have been a devoted Internet user since.

Internet Applications

Travel

Travel can either be an exciting part of your new academic life or a horror story. Not too many years ago if you wanted to travel you called a travel agent to book your flight. You never knew the type of plane, your seat assignment, or other options for different flights. The Internet can give you a very good preview of the locations you are traveling to. I like to search the local attractions in a city where I must travel for a convention or other business. Knowing what to expect and what to have fun exploring in a new city is a very exciting aspect of travel.

Internet Travel Tickets

Now you can use any number of methods to search the Internet to find all the options for a flight. I usually go directly to the airline's home page and search for time and dates. I can also go to discount brokers to see if they can fill my particular needs. If not, then I buy direct from the airline. You know the type of plane, the flight times, the connection times, and your seat number. You are in control - not the travel agent as in the recent past. Be sure to sign up for airline frequent flyer programs; there are many benefits, including free tickets. Check with your departmental administrator whether you our or the school keeps the frequent flyer miles.

Lodging: Look before You Buy

You are traveling to a strange city and you really have no idea where to stay. The Internet can help. Look at several hotel home pages and compare. I usually go either to a discount broker or the local chamber of commerce as a starting point. If you have a particular hotel chain you like, go to their homepage. First, see what accommodations are available and shop by price. Most discount brokers have a client hotel rating service. With this service you can look at the experiences of real travelers at specific hotels. I have not stayed in a hotel because of these poor ratings and I have contributed both positive and negative comments after my stays. There's nothing worse than showing up late at night at a bad hotel with no options available.

Transportation after the Airport

So you want a red convertible? Easy. Go to any of the rental car homepages and make your selection based on price. Limo or cab to and from the airport? Locate schedules and costs on the Internet.

Conventions

A major part of your new research and teaching will be attending conventions in your area of interest. You can find convention programs and participants listed on the Internet. If you are planning to attend, this is helpful in scheduling your time at the meeting. If you are not attending, this is helpful in requesting reprints from the talks and posters.

You should see what is going on after convention hours. There may be professional sporting events to attend, world famous golf courses, or the beach outside of the convention hotel to visit. Use the Internet to help schedule your free time.

Leaving an E-Trail

E-Mail

A cautionary note when you send or receive e-mail on your work computer: you have no expectation of an envelope. That means your employer can read your e-mail. The specific rules that govern the use of your computer and the e-mail you produce are included in your faculty handbook.

E-mail can greatly impact your career. In the not too distant past, a letter from Bozeman, Montana would take 4-5 days to reach a destination in the United States, often weeks overseas. Now via e-mail this time is cut to seconds. If you have a question concerning some aspect of teaching, the textbook, or your research, simply e-mail the individual. If he or she is at the computer, you could receive a reply in minutes, not weeks. In our department all the faculty use e-mail and most of the departmental business is conducted via this paper-less mode. Memos between the head and the faculty are sent via e-mail, and meeting times and assignments are likewise sent via e-mail. All communications are stored on the hard disk of our computers, not in a space-wasting filing cabinet.

There are many different types of e-mail interfaces your department or computer center can provide, as well as the necessary address and software. I set my e-mail to check every 15 minutes for new messages. I like getting information all day long.

Critical departmental information on meetings and other "must attend to" memos are constantly arriving by e-mail, as well as research, teaching, student questions, and convention news. You cannot function at your new job without e-mail.

You may receive messages from your colleagues about meetings, your thoughts, social events, or questions about your area of expertise.

I like e-mail for student communication because it creates a record of the time and date of the communication. If there is any doubt about what you told a student, just bring up the message.

Depending on your school's technical support you might have video computer conferencing available. It is a nice way to interact with colleagues in distant places, and it is free.

Beware of spam—unwanted solicitations on e-mail—much like junk mail in the snail mail. If you get something unsolicited, delete it. If it arrives several times, set your spam filter to delete it. New and more noxious viruses are being spread by e-mail, so be careful.

Electronic Journals

Most journals are currently available electronically, and an increasing number are now being added. Some of these journals are, and will be, only available electronically.

The computer revolution has had a tremendous impact on the libraries at your school. If you are not familiar with the electronic media, see your reference librarian.

Databases

Several methods of searching databases are also available. Some are free and some require a subscription fee. These include services such as PsychLit, Current Contents, GreatfulMed, Carl Uncovered, and ERIC. By browsing or searching the Internet, you can receive information on these services. See your library for access and fees associated with these services.

Leaving a Paper Trail

United Parcel Service and Federal Express

I am still amazed that I can deposit a parcel at 5 p.m. in Bozeman, Montana, and it will be delivered virtually anywhere in the United States the next morning by 10:00 AM, for under fifteen dollars! What a deal! If you really want it fast, early AM service, which delivers by 8AM, is also available in many locations. The U.S. mail still requires 4-5 days to many locations and has no method of tracking your letter. This increase in the level and speed of communication time takes weeks off of correspondence between individuals. There are other services, but UPS and FedEx are the major providers.

The Fax

The fax machine is still useful and is the fastest and often least expensive method of sending documents that do not require an original. Locate your department fax and review the operation and billing procedures. PDF technology is replacing fax technology.

Snail Mail

Snail mail via the USPS is still available, but used less and less. If you have to send something, send it priority for 2-3 day delivery. It is still fun to open endless junk mail and bills. Latest news is that the USPS will guarantee that they will not deliver any mail in one day, nice.

Traditional Paper Teaching Journals

Two of the Best Are:

Teaching of Psychology, Lawrence Erlbaum Associates, Publishers, 365 Broadway, Hillsdale, NJ 07642

The Teaching Professor, Magna Publications, Inc., 2718 Dryden Drive, Madison, WI 53704.

Chapter 12

Electronic Media in College Teaching

Electronic Media in the Classroom

The changes since I started teaching have been tremendous in the area of media in the classroom. Not too many years ago I used to carry a 16mm film projector to the classroom to show movies. These were very dated and worn films that were of little value. I often joked with my students that my right arm was 2 inches longer than my left from carrying the 35-pound projector across campus.

When I started teaching overhead transparencies were the norm. Most ancillary packages included overhead transparencies for the instructor, some were even in color. These were of varying quality and usefulness, but I amassed a collection of the best samples over the years. The students spent much of the class period copying the material from the overhead transparencies to their notes.

For the really die-hard instructors, there was the chalkboard, but even more high tech is the whiteboard with erasable colored ink. I believe these are used mostly by math and engineering departments that need to show a proof or explain in detail the steps of a process.

In the Classroom

Smart Podium

At my school the computer center developed smart podiums for several of the large lecture halls on campus ten years ago. Most of the larger rooms on campus have been upgraded but a number of smaller rooms remain without a dedicated smart podium. The smart podium is a four foot by six foot by four foot high box on wheels that has a computer for presentation software, a projection unit, video/DVD player, CD-ROM, and sound system. This podium has Internet access and is as good as it gets for presenting multimedia materials. Depending on your school, you may have a Local Area Network (LAN) connection to download activities and demonstrations. This LAN can also be useful in transferring grades from the computer scoring center to your office computer.

In the intervening years since the first smart podium my school has upgraded many classrooms to multimedia status with portable multimedia carts. It is n now an expectation by the students that you use presentation slides in your lectures.

Presentation Software (PowerPoint)

PowerPoint, or other presentation software, is the current wave of presenting lectures. Students enjoy this type of presentation. You can use motion and sound for your slides, keeping the interest level up. You can have direct access to the Internet for links to live demonstrations and activities. Films no longer require a projector, all of the material is now on VHS tape or DVDs; lightweight and easy to use, and my arms are after many years of equal length again.

There are pitfalls to PowerPoint. Too much information, too many graphics, sounds, and other features that distract from the basic intent of PowerPoint. Ask your departmental mentor for advice on how to construct a good PowerPoint lecture series for your class. Also ask others in the department for samples of their PowerPoint lectures, as well as your textbook publisher. The latest generation of publisher provided slides are great. No need to start from scratch anymore. Get the slides for the book and modify them. The question of whether to post your slides on your course page or not is discussed in Chapter 2.

Internet Usage Outside of the Classroom

You should develop a homepage for each of your classes. Some schools provide a template and Webmaster to help with this process. WebCT, Blackboard or D2L have this feature and can save you valuable time. On each course homepage you should post at least the course syllabi to help students who have misplaced the paper copy you passed out the first day of class. This posting allows everyone access to these materials on demand. You can post your notes and presentation slides on the homepage. Presentation slides posted to your home page prevent students from wasting time copying materials during class, (see Chapter 2). Students that miss class can get the basic concepts from this site. If your school permits, you can post class grades on the homepage. Students are always interested in grades. Homework assignments can also be posted and updated easily. I also post any practice tests or old tests that students can use as study aids.

Electronic Student Study Guides

Many publishers have student study guides and testing materials at their text homepage. Some are password protected, but if you adopt the text, they are typically free to the students. Other publishers supply CD-ROMs with the text for student study aids. With the advent of more comprehensive student and instructor web sites by publisher much of the material need by students and instructors can be found at one place.

Chat Rooms

You can either set up your own or use a publisher's site for a chat room on a topic from your class. You can use this device to facilitate discussion of current and controversial related topics. Some distance programs use chat rooms extensively in the course presentation.

Internet Links

On my class home page I have several URL links to additional interesting material on varying topics in the course or required material from my school. I change these links throughout the term and encourage students to submit new links to me for consideration. Check these links before the start of each semester to make sure they are still active and current.

TIPS Network

You can subscribe to the TIPS Network, see Chapter 11 for details. This and other discussion groups on teaching can be very helpful to a new instructor with problems that arise either with content issues or concerning student interactions. The TIPS network is well worth the time and is a great resource.

Internet Guides

Many publishers have guides to the Internet in their ancillary package for your text. These are very handy when planning Internet classroom activities. Many of the guides are specific to the text and a variety of guides are available for different courses.

Distance and e-Instruction

Distance and online learning continue to be an area of interest not only to the instructor but the school administrators. Schools go through phases when they are emphasizing distance learning. Instructors like it because once they have the class done it is relatively easy to update the material and the number of students served can be very large. Administrators like distance learning because they think once the class is prepared then all that is necessary is to enroll students and turn on the class. Administrators are primarily looking at the savings of not having to build more brick and mortar to accommodate more students. Areas of major concern for the instructor are: who owns the copyright to the course material? Who gets paid to develop the material? Who receives compensation each time the class is presented? See chapter 3 for further discussion.

Technology in the Classroom

Recent research suggests that students not only use technology in their educational pursuits, but also expect technology to be involved the classroom.

Student Demographics

The following are some interesting data about computer and technology use by students:

Most students come to campus with multiple technology devices and a majority have a dozen or more
87% of students own laptop computers
Community college students are more likely to have less mobile technology devices (e.g., desktop computers)

For undergraduates, technology is primarily about communication:

93% use text messaging
90% use social networking sites (primarily Facebook), and most do so several times a day
81% use instant messaging
37% have used an iPhone or other smartphone for academic activities

Primary student-reported benefits of technology:

Ease of access to resources
Ability to track academic progress
Increase productivity
Help them feel connected
Can help make learning more engaging and relevant

Source: THE ECAR STUDY OF UNDERGRADUATE STUDENTS AND INFORMATION TECHNOLOGY, 2011. Available at http://www.educause.edu/ecar

---

Digital Natives

Many of today's college students are Digital Natives. This is defined as the first generation of students to grow up surrounded by and using technology (Prensky, 2001).
Digital Natives have grown up using computers and other technological tools. Many haven't experienced educational experiences *without* technology.

Notebook Computers

New, very small and lightweight computers with the features you want, like Internet and e-mail access. These can be very inexpensive, under 300 dollars. Great for traveling and student use. Some schools have been including a computer as part of the entering Freshperson's fees and tuition. The introduction of tablet technology (iPad) has mostly eliminated the note book market.

Podcasting

Use http://www.how-to-podcast-tutorial.com/00-podcast-tutorial-four-ps.htm or http://www.podcasting-tools.com/how-to-podcast.htm as starting places to learn the art of developing podcasts.

Podcast Uses in the Classroom

Instructor-assigned podcasts:

Topic review, application, case studies, etc.
Topic-based podcasts created by instructor
Student identification of topic-related podcasts
Podcasts created by students

Out of Class

Time-shifting of supplemental materials or class information
Assigned podcasts and related assignments (e.g., personal reaction papers)

In Class

iPods can be used in class for review, quizzes, other reference information

---

Classroom Response Systems (aka "clickers")

Using clickers in large classes can have several advantages. First, you can easily obtain class attendance by having the student initialize their clickers by pushing a response key. Taking attendance was almost impossible in large class in the past, but now it is easy. Secondly, you can give short quizzes at the beginning of the class, which allows students who are attending to get course points. This method also helps encourage students to read the text in advance of the lecture.

Thirdly, you can use clickers for exams. Display your exam questions one at a time for 45 seconds using your presentation software, have the students respond with their clickers. This will save lots of paper and thus money for your department. Students generally like clickers and believe that they enhance the classroom experience.

Class & Classroom Management

Record attendance
Facilitate active student engagement
Formative assessment
Summative Assessment

Audio and Video Conferencing

All of the following are sites that will facilitate audio and video conferencing with your students:

AOL Instant Messenger http://dashboard.aim.com/aim
iChat http://www.apple.com/macosx/features/ichat.html
Google Talk http://www.google.com/talk/
Windows Live Messenger http://get.live.com/messenger/overview
Elluminate vRoom http://www.elluminate.com/vroom
GoToMeeting http://gotomeeting.com

Texting

Can be used in the following areas of teaching:

Virtual office hours
Study/review sessions
Group assignments

Facebook or MySpace

An interesting article on the use of Facebook at UCLA:
http://dailybruin.com/stories/2008/mar/10/instructors-use-tech-reach-students/

An article on MySpace and teaching can be found at:
http://pedagogy.cwrl.utexas.edu/?q=node/162

YouTube and Google Video

For class assignments with YouTube and Google Video students can identify clips that depict various concepts from psychology, and use clips for papers, in-class discussions, and PowerPoint presentations.

The above discussions are inspired by and used with permission of Noland White, Georgia College & State University.

WebCT, BlackBoard, and Desire2Learn

WebCT, Blackboard, and Desire2Learn include all of your instructional materials in a single site. Many schools have license agreements that allow for the use of these tools. More recently, major text book publishers have begun to develop their own programs that are keyed to their texts. Many times these publisher sites integrate the student study guide with on-line testing and study materials. Additionally, they will have test item files for the instructor.

The following sites will be helpful in developing your course using platforms designed to help the electronic interface with students:

http://www.blackboard.com/
http://en.wikipedia.org/wiki/WebCT
http://www.aboutus.org/DesireToLearn.com

Blogs

The use of the blog in the classroom can be very useful. You can develop an interesting interaction with student through the use of a blog.

Free blogging sites:

http://www.blogsome.com/
http://blog.com/
http://www.livejournal.com/
https://www.blogger.com/start

Kindle (Fire)

A new technology, the Kindle Fire, was released in the United States in 2011. This is essentially puts a traditional book in an e-format - the pages turn, and it looks like the text complete with pictures and graphics. The Kindle allows you to have a tremendous number of books in a very small space. Application in the classroom could be having the student keep all of their texts in this format for the entire school. So much for the bookstore - just hats and beer mugs. Search "Kindle college" for some very interesting material on the Kindle's penetration into the college market.

Reed College is a test platform for the new Kindle technology, along with five other schools, including Pace University, Arizona State University, Case Western Reserve, Princeton University, and the University of Virginia.

The market might be very large with major publishers McGraw-Hill and Pearson announcing major efforts to use the Kindle technology.

Twitter

Twitter has yet to be used with much success in the classroom. Creative instructors will surely find a use for the format in the classroom soon.

Uses of the Multimedia Classroom

Once you have invested the time to develop presentation slides, you can very easily change or modify them. Many publishers are developing rather good presentations slides in outline forms for your text. Ask for a copy before you adopt the text; much of your work will already be done.

Department Website

Before you interview or apply for a position at a school, you should explore the department's homepage. You can learn a lot about the faculty, students, research interests, and the general tone of the department. You can also indirectly see how cutting edge the department appears to be at least in their homepage interface. Homepages that are bland, sterile, uninteresting, and technologically simple may be a good indicator of the multimedia capabilities of the department.

You can make the name/face associations of the faculty you may be working with and get a feel for their research interests and how you might fit in from the departmental homepage.

The Publisher's Internet Site

Ordering Text Books

You can quickly order a desk copy of the text or replace a test item file using the publisher's Internet site. Check this site for the status of your textbook order and find the estimated completion dates for important ancillary items like the test item file and student study guide.

Look at the Ancillary Package

You can preview the ancillary package for several texts prior to an adoption decision. The ancillary packages have grown very large in the last five years; most of the materials are interesting. You can choose the materials you need and order them at this site.

What's New?

You can see what the publisher is planning, in the next copyright year, and preview any new texts. If your favorite text is being revised you might like a new copy as soon as possible.

Communicating with Publishers

One of the fastest methods of communication with a publisher is to use the e-mail address associated with the Internet site. The sales department personnel will respond rapidly to your questions.

Chapter 13

Summation and Final Thoughts

The Big Three

Major consideration must be given to how you will distribute the finite energy that you have during your first years as a faculty member. In most schools there are three components to a successful faculty member: research, teaching, and service, often in this order. Depending on the size and emphasis of your school, these three components must be adjusted. As you progress through your career you might change the emphasis of each component.

Teaching

How to teach is what you probably were not taught in graduate school. Teaching is what many of us want to do and your school would like you to be at least competent. This book attempts to help you on this journey into teaching. At many research institutions, teaching comes in a distant second place in importance. You can be the best teacher in your school and never be promoted to full professor. But at the same time, you must be an adequate teacher to become tenured. The mix between research and teaching can be interesting; the best researchers get grants and buy out of teaching. They can be the best teachers, but they are also the funded researchers. In some cases, teaching faculty are deemed to be at a lower level than research faculty.

Research

Research is what most of us are taught to do in graduate school. Your specialty can be in any field; this is your expertise. Along with research comes the most important area to many schools—grants. If you can secure some grant funding in the beginning of your career, you will have a substantial head start on other new faculty members. Many public universities are morphing into hybrid public/grant-funded institutions. At my university in the past eight years, the research funding increased from 40 million dollars a year to over 110 million dollars a year. Reliance on grant funding to back-fill the ever-shrinking funding from the public sector is a common scenario in state funded higher education.

With the "Great Recession" impacting the budgets of states in a dramatically negative way, states are slashing budgets. The easiest budgets to slash are often in education, particularly higher education. The common joke in my school is the only state funded program with a lower priority than higher education is the mental hospital. The use of these funds at an ever-increasing rate to fulfill the mission of the school is an interesting reality. Individuals with grant funding are in a position to receive special consideration when it comes to tenure and promotion. If you can get funding early, and in a substantial amount, you are in a good position.

Publishing

Publishing research material can be accomplished at various levels. The following is a rough estimation of the importance of different venues for publishing in descending order of importance. Use this as a guideline in your targeting venues for publications.

An original scholarly book published by a leading academic publisher.

A refereed journal article of single authorship in a leading journal in your field.

A single authorship of scholarly monograph or a major technical report.

A refereed journal article of multiple authorship in a leading journal in your field. Name placement is sometimes considered important, but varies by discipline.

A multiple authorship of scholarly monograph or a major technical report.

A critical essay, research analysis, or interpretive study published in a refereed scholarly journal. Meta-analysis is a good example.

An edited anthology or collection of essays or research studies on a specific topic released through a well known academic press or a major trade publisher.

An original textbook published by a reputable publisher (not vanity press). The importance of this activity differs greatly from school to school and discipline to discipline.

A contributed chapter in a refereed scholarly book.

A contributed chapter in an invited scholarly book.

A major invited essay in a leading academic or professional journal.

A refereed paper appearing in a published collection of conference proceedings, posters and presentations at scholarly conferences.

An article or essay appearing in a nonrefereed journal.

A publication appearing in a semi-professional or general-circulation magazine.

A book review.

School level papers, reports, and articles.

Departmental level papers, reports, and articles.

(Influenced by Lucas and Murry 2002)

Service

This is the area in which many of us like to spend our time. Service can be to the school in the form of committee assignments, directors of programs, search committees, tenure and promotion committees, faculty advisor to honor societies, or faculty governance body—all the things you do without monetary consideration. In the community, this service can be in the form of volunteer work for nonprofit agencies, free clinics, youth organizations, or charitable organizations that enhance the community.

Often individuals believe that this service commitment is an important commitment not only to the school, but the community. However, in some cases, the school does not have the same perspective. Many faculty members have not been promoted or tenured because they invested energies in the service area at the expense of research and teaching areas. Remember, service is almost always secondary to research and teaching. Learn when and how to say no to a service overload. You can enlist your departmental mentor to help you resist too much service.

The following is a list of reasons to say yes to service and a list of reasons to say no. Use these as an additional guideline in your decisions.

When to Agree to a Service Request

When the invitation comes directly from the dean or some other high-ranking administrative official.

When the invitation comes directly from your departmental chair.

When the nature of the assignment is congruent with one of your major professional interests.

When it is clear the committee assignment will not be overly burdensome or excessively time-consuming. Be very careful here—as a new faculty member you might not be a good judge of the time required.

When the committee in question will allow you to network with, and become better known by, colleagues with whom you anticipate working in future. Try to not spend too much time on this if you are just starting your academic career.

When the committee or task force has a clear charge and a proven track record of effectiveness in dealing with significant issues or problems, thus affording you the prospect of helping to make a significant, positive contribution to the institution. Again, good luck; any committee will strive for this, but few reach the goal.

When to Disagree to a Service Request

When it is obvious nobody else wants the job, there's probably a good reason for the general disinterest.

When the committee's focus is far removed from your own interests and concerns.

When it is evident that the assignment will call for a significant expenditure of time and effort. Research and teaching are much more important at the beginning of your career.

When the assignment will place you into the middle of some divisive controversy or a highly-charged political dispute that is unlikely to be resolved to everyone's satisfaction anytime soon. Remember: in the beginning of your career you want to be stealth; do your work and wait until you are a full professor before venturing into this type service commitment.

(Influenced by Lucas and Murry 2002)

Time Management Strategies

The following are some techniques that you can use to maximize your limited time. If you are a new faculty member on a tenure track line, the clock starts the day your contract starts and you have a tremendous amount of work to do in a very short time period. As an undergraduate and graduate student you have probably adopted some of the following techniques, but try to augment your methods with this list.

Arrival Time/Departure Time

Begin work early when there are fewer people around. I like to be in my office and settled an hour before anyone else enters the building. I get more done in that hour than the rest of the day.

If you are a more nocturnal type, stay late after everyone else has left. This might hurt your social life, but in a new job you will not have much of one anyway.

Setting Priorities

Establish priorities and give important tasks the most attention. I review my list each morning and re-order when necessary. I will have a written list of things to do and cross off each task as completed.

Making Deadlines

Make it a habit to complete tasks well before their deadlines. I am compulsive about deadlines. Whether it is a major book project or completing an examination for copying, I am always ahead of schedule.

Office Hours

Maintain scheduled office hours for appointments as well as drop-ins. I always schedule the hour before class as an office hour I can review my notes and update my presentation slides during this time. Have a sign up sheet for your office hours with 15 minute segments per visit. When the schedule is over, close your door. Tell the administrative assistant and faculty you are in but stop the constant student drop-ins; they will lower your productivity.

Block of Time

Uninterrupted time is essential. Keep the office door closed and ask the administrative assistant's help in screening calls, receiving messages, and barring drop-in visitors. To help facilitate this many faculty "work from home", there are advantages like no student will ever interrupt you—see below. In your syllabus and the first day of class inform your students of your office hours and as well as other times you will be available. . Fill out and post (the bigger the better) a weekly time schedule which should include a teaching schedule, office hours, and large blocks of "I am not here" time.

Limit Service Commitments

Be assertive with others about time; limit the duration of conferences and meetings when possible. (See the discussion above about service commitments.)

Multi Tasking?

You probably think you are good at this, but when accuracy is essential, focus on doing one thing at a time.

Taking Breaks and Collegiality

Avoid excessive isolation; do not become a hermit. Take short breaks to converse with colleagues and staff members. Walk across campus for a cup of coffee with colleagues. More important decisions have been made on these informal walks than you might think. Be part of this process.

Work at Home

A selfish trend on the part of some faculty is to reserve some portion of a day or two per week to accomplish work at home that cannot be done in the office. This will help you, but lowers you collegiality index and shifts the burden of some work to other faculty that are in the department on a more regular basis. Be careful not to be too selfish particularly when you are a new faculty member.

Major Projects

When beginning work on a large or long-term project or task, break it down into parts and work on one part at a time. Writing a book or journal article may seem like an impossible task until you take the time to analyze a strategy. I always believe that the hardest part of any project is setting the formats for the work and then starting. Starting can be the most difficult aspect of a very long-term project.

Poor Planning

You can not afford poor planning anymore; you have way too much to do and little time to waste. Maintain a day planner, either computer or paper to plan each hour of each day, from teaching to office hours, lunch and writing/research. If you plan well your progress will be much greater than if you do not.

(Influenced by Lucas and Murry 2002)

Balancing the Big Three

The balancing of research, teaching, and service depends on your school. If you are at a large university, this is fairly easy: research, teaching, and service in that order. A small private liberal arts college? A two-year college? Then what? Look at what most of the younger faculty do with their time. Ask your chair or you mentor for some direction. Ask your colleagues in the department. Get as many opinions from diverse sources as you can. Your department will have some sort of promotion and tenure document that will give you official/formal requirements. Know the parameters and adjust your mix suitably. This is a critical juncture for your departmental mentor. He/she can help you adjust your big three to align with the departmental expectations. Keep your eyes wide open and see what behaviors are actually rewarded in your department.

The End

I hope the task of teaching will be easier after reading this book, which describes the navigation process through the maze of academia. Throughout this book, I have attempted to share my experiences in teaching with the hope that this knowledge will provide shortcuts to becoming the good instructor you want to be.

Take the time to plan your course and present your best effort. Take the time to evaluate the content and style of your course; after this evaluation make every effort possible to improve your mistakes and strengthen your weaknesses. The next time you teach this course, it should be much improved.

Pass on the experiences of your education to the next generation of students. Some of your first students could be your colleagues in the future.

Good luck with your teaching career and remember, Have Fun!

Appendix A

Psychology 1001S

Fall 2013

F. W. Whitford

General Information

Office	
Office Hours	and by appointment
Telephone	
E-mail	
Course Home Page	http://

Texts Required for this course:
Ancillary Package:

If you have a documented disability for which you are or may be requesting an accommodation(s), you are encouraged to contact your instructor and Disabled Student Services as soon as possible.

This class will introduce you to the major methods of and approaches to psychology which are summarized in the following table:

Topic	*Approximate Dates**	*Readings*
Introduction to Course	August 30	
History and Methods	September 1-13	Chapter #1
Biology and Behavior	September 15-22	Chapter #2
Sensation and Perception	September 27-29	Chapter #3
Learning	October 4-11	Chapter #5
Memory	October 13-20	Chapter #6
Cognition	October 25-27	Chapter #7
Social Psychology	November 1-10	Chapter #14
Psychological Disorders	November 15-29	Chapter #12
Therapy	December 1-6	Chapter #13
Course Summation	December 10	

*could vary by one class session

Schedule of Important Dates

Examination #1	October 1	Chapters 1, 2 & 3
Examination #2	October 29	Chapters 5, 6 & 8
Examination #3	December 8	Chapters 14, 12 & 13
Final Examination	December 13	Groups 1, 2, 3, or 4

Final Exam 8pm-10pm

No one admitted to final examination after 8:15pm.

University Holidays

September 6	Labor Day
November 11, 25 & 26	Veteran's Day and Thanksgiving

Recitation Section Activities

Week of
Journal

Activity

September 6-10	#1 Ice Breaker	None
September 13-17	#2 Experimental Design	#1
September 20-24	#3 Physiological Jeopardy	#2
Sept/Oct 27-1	#4 Sensation and Perception	#3
October 4-8	#5 Learning	#4
October 11-15	#6 Memory	#5
October 18-22	#7 Intelligence and Creativity	#6
November 1-5	#8 Social Psychology	#7
November 15-19	#9 Abnormal	#8
Nov/Dec 29-3	#10 Treatment	#9
December 6-10	#11 Summary/Evaluation	None

Recitation First Meeting and Journal

First Recitation Meeting	September 6-10
Group #1 Journals Due	September 13-17

Course Questions

All challenges to specific items on the examinations will be submitted in writing to Fred Whitford, Room 306 Traphagen, no later than onc (1) week after the examination. No challenges will be accepted after this deadline. These challenges will be evaluated and posted on the final grade roster. Any make-up tests must be completed within one (1) week of the examination. Challenges, grade changes, and make-up test scores **will not** appear on the regular grade posting throughout the semester.

If you have any questions, comments, or concerns about the course or course points, you should first discuss these with your recitation leader, then with the Psychology 100 coordinator, Room 410 Traphagen. If you are still not satisfied, you may then discuss the problem with Fred Whitford, Room 306 Traphagen. Do not ask the Psychology department secretaries for assistance with course points or grading matters; they will not be able to assist you.

Summary Course of Points and Grading System

Content Module: 200 points maximum, determined by the number of correct answers on three exams (50 points each), 150 points and doubling your highest exam score. These tests are multiple choice with 50 items.

Journal Module: 54 points maximum, 2 points per acceptable entry based on the number of acceptable entries up to a maximum of 27; no credit for fewer than 13 entries, regardless of quality.

Attendance and Participation at Recitation Sections: 44 points maximum, 4 points per meeting (11 meetings) will be given by your recitation group leader. Participation in discussions and exercises is required.

Individual Reading Module: 50 points maximum, based on an objective test over a group of two chapters which you read and study on your own time. This test is multiple choice with 50 items.

Determination of Course Grade

Total Points Possible: 348

Grade Cut-Off Scores

A = 313 or more points (90% or more)

B = 278 - 312 points (80% - 89%)

C = 244 - 277 points (70% - 79%)

D = 209 - 243 points (60% - 69%)

F = 208 or fewer points (less than 60%)

Any student caught cheating by any method will receive a grade of zero on the examination they are caught cheating on, no exceptions. For a detailed explanation see, the course workbook.

***If you have a documented disability for which you are or may be requesting an accommodation(s), you are encouraged to contact your instructor and Disabled Student Services as soon as possible.

Appendix B

General Academic and Teaching References

Abrami, P. (1995). Classroom connections: Understanding and using cooperative learning. Toronto, CAN: Harcourt Brace.

Adam B. & Roberts, A. (1993). Differences among the disciplines, in Robert M. Diamond and Bronwyn E. Adam, eds., Recognizing faculty work: reward systems for the Year 2000. New Directions for Higher Education.

Adams, A., Carnine, D., & Gersten, R. (1982). Instructional strategies for studying content area texts in the intermediate grades. Reading Research Quarterly, 18.

Adams, M. (Ed.). (1992). Promoting diversity in college classrooms: Innovative responses for the curriculum, faculty, and institutions. San Francisco, CA: Jossey-Bass.

Aiken, W. M. (1942). Story of the eight-year study. New York, NY: Harper.

Akin, J.N. (1985). Teacher supply/demand 1985. Madison, WI: Association for School, College, and University Staffing.

Alderman, D.L., & Powers, D.E. (1980). The effects of special preparation on SAT-verbal scores. American Educational Research Journal, 17.

Alderman, D.L., Appel, L.R., & Murphy, R.T. (1978). PLATO and TICCIT: An evaluation of CAI in the community college. Educational Technology, 18.

Alderman, M.K. (1985). Achievement motivation and the preservice teacher. In M. Alderman & M. Cohen (Eds.), Motivation theory and practice for preservice teachers. Washington, DC: Eric Clearinghouse on Teacher Education.

Aleamoni, L. (Ed.). (1987). Techniques for evaluating and improving instruction. New Directions for Teaching and Learning, No. 31. San Francisco, CA: Jossey-Bass.

Alessi, S.M., & Trollip, S.R. (1985). Computer-based instruction: Methods and development. Englewood Cliffs, NJ: Prentice Hall.

Alexander-Snow, M. & Johnson, B. (1999). Perspectives from faculty of color, in faculty in new jobs, ed. Robert Menges, et al. San Francisco, CA.: Jossey-Bass.

Allen, R. & Pilnick, S. (1973). Confronting the shadow organization: How to detect and defeat negative norms. Organizational Dynamics.

Allen, R., & Rueter, T. (1990). Teaching assistant strategies: An introduction to college teaching. Dubuque, IA: Kendall/Hunt.

Alwain, D., & Thornton, A. (1984). Family origins and schooling processes: Early versus late influence of prenatal characteristics. American Sociological Review, 49.

American Association of University Professors, A Statement of the Association's Council: Freedom and Responsibility, AAUP Policy Documents and Reports.

American Association of University Professors, Joint Statement on Rights and Freedoms of Students, AAUP Policy Documents and Reports.

American Association of University Professors, Statement on Professional Ethics. (1990). AAUP Policy Documents and Reports. Washington, DC: American Association of University Professors.

American Educational Research Association, Committee on the Criteria of Teaching Effectiveness. (1953). Journal of Educational Research (2nd Rep.), 46.

Ames, C. (1985). Attributions and cognition in motivation theory. In M. Alderman & M. Cohen (Eds.), Motivation theory and practice for preservice teachers. Washington, DC: Eric Clearinghouse on Teacher Education.

Ames, R. & Lau, S. (1982). An attributional analysis of student help-seeking in academic settings. Journal of Educational Psychology, 74.

Anand, P., & Ross, S.M. (1987). Using computer-assisted instruction to personalize math learning materials for elementary school children. Journal of Educational Psychology, 79.

Anastasi, A. (1988). Psychological testing (6th ed.). New York, NY: Macmillan.

Anderson, C. (1989). The role of education in the academic disciplines in teacher education. In A. Woolfolk (Ed.), Research bases for the graduate preparation of teachers. Englewood Cliffs, NJ: Prentice Hall.

Anderson, E. & Lucasse, A. (1988). Toward a conceptualization of mentoring. Journal of Teacher Education 39.

Anderson, J.R. (1985). Cognitive psychology and its implications (2nd ed.). San Francisco, CA: W. H. Freeman.

Anderson, L.M. (1985). What are students doing when they do all that seatwork? In C. Fisher & D. Berliner (Eds.:), Perspectives on instructional time. New York, NY: Longman.

Anderson, R.E., Klassen, D.L., & Johnson, D.C. (1986). In defense of a comprehensive view of computer literacy—A reply to Luehrmann. In T. R. Cannings & S.W. Brown (Eds.), The information-age classroom: Using the computer as a tool. Irvine, CA: Franklin, Beedle & Associates.

Andre, R., & Frost, P. (1997). Researchers hooked on teaching. Thousand Oaks, CA: Sage.

Andrews, J. (Ed.). (1985). Strengthening the teaching assistant faculty. San Francisco, CA: Jossey-Bass.

Angelo, T. A., & Cross, K. P. (1993). Classroom assessment techniques: A handbook for college teachers (2nd ed.). San Francisco, CA: Jossey-Bass.

Angelo, Thomas A., and K. Patricia Cross. Classroom Assessment Techniques: A Handbook for College Teachers. 2nd edition. San Francisco: Jossey-Bass, 1994.

Apple, M. (1995). Education and power. Boston, MA: Ark Paperbacks.

Argon, J. (1995). Securing funding from federal sources. in The Academic Handbook, 2nd ed., ed. Deneef, A. and Craufurd, D. Goodwin. Durham, NC: Duke University Press, 220.

Arlin, M. (1984). Time, equality, and mastery learning. Review of Educational Research, 54.

Armbruster, B.B., & Anderson, T.H. (1981). Research synthesis on study skills. Educational Leadership, 39.

Arreola, R. (1995). Developing a comprehensive faculty evaluation system: A handbook for college faculty and administrators on designing and operating a comprehensive faculty evaluation system. Bolton, MA: Anker.

Ashton-Warner, S. (1963). Teacher, New York, NY: Simon & Schuster.

Astin, A. (1977). Four critical years: Effects of college on beliefs, attitudes, and knowledge. San Francisco, CA: Jossey-Bass.

Astin, A. (1993). What matters in college? Four critical years revisited. San Francisco, CA: Jossey-Bass.

Atkinson, J.W. (1964). An introduction to motivation. Princeton, NJ: Van Nostrand.

Atkinson, R.C. (1975). Mnemotechnics in second-language learning. American Psychologist, 30.

Atkinson, R.C., & Raugh, M.R. (1975). An application of the mnemonic keyword method to the acquisition of Russian vocabulary. Journal of Experimental Psychology: Human Learning and Memory, 104.

Atkinson, R.C., & Shifferin, R.M. (1968). Human memory: A proposed system and its control processes. In K. Spence & J. Spence (Eds.), The psychology of learning and motivation (Vol. 2). New York, NY: Academic Press.

Austin, A. 1990. Faculty cultures, faculty values, New Directions for Institutional Research 68.

Ausubel, D.P. (1963). The psychology of meaningful verbal learning. New York, NY: Grune and Stratton.

Ausubel, D.P. (1977). The facilitation of meaningful verbal meaning in the classroom. Educational Psychologist, 12.

Axelrod, J. (1979). The university teacher as artist. San Francisco, CA: Jossey-Bass.

Babad, E.Y., Inbar, J., & Rosenthal, R. (1982). Pygmalion, Galatea, and the Golem: Investigations of biased and unbiased teachers. Journal of Educational Psychology, 74.

Backman, M. (1972, Winter). Patterns of mental abilities: Ethnic, socioeconomic, and sex differences. American Educational Research Journal, 9(1),

Baiocco, S., & DeWaters, J. (1998). Successful college teaching. Boston, MA: Allyn and Bacon.

Baker, G., Dudziak, J., & Tyler, P. (1994). A handbook on the community college in America: Its history, mission, and management. Westport, CN: Greenwood Press.

Baker, L., & Brown, A. L. (1984). Cognitive monitoring in reading. In J. Flood (Ed.), Understanding reading comprehension. Newark, DE: International Reading Association.

Baker, L., & Brown, A.L. (1984). Metacognitive skills and reading. In P. D. Pearson, M. Kamil, R. Barr, & P. Mosenthal (Eds.), Handbook of reading research. New York, NY: Longman.

Baldwin, J.D., & Baldwin, J.I. (1986). Behavioral principles in everyday life (2nd ed.). Englewood Cliffs, NJ: Prentice Hall.

Balsmeyer, B., Haubrich, K. & Quinn, C. (1966). Defining Collegiality within the Academic Setting, Journal of Nursing Education 35.

Bandura, A. (1973). Aggression: A social learning analysis. Englewood Cliffs, NJ: Prentice Hall.

Bandura, A. (1977). Social learning theory. Englewood Cliffs, NJ: Prentice Hall.

Bandura, A. (1978). The self-system in reciprocal determinism. American Psychologist, 33.

Bandura, A. (1986). Social foundations of thought and action. Englewood Cliffs, NJ: Prentice Hall.

Bandura, A., Ross, D., & Ross, S.A. (1963). Vicarious reinforcement and imitative learning. Journal of Abnormal and Social Psychology, 67.

Banner, J., & Cannon, H. (1997). The elements of teaching. New Haven: Yale University Press.

Banner, James, and Harold C. Cannon. The Elements of Teaching. New Haven: Yale University Press, 1999.

Barber, B. (1992). An Aristocracy of Everyone: The politics of education and the future of america. New York, NY: Ballantine.

Barger, R. (1984). Computer literacy: Toward a clearer definition. In J. H. Tashner (Ed.), Computer literacy for teachers: Issues, questions and concerns. Phoenix, AZ: The Oryz Press.

Barr R. & Tagg, J. (1995). From teaching to learning: A new paradigm for undergraduate education. Change 27.

Barron, F., & Harrington, D.M. (1981). Creativity, intelligence, and personality. In M. Rosenzweig & L. W. Porter (Eds.), Annual Review of Psychology. Palo Alto, CA: Annual Reviews, Inc.

Bartlett, F. C. (1932). Remembering: A study in experimental and social psychology. New York, NY: Macmillan.

Barton, E.J. (1981). Developing sharing: An analysis of modeling and other behavioral techniques. Behavior Modification, 5.

Barzun, J. (1991). Begin Here: The Forgotten conditions of teaching and learning, Chicago, IL, IL: University of Chicago, IL Press.

Bean, J. (1996). Engaging ideas: The professor's guide to integrating writing, critical thinking, and active learning in the classroom. San Francisco, CA: Jossey-Bass.

Beard, R., & Hartley, J. (1984). Teaching and learning in higher education (4th ed.). New York, NY: Harper & Row.

Becker, W.C., Engelman, S., & Thomas, D.R. (1975). Teaching 1: Classroom management. Chicago, IL: Science Research Associates.

Beidler, P. (Ed.). (1986). Distinguished teachers on effective teaching. San Francisco, CA: Jossey-Bass.

Belcher B.&. Jacobson, J. (1992). From idea to funded project grant proposals that work, 4th ed. Phoenix, AZ: Oryx Press.

Belenky, M., & Clinchy, B. (1986). Women's ways of knowing: The development of self, voice, and mind. NY: Basic Books.

Benbow, C.P., & Stanley, J.C. (1980). Sex differences in mathematical ability: Fact or artifact? Science, 210.

Benbow, C.P., & Stanley, J.C. (1983). Differential course-taking hypothesis revisited. American Educational Research Journal, 20.

Benjamin, L. T., & Lowman, K. D. (Eds.) (1981). Activities handbook for the teaching of psychology. Washington, DC: American Psychological Association.

Benjamin, L., Daniel, R., & Brewer, C. (Eds.). (1985) Handbook for teaching introductory psychology. Hillsdale, NJ: Lawrence Erlbaum.

Berger, K.S. (1983). The developing person through the life span. New York, NY: Worth.

Bergquist, W., & Phillips, S. (1975). A handbook for faculty development. Washington, D.C.: Council for the Advancement of Small Colleges, 3 vols.

Bergquist, W., Gould, R., & Greenberg, R. (1981). Designing undergraduate education. San Francisco, CA: Jossey-Bass.

Berliner, D. (1983). Developing concepts of classroom environments: Some light on the T in studies of ATI. Educational Psychologist, 18.

Berliner, D. (1987). But do they understand? In V. Richardson-Koehler (Ed.), Educators' handbook: A research perspective. New York, NY: Longman.

Berliner, D. (1988). Simple views of effective teaching and a simple theory of classroom instruction. In D. Berliner & B. Rosenshine (Eds.), Talks to teachers. New York, NY: Random House.

Berliner, D., & Biddle, B. (1995). The manufactured crisis. Reading, MA: Addison-Wesley.

Berman, L., Hultgren, F., Lee, D., Rivkin, M., & Rodereck, J. (1991). Toward a curriculum for being: Voices of educators. Albany, NY: SUNY Press.

Bernstein, H. (1976). Manual for teaching. Ithaca, NY: Cornell University.

Bess, J. (Ed.) (1997). Teaching well and liking it: Motivating faculty to teach effectively. Baltimore, MD: Johns Hopkins Press.

Bess, J. Collegiality: (1987). Toward a clarification of meaning and function, in higher education. Handbook of Theory and Research, New York, NY: Agathon Press.

Beyer, B.K. (1984). Improving thinking skills: Practical approaches. Phi Delta Kappan, 65.

Beyer, B.K. (1985). Practical strategies for the direct teaching of thinking skills. In A. Costa (Ed.), Developing minds: A resource book for teaching thinking. Alexandria, VA: Association for Supervision and Curriculum Development.

Beyer, B.K. (1997). Improving student thinking: A comprehensive approach. Boston, MA: Allyn and Bacon.

Bieber, J. (1997). Faculty work and public trust: restoring the value of teaching and public service in American academic life. Journal of Higher Education 68.

Black, B., Gach, M., & Kotzian, N. (1996). Guidebook for teaching labs. Ann Arbor: Center for Research on Learning and Teaching.

Blackburn, T. &. Lawrence, J. (1995). Faculty at work, motivation, expectation, satisfaction. Baltimore, MD, MD: The Johns Hopkins University Press.

Blackman, S., & Goldstein, K. (1982). Cognitive styles and learning disabilities. Journal of Learning Disabilities, 15.

Bligh, Donald A. What's the Use of Lectures? San Francisco: Jossey-Bass, 2000..

Bloom, B.S. (1968). Learning for mastery. Evaluation Comment, 1(2). Los Angeles, CA: University of California, Center for the Study of Evaluation of Instructional Programs.

Bloom, B.S. (1973). Individual differences in achievement. In L. J. Rubin (Ed.), Facts and feelings in the classroom. New York, NY: Viking.

Bloom, B.S. (1976). Human characteristics and school learning. New York, NY: McGraw-Hill.

Bloom, B.S. (Ed.). (1956). Taxonomy of educational objectives: The classification of educational goals. Handbook I: Cognitive domain. NY: Longman.

Bloom, B.S., Engelhart, M.D., Frost, E.J., Hill, W.H., & Krathwohl, D.R. (1956). Taxonomy of educational objectives. Handbook I: Cognitive domain. New York, NY: McGraw-Hill.

Bloom, B.S., Hastings, J.T., & Madaus, G.F. (1971). Handbook on formative and summarized evaluation of student learning. New York, NY: McGraw-Hill.

Bloom, R., & Bourdon, L. (1980). Types and frequencies of teachers' written instructional feedback. Journal of Educational Research, 74.

Bode, R. (1986). Mentoring and collegiality, in faculty in new jobs: A guide to settling in, becoming established, and building institutional support, 8th ed. Lexington, MA.: D.C. Heath & Company.

Boice, B. (2000). Advice for new faculty members. Needham Heights, MA: Allyn & Bacon.

Boice, R. (1992). The new faculty member: Support and fostering professional development. San Francisco, CA: Jossey-Bass.

Boice, R. (1996). First-order principles for college teachers. Bolton, MA: Anker Publishing.

Boice, Robert. Advice for New Faculty Members. Boston: Allyn and Bacon, 2000.

Bonwell, C., & Eison, J. (1991). Active learning: Creating excitement in the classroom. ASAHE-ERIC Higher Education Report No. 1.

Bork, A. (1978). Machines for computer-assisted learning. Educational Technology, 18.

Bork, A. (1984). Computers in education today—and some possible futures. Phi Delta Kappan, 66.

Bork, A., & Franklin, S. (1979). Personal computers in learning. Educational Technology, 19.

Borko, H. (1989). Research on learning to teach: Implications for graduate teacher preparation. In A. Woolfolk (Ed.), Research perspectives on the graduate preparation of teachers. Englewood Cliffs, NJ: Prentice Hall.

Borkowski, J.G., Johnston, M.B., & Reid, M.K. (1986). Metacognition, motivation, and the transfer of control processes. In S. J. Ceci (Ed.), Handbook of cognition: Social and neurological aspects of learning disabilities. Hillsdale, NJ: Erlbaum.

Bornstein, P.H. (1985). Self-instructional training: A commentary and state-of-the-art. Journal of Applied Behavior Analysis, 18.

Boud, D. (Ed.). (1988). Developing student autonomy in learning. NY: Kogan Page and Nichols.

Bourne, L.E., Dominowski, R.L., Loftus, E.F., & Healy, A. (1986). Cognitive processes (2nd ed.). Englewood Cliffs, NJ: Prentice Hall.

Bower, G.H., & Hilgard, E.L. (1981). Theories of learning. Englewood Cliffs, NJ: Prentice Hall.

Bowser, B., Auletta, G., & Jones, T. (1993). Confronting diversity issues on campus. Newbury Park, CA: Sage.

Bowser, B., Jones, T., & Young, G. (Eds.). (1995). Toward the multicultural university. Westport, CT: Praeger.

Boyer, E. (1987). College: The undergraduate experience in America. NY: Harper and Row.

Boyer, E. L. (1990). Scholarship reconsidered: Priorities of the professoriate. Princeton, NJ: Carnegie Foundation for the Advancement of Teaching.

Boyle, P. and Boice, B. (1998). Systematic mentoring for new faculty teachers and graduate teaching assistants. Innovative Higher Education 22.

Bozeman, W., & House, J. (1988). Microcomputers in education: The second decade. T. H. E. Journal, 15(6).

Bransford, J.D., Stein, B.S., Vye, N.J., Franks, J.J., Auble, P.M., Mezynski, K.J., & Perfetto, G.A. (1982). Differences in approaches to learning: An overview. Journal of Experimental Psychology: General, 111.

Braun, C. (1976). Teacher expectation: Sociopsychological dynamics. Review of Educational Research, 46(2).

Brenner, L.P., & Agee, C.C. (1979). The symbiosis of PLATO and microcomputers. Educational Technology, 19.

Brent, R. and Felder, R. (1999). It's a start. College teaching, 47.

Brewer, W.F. (1974). There is no convincing evidence for operant and classical conditioning in humans. In W. B. Weimer & D. S. Permo (Eds.), Cognition and symbolic processes. Hillsdale, NJ: Erlbaum.

Brookfield, S. (1990). The skillful teacher. San Francisco, CA: Jossey-Bass.

Brookfield, S. D. (1995). Becoming a critically reflective teacher. San Francisco, CA: Jossey-Bass.

Brophy, J. (1998). Motivating students to learn. Boston, MA: McGraw-Hill.

Brophy, J.E. (1988). On motivating students. In D. Berliner & B. Rosenshine (Eds.), Talks to teachers. New York, NY: Random House.

Brophy, J.E. (1973). Stability of teacher effectiveness. American Educational Research Journal, 10.

Brophy, J.E. (1981). Teacher praise: A functional analysis. Review of Educational Research, 51.

Brophy, J.E., & Evertson, C. (1976). Learning from teaching: A developmental perspective. Boston, MA: Allyn & Bacon.

Brophy, J.E., & Evertson, C. (1978). Context variables in teaching. Educational Psychologist, 12.

Brophy, J.E., & Good, T. (1986). Teacher behavior and student achievement. In M. Wittrock (Ed.):, Handbook of research on teaching (3rd ed.). New York, NY: Macmillan.

Brophy, J.E., & Kher, N. (1986). Teacher socialization as a mechanism for developing student motivation to learn. In R. Feldman (Ed.), Social psychology applied to education. New York, NY: Cambridge, MA University Press.

Brown, A.L., Bransford, J.D., Ferrara, R.A., & Campione, J.C. (1983). Learning, remembering, and understanding. In P. Mussen (Ed.), Carmichael's manual of child psychology. Vol. 3: Cognitive development (E. Markman & J. Flavell, Volume Eds.). New York, NY: Wiley.

Brown, A.L., Compione, J.C., & Day, J.D. (1981). Learning to learn: On training students to learn from tests. Educational Researcher, 9.

Brown, G. (1978). Lecturing and explaining. New York, NY: Methuen.

Brown, G., & Alkins, M. (1988). Effective teaching in higher education. NY: Methuen.

Brown, J., & Thornton, J. (1971). College teaching: A systematic approach. NY: McGraw.

Brown, J.S., & Burton, R.R. (1979). Diagnostic models for procedural bugs in basic mathematical skills. Cognitive Science, 2.

Brown, R., & McNeill, D. (1966). The "tip-of-the-tongue" phenomenon. Journal of Verbal Learning and Verbal Behavior, 5.

Brown, S., Race, P., & Smith, B. (1996). 500 tips on assessment. London: Kogan Page.

Bruffee, K. (1993). Collaborative learning: Higher education, interdependence and the authority of knowledge. Baltimore, MD: Johns Hopkins Press.

Bruner, J.S. (1960). The process of education New York, NY: Vintage Books.

Bruner, J.S. (1962). The process of education. Cambridge, MA: Harvard University Press.

Bruner, J.S. (1966). Toward a theory of instruction. New York, NY: Norton.

Bruner, J.S. (1973). Beyond the information given: Studies in the psychology of knowing. New York, NY: Norton.

Burbach, H.J. (1981). The labeling process: A sociological analysis. In J. Kauffman & D. Hallahan (Eds.), Handbook of special education. Englewood Cliffs, NJ: Prentice Hall.

Burton, R.V. (1963). The generality of honesty reconsidered. Psychological Review, 70.

Butler, R., & Nisan, M. (1986). Effects of no feedback, task-related comments, and grades on intrinsic motivation and performance. Journal of Educational Psychology, 78.

Buxton, C. (1956). A guide to college teaching. New York, NY: Harcourt Brace Jovanovich.

Byrd, M. (Spring 1995). Academic Advising Ain't What It Used to Be: Strangers in the University. NACADA Journal 15.

Cahn, S. (1986). Saints and scamps: Ethics in academia. Totowa, NH: Rowman & Littlefield.

Campbell, B., & Smith, K. (Eds.). (1997). New paradigms for college teaching. Edina, MN: Interaction Book Company.

Canter, L., & Canter, M. (1976). Assertive discipline: A take-charge approach for today's educator. Los Angeles, CA: Lee Canter and Associates.

Cantrell, R.P., Stenner, A.J., & Katzenmeyer, W.G. (1977). Teacher knowledge, attitudes, and classroom teaching correlates of student achievement. Journal of Educational Psychology, 69.

Carbone, E. (1998). Teaching large classes: Tools and strategies. Thousand Oaks, CA: Sage Publications.

Carley S. and Scheinborg, C. (2000). Proposal Writing, 2nd ed. Thousand Oaks, CA: Sage Publications.

Carter, K. (1984). Do teachers understand principles of writing tests? Journal of Teacher Education, 35.

Casanova, U. (1987). Ethnic and cultural differences. In V. Richardson-Koehler (Ed.), Educators' handbook: A research perspective. New York, NY: Longman.

Case, R. (1978). Developmentally-based theory and technology of instruction. Review of Educational research, 48.

Case, R. (1978). Piaget and beyond: Toward a developmentally-based theory and technology of instruction. In R. Glaser (Ed.)., Advances in instructional psychology (Vol. 1). Hillsdale, NJ: Erlbaum.

Case, R. (1980). Intellectual development: A systematic reinterpretation. In F. Farley & N. J. Gordon (Eds.), Psychology and education: The state of the union. Berkeley, CA: McCutchan.

Case, R. (1985). A developmentally-based approach to the problem of instructional design. In R. Glaser, S. Chipman, & J. Segal (Eds.), Teaching thinking skills (Vol. 2) Hillsdale, NJ: Erlbaum.

Cattell, R.B. (1963). The fluid and crystallized intelligence: A critical experiment. Journal of Educational Psychology.

Cawelti, G. (1995). Handbook on research on improving student achievement. Arlington, VA: Educational Research Services.

Cazden, C.B. (1988). Classroom discourse: The language of teaching and learning. Portsmouth, NH: Heinemann.

Centra, J. (1972). Strategies for improving college teaching. Washington: ERIC Clearinghouse on Higher Education.

Centra, J. (1979). Determining faculty effectiveness. San Francisco, CA: Jossey-Bass.

Centra, J. (1993). Reflective faculty evaluation: Enhancing teaching and determining faculty effectiveness. San Francisco, CA: Jossey-Bass.

Change Magazine. (1978). Guide to effective teaching. New York, NY: Change Magazine Press.

Chapman, D.W., & Hutcheson, S.M. (1982). Attrition from teaching careers: A discriminant analysis. American Educational Research Journal, 19.

Charles, C. M. (1992). Building classroom discipline (4th ed). White Plains, NY: Longman.

Charles, C.M. (1981). Building classroom discipline: From models to practice (2nd ed.). New York, NY: Longman.

Chase, C.I. (1978). Measurement for educational evaluation (2nd ed.). Reading, MA: Addison-Wesley.

Chickering, A. (1993). Education and identity (2nd ed.). San Francisco, CA: Jossey-Bass.

Chickering, A., & Gamson, Z. (1987). Seven principles for good practice in undergraduate education. The Wingspread Journal, 9, No. 2

Chickering, A., & Gamson, Z. (Eds.). (1991). Applying the seven principles for good practice in undergraduate education. New Directions for Teaching and Learning 47. San Francisco, CA: Jossey-Bass..

Chickering, A., et al. (1994). The modern American college. San Francisco, CA: Jossey-Bass. 1981 edition

Chism, N. (1999). Peer review of teaching: A sourcebook. Bolton, MA: Anker.

Chomsky, N. (1965). Aspects of a theory of syntax. Cambridge, MA: MIT Press.

Christensen, C. (1987). Teaching and the case method: Text, cases, and readings. MA: Harvard Business School.

Christensen, C. Roland, David A. Garvin, and Ann Sweet, eds. Education for Judgment: The Artistry of Discussion Leadership. Boston: Harvard Business School Press, 1991.

Clairborn, W.L. (1969). Expectancy effects in the classroom: A failure to replicate. Journal of Education Psychology, 60.

Clarizio, H.F. (1971). Toward positive classroom discipline. New York, NY: Wiley.

Clark, B. R. (1987). The academic life: Small worlds, different worlds. Princeton, NJ: Carnegie Foundation for the Advancement of Teaching, Princeton University Press.

Clark, C., & Yinger, R. (1988). Teacher planning. In D. Berliner & B. Rosenshine (Eds.), Talks to teachers. New York, NY: Random House.

Clark, C.M. & Peterson, P.L. (1986). Teachers' thought processes. In M. Wittrock (Ed.), Handbook of research on teaching (3rd ed.). New York, NY: Macmillan.

Clark, C.M., Gage, N.L., Marx, R.W., Petersonn, P.L., Staybrook, N.G., & Winnie, P.H. (1979). A factorial experiment on teacher structuring, soliciting, and reacting. Journal of Educational Psychology, 71.

Clark, R.E. (1983). Reconsidering research on learning from media. Review of educational Research, 53.

Clark, R.E. (1984). Research on student thought processes during computer-based instruction. Journal of Instructional Development, 7.

Clark, R.E. (1985). Evidence for confounding in computer-based instruction studies: Analyzing the meta-analyses. Educational Communication and Technology Journal, 33.

Clements, D.H., & Gullo, D.F. (1984). Effects of computer programming on young children's cognition. Journal of Educational Psychology, 76.

Clifford, M.M. (1979). Effects of failure: Alternative explanations and possible implications. Educational Psychologist, 14.

Clifford, M.M. (1984). Educational psychology. In Encyclopedia of education. New York, NY: Macmillan.

Clifford, M.M. (1984). Thoughts on a theory of constructive failure. Educational Psychologist, 19.

Clift, J., & Irmrie, B. (1981). Assessing students, appraising teaching. NY: Wiley.

Coates, J.F. (1978). Population and education: How demographic trends will shape the U.S. The Futurist, 12.

Coates, T.J., & Thoresen, C.E. (1979). Behavioral self-control and educational practice or do we really need self-control? In D. C. Berliner (Ed.), Review of research in education, (Vol. 7). Itasca, IL: F. E. Peacock.

Coburn, P., Kelman, P., Roberts, N., Snyder, T.F.F., Watt, D.H., & Weiner, C. (1985). Practical guide to computers in education. Reading, MA: Addison-Wesley.

Cohen, A., & Brawer, F. (1987). The collegiate function of community colleges: Fostering higher learning through curriculum and student transfer. San Francisco, CA: Jossey-Bass.

Colbeck, C. (1998). Merging In A Seamless Blend: How Faculty Integrate Teaching and Research. Journal of Higher Education.

Cole, N.S. (1981). Bias in testing. American Psychologist, 36.

Coleman, J.S., Campbell, J., Wood, A.M., Weinfeld, F.D., & York, R.L. (1966). Equality of educational opportunity. Washington, DC: United States Department of Health, Education and Welfare, Office of Education.

College Teaching. Washington, D.C.: HELDREF Publications.

Collins, A., & Smith, E. (1980). Teaching the process of reading comprehension (Tech. Rep. No. 182). Urbana-Champaign, IL: University of Illinois, Center for the Study of Reading.

Collins, A., & Smith, E. (1982). Teaching the process of reading. In D. K. Detterman & R. J. Sternberg (Eds.), How and how much can intelligence be increased. Norwood, NJ: Ablex.

Committee on Undergraduate Science Education. (1997). Science teaching reconsidered: A handbook. Washington, DC: National Academy Press.

Cooper, G., & Sweller, J. (1987). Effects of schema acquisition and rule automation on mathematical problem-solving transfer. Journal of Educational Psychology, 79.

Cooper, H. (1979). Pygmalion grows up: A model for teacher expectation communication and performance influence. Review of Educational Research, 49.

Cooper, H.M., & Good, T. (1983). Pygmalion grows up: Studies in the expectation communication process. New York, NY: Longman.

Cooper, J., Prescott, S., Cook, L., Smith, L., Meuck, R., & Cuseo, J. (1990). Coperative learning and college instruction. Effective use of student learning teams. Carson, CA: California State University Foundation.

Cooper, J., Robinson, P., & McKinney, M. (1994). Coperative learning in the classroom. In D. Halpern (Ed.). Changing college classrooms: New directions and learning strategies for an increasingly complex world. San Francisco, CA: Jossey-Bass.

Copeland, J. and Murry, J. (1996): Getting tossed from the ivory tower: The legal implications of evaluating faculty performance. Missouri Law Review 61(2).

Copi, I.M. (1961). Introduction to logic. New York, NY: Macmillan.

Cornesky, R. (1991). The quality professor: Implementing TQM in teaching. Madison, WI: Magna Pub.

Corno, L. (1988). Teaching and self-regulated learning. In D. Berliner & B. Rosenshine (Eds.:), Talks to teachers. New York, NY: Random House.

Corno, L., & Snow, R.E. (1986). Adapting teaching to individual differences in learners. In M. Wittrock (Ed.), Handbook of research on teaching (3rd ed.). New York, NY: Macmillan.

Costa, A.L. (Ed.). (1985). Developing minds: A resource book for teaching thinking. Alexandria, VA: Association for Supervision and Curriculum Development.

Covey, A. et al., (1994). First things first. New York, NY: Simon & Schuster.

Covey, S. (1989). The seven habits of highly effective people. New York, NY: Fireside/Simon & Schuster.

Covington, M. (1984). Strategic thinking and the fear of failure. In J. Segal, S. Chipman, & R. Glaser (Eds.), Thinking and learning skills: Relating instruction to basic research. Hillsdale, NJ: Erlbaum.

Covington, M. (1992). Making the grade. Cambridge, MA: Cambridge, MA University Press.

Covington, M., & Omelich, C. (1987). "I knew it cold before the exam": A test of the anxiety-blockage hypothesis. Journal of Educational Psychology, 79.

Covington, M.V., & Omelich, C.L. (1984). An empirical examination of Weiner's critique of attribution research. Journal of Educational Psychology, 76.

Cox, C.C. (1926). The early mental traits of three hundred geniuses. In L. M. Terman (Ed.), Genetic studies of genius (Vol. 2). Stanford, CA: Stanford University Press.

Cox, W.F., & Dunn, T.G. (1979). Mastery learning: A psychological trap? Educational Psychologist, 14.

Craig, G. (1986). Human development (4th ed.). Englewood Cliffs, NJ: Prentice Hall.

Craik, F.I.M. (1979). Human memory. Annual Review of Psychology, 30.

Craik, F.I.M., & Lockhart, R.S. (1972). Levels of processing: A framework for memory research. Journal of Verbal Learning and Verbal Behavior, 11.

Cranton, P. (1989). Planning instruction for adult learners. Toronto, CAN: Wall and Emerson, Inc.

Crockover, G. (1991). Reflections on professorial mentorships, Teaching Education 3.

Cronbach, L., & Snow, R. (1977). Aptitudes and instructional methods. New York, NY: Irvington.

Cross, P. (1976). Accent on learning. San Francisco, CA: Jossey-Bass.

Cross, P. (1981). Adults as learners: Increasing participation and facilitating learning. San Francisco, CA: Jossey-Bass.

Cross, P., & Steadman, M. (1996). Classroom research: Implementing the scholarship of teaching. San Francisco, CA: Jossey-Bass.

Crouse, J.M. (1971). Retroactive interference in reading prose materials. Journal of Educational Psychology, 62.

Dahlstrom, E., de Boor, T., Grunwald, P., & Vockley, M. (2011). The ECAR Study of Undergraduate Students and Information Techology, 2011 (Research Report). Boulder, CO: EDUCAUSE Center for Applied Research, available from http://www.educause.edu/ecar.

Daiute, C. (1985). Writing and computers. The Harvard Education Letter, 1(4).

Daloz, L. (1986). Effective teaching and mentoring. San Francisco, CA: Jossey-Bass.

Dansereau, D.F. (1985). Learning strategy research. In J. Segal, S. Chipman, & R. Glaser (Eds.), Thinking and learning skills. Vol. 1: Relating instruction to research. Hillsdale, NJ: Erlbaum.

Darley, J., & Fazio, R. (1980). Expectancy confirmation processes arising in the social interaction sequence. American Psychologist, 35.

Darling-Hammond, L. (1984). Beyond the commission reports: The coming crisis in teaching. Santa Monica, CA: Rand.

Daurio, S.P. (1979). Educational enrichment versus acceleration: A review of the literature. In W. George, S. Cohn, & J. Stanley (Eds.), Educating the gifted: acceleration and enrichment. Baltimore, MD: Johns Hopkins Press.

Davidson, C. & Ambrose, A. (1994). The new professor's handbook: A guide to teaching and research in engineering and science. Bolton, MA: Anker Publishing Company, Inc.

Davis, B. G. (1993). Tools for teaching. San Francisco, CA: Jossey-Bass.

Davis, J. (1976). Teaching strategies for the college classroom. San Francisco, CA: Jossey-Bass.

Davis, J. (1996). Better teaching, more learning: Strategies for success in postsecondary settings. Phoenix, AZ: American Council on Education and Oryx Press.

Davis, S. F., & Buskist, W. (Eds.). (2002). The teaching of psychology: Essays in honor of Wilbert J. McKeachie and Charles L. Brewer. Mahwah, NJ: Erlbaum.

De Charms, R. (1968). Personal causation. New York, NY: Academic Press.

De Charms, R. (1976). Enhancing motivation: Change in the classroom. New York, NY: Irvington.

De Charms, R. (1983). Intrinsic motivation, peer tutoring, and cooperative learning: Practical maxims. In J. Levine & M. Wang (Eds.):, Teacher and student perceptions: Implications for learning. Hillsdale, NJ: Erlbaum.

De Lisi, R., & Staudt, J. (1980). Individual differences in college students' performances on formal operations tasks. Journal of Applied Developmental Psychology, 1.

Deci, E. (1975). Intrinsic motivation. New York, NY: Plenum.

Deci, E., & Ryan, R.M. (1985). Intrinsic motivation and self-determination in human behavior. New York, NY: Plenum.

Deiderich, P.B. (1973). Short-cut statistics for teacher-made tests. Princeton, NJ: Educational Testing Services.

Dellow, D.A., & Ross, S.M. (1982). Implications of personal computers for social science faculty. Community College Social Science Journal, 4.

Dempster, F.N. (1981). Memory span: Sources of individual and developmental differences. Psychological Bulletin, 89.

Deneef, L. Craufurd, D. & Goodwin, eds. (1995). The academic handbook, 2nd ed. Durham, NC: Duke University Press.

Denham, C., & Lieberman, A. (1980). Time to learn. Washington, DC: National Institute of Education.

Derry, S.J., & Murphy, D.A. (1986). Designing systems that train learning ability: From theory to practice. Review of Educational Research, 56.

Devine, T. (1981). Teaching study skills. Boston, MA: Allyn and Bacon.

Diamond, R. (1989). Designing and improving courses and curricula in higher education. San Francisco, CA: Jossey-Bass.

Dillon, J. (1983). Teaching and the art of question. Bloomington, IN: Phi Delta Kappa Educational Foundation.

Dinnel, D., & Glover, J.A. (1985). Advance organizers: Encoding manipulations. Journal of Educational Psychology, 77.

Diogenes, R., & Vestal, L. B., (1994). Prentice Hall critical thinking resource manual for psychology. Upper Saddle River, NJ: Prentice Hall.

Doctorow, M., Wittrock, M.C., & Marks, C. (1978). Generative processes in reading comprehension. Journal of Educational Psychology, 70.

Donald, J. (1997). Improving the environment for learning. San Francisco, CA: Jossey-Bass.

Donald, J., & Sullivan, A. (Eds.). (1985). Using research to improve teaching. New Directions for Teaching and Learning. San Francisco, CA: Jossey-Bass.

Douglas, G. (1992). Education without impact, how our universities fail the young. New York, NY: Carol Publishing Group.

Doyle, W. (1977). The uses of nonverbal behaviors: Toward an ecological model of classrooms. Merrill-Palmer Quarterly, 23.

Doyle, W. (1979). Making managerial decisions in classrooms. In D. Duke (Ed.), Classroom management: 78th Yearbook of the National Society for the Study of Education (Part 2). Chicago, IL: University of Chicago Press.

Doyle, W. (1980). Classroom management. West Lafayette, IN: Kappa Delta Pi.

Doyle, W. (1983). Academic work. Review of Educational Research, 53.

Doyle, W. (1985). Recent research on classroom management: Implications for teacher preparation. Journal of Teacher Education, 85.

Doyle, W. (1986). Classroom organization and management. In M. Wittrock (Ed.), Handbook of research on teaching (3rd ed.). New York, NY: Macmillan.

Doyle, W., & Ponder, G. (1978). The practicality ethic in teacher decision making. Interchange, 8(3).

Dreikurs, R., Grunwald, B.B., & Pepper, F.C. (1971). Maintaining sanity in the classroom: Illustrated teaching techniques. New York, NY: Harper and Row.

Dressel, P., & Marcus, D. (1982). On teaching and learning in college. San Francisco, CA: Jossey-Bass.

Dressel, P.L. (1977). The nature and role of objectives in instruction. Educational Technology, 17.

Druckman, D., & Bjork, R. (Eds.). (1994). Learning, remembering, believing. Washington, D.C.: National Academy Press.

Duchastel, P. (1979). Learning objectives and the organization of prose. Journal of Educational Psychology, 71.

Duffy, D., & Jones, J. (1995). Teaching within the rhythms of the semester. San Francisco, CA: Jossey-Bass.

Duffy, G., Roehler, L.R., Meloth, M.S., & Vavrus, L.G. (1986). Conceptualizing instructional explanation. Teaching and Teacher Education, 2.

Duncker, K. (1945). On solving problems. Psychological Monographs, 58, (5, Whole No. 270).

Dunkel, N. & Schuh, J. (1998). Advising student groups and organizations. San Francisco, CA: Jossey-Bass.

Dunkin, M.J., & Biddle, B.J. (1974). The study of teaching. New York, NY: Holt, Rinehart & Winston.

Dunn, K., & Dunn, R. (1978). Teaching students through their individual learning styles. Reston, VA: Reston.

Dunn, K., & Dunn, R. (1987). Dispelling outmoded beliefs about student learning. Educational Leadership, 44(6).

Dunn, R., Dunn, K., & Price, G.E. (1984). Learning style inventory. Lawrence, KS: Price Systems.

Dush, D.M., Hirt, M.L., & Schroider, H. (1983). Self-management modification with adults: A meta-analysis. Psychological Bulletin, 94.

Dweck, C. (1983). Theories of intelligence and achievement motivation. In S. Paris, G. Olson, & H. Stevenson (Eds.), Learning and motivation in the classroom. Hillsdale, NJ: Erlbaum.

Dweck, C.S. (1986). Motivational processes affecting learning. American Psychologist, 41.

Eatonn, S., & Olson, J. (1986). "Doing computers?" The micro in the elementary curriculum. Journal of Curriculum Studies, 18(3).

Eble, K. (1972). Professors as teachers. San Francisco, CA: Jossey-Bass.

Eble, K. (1983). The aims of college teaching. San Francisco, CA: Jossey-Bass.

Eble, K. (1990). The craft of teaching. San Francisco, CA: Jossey-Bass,

Eccles, J., & Wigfield, A. (1985). Teacher expectations and student motivation. In J. Dusek (Ed.), Teacher expectancies. Hillsdale, NJ: Erlbaum.

Edgerton, R. (1993). The re-examination of faculty priorities. Change 25.

Edgerton, Russell, Patricia Hutchings, and Kathleen Quinlan. The Teaching Portfolio: Capturing the Scholarship in Teaching. Washington, D. C.: American Association for Higher Education, 1991.

Edington, S., & Hunt, C. (1996). Teaching consultation process sourcebook. Stillwater, OK: New Forums Press.

Eisner, E. (1983, January). The art and craft of teaching. Educational Leadership, 40.

Eisner, E. (1986). A secretary in the classroom. Teaching and Teacher Education, 2.

Elashoff, J.D., & Snow, R.E. (1971). Pygmalion reconsidered. Worthington, OH: Charles A. Jones.

Elawar, M.C., & Corno, L. (1985). A factorial experiment in teachers' written feedback on student homework: Changing teacher behavior a little rather than a lot. Journal of Educational Psychology, 77.

Electronic Learning (1987). Educational technology 1987: A report on EL's seventh annual survey of the states. Electronic Learning. 7(2).

Elkind, D. (1981). Obituary—Jean Piaget (1896-1980). American Psychologist, 36.

Emmer, E.T., & Evertson, C.M. (1981). Synthesis of research on classroom management. Educational Leadership, 38.

Emmer, E.T., & Millett, JG. (1970). Improving teaching through experimentation: A laboratory approach. Englewood Cliffs, NJ: Prentice Hall.

Epstein, H. (1970). A strategy for education. Fair Lawn, N.J.: Oxford University Press.

Erickson, B., & Strommer, D. (1991). Teaching college freshmen. San Francisco, CA: Jossey-Bass.

Erickson, Bette LaSere, Calvin B. Peters, and Diane Weltner Strommer. Teaching College Freshmen. 2nd ed. San Francisco: Jossey-Bass, 2006.

Erickson, JF., & Shultz, J. (1977). When is context? Some issues and methods in the analysis of social competence. Quarterly Newsletter for the Institute for Comparative Human Development, 1(2).

Erickson, S. (1974). Motivation for learning. Ann Arbor, MI: University of Michigan Press.

Erickson, S. (1984). The essence of good teaching. San Francisco, CA: Jossey-Bass.

Evans, E.D. (1976). Transition to teaching. New York, NY: Holt, Rinehart & Winston.

Evans, N., Forney, D., & Guido-DiBrito, F. (1998). Student development in college: Theory, research and practice. San Francisco, CA: Jossey-Bass.

Evertson, C.M. (1988). Managing classrooms: A framework for teachers. In D. Berliner & B. Rosenshine (Eds.), Talks to teachers. New York, NY: Random House.

Evertson, C.M., & Green, J. (1986). Observation as inquiry and method. In M. Wittrock (Ed.), Handbook of research on teaching (3rd ed.). New York, NY: Macmillan.

Faw, H.W., & Waller, T.G. (1976). Mathemagenic behaviors and efficiency in learning from prose. Review of Educational Research, 46.

Feiman-Nemser, S. (1983). Learning to teach. In L. Shulman & G. Sykes (Eds.), Handbook of teaching and policy. New York, NY: Longman.

Feitler, F., & Tokar, E. (1982). Getting a handle on teacher stress: How bad is the problem? Educational Leadership, 39.

Feldman, K., & Newcomb, T. (1969). The impact of college on students (Vol. 2). San Francisco, CA: Jossey-Bass.

Feldman, K., & Paulsen, M. (1994). Teaching and learning in the college classroom. Needham Heights, MA: Ginn Press.

Fennema, E., & Sherman, J. (1977). Sex-related differences in mathematics achievement, spatial visualization and affective factors. American Educational Research Journal, 14(1).

Ferguson, D.L., Ferguson, P.M., & Bogdan, R.C. (1987). If mainstreaming is the answer, what is the question? In V. Richardson-Koehler (Ed.), Educators' handbook: A research perspective. New York, NY: Longman.

Ferster, C.B., & Skinner, B.F. (1957). Schedules of reinforcement. New York, NY: Appleton Century Crofts

Feurerstein, R. (1979). The dynamic assessment of retarded performers: The Learning Potential Assessment Device, theory, instruments, and techniques. Baltimore, MD: University Park Press.

Fink, L. Dee. Creating Significant Learning Experiences: An Integrated Approach to Designing College Courses. San Francisco: Jossey-Bass, 2003.

Finn, J. (1972). Expectations and the educational environment. Review of Educational Research, 42.

Fisch, L. (1996). The chalk-dust collection. Stillwater, OK: New Forums Press.

Fisher, C. (Ed.). (1996). Education and technology: Reflections on computing in classrooms. San Francisco, CA: Jossey-Bass.

Fiske, D. and Fogg, L. (1990). But the reviewers are making different criticisms of my paper! American Psychologist, 45.

Fiske, E.B. (1981). Teachers reward muddy prose, study finds. The New York Times.

Fiske, E.B. (1988). America's test mania. The New York Times (Education Life Section).

Flavell, J.H. (1976). Metacognitive aspects of problem solving. In L. Resnick (Ed.), The nature of intelligence. Hillsdale, NJ: Erlbaum.

Flavell, J.H. (1985). Cognitive development (2nd ed.). Englewood Cliffs, NJ: Prentice Hall.

Flavell, J.H., Friedrichs, A.G., & Hoyt, J.D. (1970). Developmental changes in memorization processes. Cognitive Psychology, 1.

Flood, B., & Moll, J. (1990). The professor business: A teaching primer for faculty. Medford, NJ: Learned Information, Inc.

Flournoy, D. (1972). The new teachers. San Francisco, CA: Jossey-Bass.

Fobes, R. (1993). The creative problem solver's toolbox. Corvallis, OR: Solutions Through Innovation.

Foos, K. (1987). Abstracts can enhance writing skills..

Fox, L.H. (1979). Programs for the gifted and talented: An overview. In A. Passow (Ed.), The gifted and talented: Their education and development. Chicago, IL: University of Chicago Press.

Fox, L.H. (1981). Identification of the academically gifted. American Psychologist, 36.

Frederiksen, N. (1984). Implications of cognitive theory for instruction in problem solving. Review of Educational Research, 54.

French, W. and Bell, C. (1999). Organizational Development: Behavior Science Interviews for Organization Improvement, 6th ed. Upper Saddle River, NJ: Prentice Hall.

Frender, R., Brown, B., & Lambert, W. (1970). The role of speech characteristics in scholastic success. Canadian Journal of Behavioral Science, 2.

Friedlander, B. (1985). Get your class in-line and on-line with a modem. Electronic Education.

Frost, S. (1993). Developmental Advising: Practices and Attitudes of Faculty Advisors. NACADA Journal 13.

Frostig, M., & Horne, D. (1964). The Frostig program for the development of visual perception: Teacher's guide. Chicago, IL: Follett.

Frye, B. (1994). Teaching in college: A resource for college teachers. Cleveland, OH: Info-Tech.

Fuhrmann, B., & Grasha, A. (1983). A practical handbook for college teachers. Boston, MA: Little, Brown and Company.

Fuller, F.G. (1969). Concerns of teachers: A developmental conceptualization. American Educational Research Journal, 6

Furst, E.J. (1981). Bloom's taxonomy of educational objectives for the cognitive domain: Philosophical and educational issues. Review of Educational Research, 51.

Furth, H., & Wachs, H. (1974). Thinking goes to school: Piaget's theory in practice. New York, NY: Oxford University Press.

Gaff, J., Ratcliff, J., & Associates. (1996). Handbook of the undergraduate curriculum. San Francisco, CA: Jossey-Bass.

Gaff, S., Festa, S., & Gaff, J. (1978). Professional development: A guide to resources. New Rochelle, NY: Change Magazine Press.

Gagne, E.D. (1985). The psychology of school learning. Boston, MA: Little, Brown.

Gagne, R.M. (1977). The conditions of learning (3rd ed.). New York, NY: Holt, Rinehart & Winston.

Gagne, R.M. (1985). The conditions of learning and theory of instruction (4th ed.). New York, NY: Holt, Rinehart & Winston.

Gagne, R.M., & Driscoll, M.P. (1988). Essentials of learning for instruction (2nd ed.). Englewood Cliffs, NJ: Prentice Hall.

Gagne, R.M., & Smith, E. (1962). A study of the effects of verbalization on problem solving. Journal of Experimental Psychology, 63.

Gall, M.D. (1970). The use of questions in teaching. Review of Educational Research, 40.

Gall, M.D. (1984). Synthesis of research on teachers' questioning. Educational Leadership, 41.

Gallini, J.K. (1989). Schema-based strategies and implications for instructional design in strategy training. In C. McCormick, G. Miller, & M. Pressley (Eds.), Cognitive strategies research: From basic research to educational applications. New York, NY: Springer-Verlag.

Gamson, Z. (1995). Faculty and Service. Change 27.

Gamson, Z. et al. (1984). Liberating education. San Francisco, CA: Jossey-Bass.

Gappa, J., & Leslie, D. (1993) The invisible faculty: Improving the status of part-timers in higher education. San Francisco, CA: Jossey-Bass.

Gardiner, L. (1997). Redesigning higher education: Producing dramatic gains in student learning. ASHE-ERIC Higher Education Reports, 23, (7). Washington, DC: Association for the Study of Higher Education.

Gardner, H. (1982). Developmental psychology (2nd ed.). Boston, MA: Little, Brown.

Gardner, H. (1983). Frames of mind: The theory of multiple intelligences. New York, NY: Basic Books.

Gardner, R. M. (1980). Exercises for general psychology. Minneapolis, MN: Burgess.

Garrett, S.S., Sadker, M., & Sadker, D. (1986). Interpersonal communication skills. In J. Cooper (ed.), Classroom teaching skills (3rd ed.). Lexington, MA: D. C. Heath.

Garrison, R. (1974). Implementing innovative instruction. San Francisco, CA: Jossey-Bass.

Gartner, A., & Lipsky, D.K. (1987). Beyond special education: Toward a quality system for all students. Harvard Educational Review, 57.

Gentner, D. (1975). Evidence for the psychological reality of semantic components: The verbs of possession. In D. Norman & D. Rumelhart (Eds.), Explorations in cognition. San Francisco, CA: W. H. Freeman.

Gibbs, G. (1992). Teaching more students: Problems and course design strategies. Oxford: Oxford Centre for Staff Development.

Gibbs, G. (1995). Assessing student-centered courses. Oxford: Oxford Centre for Staff Development.

Gibbs, J.W., & Luyben, P.D. (1985). Treatment of self-injurious behavior: Contingent versus noncontingent positive practice overcorrection. Behavior Modification, 9.

Gibbs, R. (1992). Improving the quality of student learning. Estover Plymouth, England: Plymouth Distributors.

Gibson, C. (1998). Distance learners in higher education: Institutional responses for quality outcomes. Madison, WI: Atwood Publishing.

Gibson, G. (1992). Good Start, A Guidebook for New Faculty in Liberal Arts Colleges. Bolton, MA: Anker Publishing Company.

Gick, M.L. (1986). Problem-solving strategies. Educational Psychologist, 21.

Gilligan, C. (1977). In a different voice: Women's conceptions of self and of morality. Harvard Educational Review, 47.

Gilligan, C. (1982). In a different voice: Psychological theory and women's development. Boston, MA: Harvard University Press.

Gilstrap, R.L., & Martin, W.R. (1975). Current strategies for teachers: A resource for personalizing education. Pacific Palisades, CA: Goodyear.

Ginsburg, H. (1985). Piaget and education. In N. Entwistle (Ed.), New directions in educational psychology. Vol. 1: Learning and teaching. Philadelphia: Falmer Press.

Ginsburg, H., & Opper, S. (1988). Piaget's theory of intellectual development (3rd ed.). Englewood Cliffs, NJ: Prentice Hall.

Glaser, R. (1981). The future of testing: A research agenda for cognitive psychology and psychometrics. American Psychologist, 36.

Gleitman, H. (1984). Introducing psychology. American Psychologist, 39.

Gleitman, H. (1987). Basic psychology (2nd Ed.). New York, NY: Norton.

Gleitman, H. (1988). Psychology (3rd ed.). New York, NY: Norton.

Goldberger, N., Clinchy, B., Belenky M., & Tarule, J. (1998). Knowledge, difference and power: Essays inspired by women's ways of knowing. New York, NY: Basic Books.

Goleman, D. (1988). An emerging theory on Blacks' I.Q. scores. The New York, NY Times.

Good, T.L. (1983). Classroom research: A decade of progress. Educational Psychologist.

Good, T.L. (1983). Research on classroom teaching. In L. Shulman & G. Sykes (Eds.), Handbook of teaching and policy. New York, NY: Longman.

Good, T.L. (1988). Teacher expectations. In D. Berliner & B. Rosenshine (Eds.), Talks to teachers. New York, NY: Random House.

Good, T.L., & Brophy, J.E. (1984). Looking in classrooms (3rd ed.). New York, NY: Harper and Row.

Good, T.L., & Marshall, S. (1984). Do students learn more in heterogeneous or homogeneous groups? In P. Peterson, L.C. Wilkinson, & M. Hallinan (Eds.):, The social context of instruction: Group organization and group processes. Orlando, FL: Academic Press.

Good, T.L., & Stipek, D.J. (1983). Individual differences in the classroom: A psychological perspective. In G. Fenstermacher & J. Goodlad (Eds.):, 1983 National Society for the Study of Education Yearbook. Chicago, IL: University of Chicago Press.

Good, T.L., Biddle, B., & Brophy, J.E. (1975). Teachers make a difference. New York, NY: Holt, Rinehart & Winston.

Good, T.L., Grouws, D., & Ebmeier, H. (1983). Active mathematics teaching. New York, NY: Longman.

Grabe, M., & Grabe, C. (1998). Integrating technology into meaningful learning (2nd ed.). Boston, MA: Houghton Mifflin.

Grabe, M., & Latta, R.M. (1981). Cumulative achievement in a mastery instructional system: The impact of differences in resultant achievement motivation and persistence. American Educational Research Journal, 18.

Grasha, T. (1995). Teaching with style. Pittsburgh, PA: Alliance Publishers.

Gray, P., Froh, R. & Diamond, R. (1992). A National Study of Research Universities: On the Balance Between Research and Undergraduate Teaching. Syracuse, NY: Center for Instructional Development, Syracuse University.

Green, B.F. (1981). A primer of testing. American Psychologist, 36.

Green, J., & Weade, R. (1985). Reading between the lines: Social cues to lesson participation. Theory into Practice, 24.

Green, M. (1995). Releasing the imagination. San Francisco, CA: Jossey-Bass.

Greenberg, H. (1974). To educate with love. New York, NY: MacMillan.

Gregorc, A.F. (1982). Gregorc style delineator: Development, technical, and administrative manual. Maynard, MA: Gabriel Systems.

Grieve, D. (Ed.). (1989). Teaching in college: A resource for college teachers. Cleveland, OH: Info-Tech.

Grieve, E. (1983). Teaching in college: A resource for adjunct and part-time faculty. Cleveland, OH: Info-Tec.

Grieve, E. (1984). A handbook for adjunct and part-time faculty. Cleveland, OH: Info-Tec.

Griffin, G. (1984). Why use research in preservice teacher education? A proposal. Journal of Teacher Education, 35(4).

Gronlund, N.E. (1977). Constructing achievement tests (2nd ed.). Englewood Cliffs, NJ: Prentice Hall.

Gronlund, N.E. (1978). Stating behavioral objectives for classroom instruction (2nd ed.). Toronto, CAN: Macmillan.

Gronlund, N.E. (1985). Measurement and evaluation in teaching (5th ed.). New York, NY: Macmillan.

Gronlund, N.E. (1988). How to construct achievement tests (4th ed.). Englewood Cliffs, NJ: Prentice Hall.

Grunert, J. (1997). The course syllabus: A learning-centered approach. Bolton, MA: Anker.

Guilford, J.P. (1967). The nature of human intelligence. New York, NY: McGraw-Hill.

Gullette, M. (Ed.). (1982). The art and craft of teaching. Cambridge, MA, MA: Harvard-Danforth Center for Teaching and Learning.

Guskey, T. (1987). Improving student learning in college classrooms. Springfield, IL: Thomas.

Guskey, T.R., & Gates, S.L. (1986). Synthesis of research on mastery learning. Education Leadership, 43.

Guttmacher (Alan) Institute (1984). Issues in brief (Vol. 4, No. 2). Washington, DC: Alan Guttmacher Institute.

Habley, W. and Morales, R. (l998). Advising Models: Goal Achievement and Program Effectiveness. NACADA Journal 18.

Halpern, D., & Associates. (1994). Changing college classrooms. San Francisco, CA: Jossey-Bass.

Hamilton, R.J. (1985). A framework for the evaluation of the effectiveness of adjunct questions and objectives. Review of Educational Research, 55.

Haney, W. (1981). Validity, vaudeville, and values: A short history of social concerns over standardized testing. American Psychologist, 36.

Hanna, G. (1993). Better teaching through better testing. Fort Worth, TX: Harcourt Brace Jovanovich.

Hansen, D.N., Ross, S.M., & Bowman, H.L. (1978, December). Cost effectiveness of navy computer-managed instruction. In T. A. Ryan (Ed.), Systems Research in Education. Columbia, SC: University of South Carolina.

Hansen, R.A. (1977). Anxiety. In S.J. Ball (Ed.), Motivation in education. New York, NY: Academic Press.

Hansford, B.C., & Hattie, J.A. (1982). The relationship between self and achievement/performance measures. Review of Educational Research, 52.

Hanson, G. & Huston, C. (1995). Academic Advising and Assessment, New Directions for Teaching and Learning. San Francisco, CA: Jossey-Bass.

Harnish, D. and Lynn ,A. (1993). Wild, mentoring: A strategy for improving instruction. AACCJournal, 64.

Harris, V.W., & Sherman, J.A. (1973). Use and analysis of the “Good Behavior Game” to reduce disruptive classroom behavior. Journal of Applied Behavior Analysis, 6.

Harrow, A.J. (1972). A taxonomy of the psychomotor domain: A guide for developing behavioral objectives. New York, NY: David McKay.

Harvard University. (1986, March). When the student becomes the teacher. Harvard Education Letter, 2(3).

Harvard University. (1988, March). Cultural differences in the classroom. The Harvard Education Letter, 4(2).

Hatfield, S. (Ed.). (1995). The seven principles in action: Improving undergraduate education. Boston, MA: Anker.

Hativa, Nira. Teaching for Effective Learning in Higher Education. Dordrecht: Kluwer Academic Publishers, 2000. T

Havighurst, R.J. (1981). Life-span development and educational psychology. In F. H. Farley & N. J. Gordon (Eds.), Psychology and education: The state of the union. Berkeley, CA: McCutchan.

Hayes, J.R., Waterman, D.A., & Robinson, C.S. (1977). Identifying relevant aspects of a problem text. Cognitive Sciences, 1.

Hayes, S.C., Rosenfarb, I., Wulfert, E., Munt, E.D., Korn, Z., & Zettle, R.D. (1985). Self-reinnforcement effects: An artifact of social standard setting? Journal of Applied Behavior Analysis, 18.

Hellriegrel, D., Slocum, J. & Woodman, R. (1989). Organizational Behavior, 5th ed. St. Paul, MN: West Publishing Company.

Henson, J. (1997). Writing for Publication, Some Perennial Mistakes. Phi Delta Kappa 78.

Henson, K. (1996). The art of writing grant proposals, Part III. Contemporary Education 68(1).

Henson, K. (1999). So you want to be published? Kappa Delta Pi Record.

Herb, D. O. (1974). What psychology is about. American Psychologist, 29.

Highet, G. (1950). The art of teaching. NY: Vintage Books.

Hill, W.F. (1985). Learning: A survey of psychological interpretations (4th ed.). New York, NY: Harper and Row.

Hiller, J.H. (1971). Verbal response indicators of conceptual vagueness. American Educational Research Journal, 8.

Hills, J.. (1976). Measurement and evaluation in the classroom. Columbus, OH: Charles E. Merrill.

Hines, C.V., Cruickshank, D.R., & Kennedy, J.J. (1985). Teacher clarity and its relation to student achievement and satisfaction. American Educational Research Journal, 22.

Hinsley, D., Hayes, J.R., & Simon, H.A. (1977). From words to equations. In P. Carpenter & M. Just (Eds.), Cognitive processes in comprehension. Hillsdale, NJ: Erlbaum.

Hirsch, D. & Lynton, E. (1995). Bridging Two Worlds: Professional Service and Service Learning. Boston, MA: University of Massachusetts, New England Center for Higher Education.

Hock, R. (1992). Forty studies that changed psychology. Upper Saddle River, NJ: Prentice Hall.

Hoffman, L.W. (1977). Changes in family roles, socialization, and sex differences. American Psychologist, 32(8).

Hoffman, M.L. (1978). Empathy: Its development and prosocial implications. In C. B. Keasey, (Ed.):, Nebraska Symposium on Motivation, 1977. Lincoln, NE: University of Nebraska Press.

Hoffman, M.L. (1979). Development of moral thought, feeling, and behavior. American Psychologist, 34.

Hoffman, M.L. (1983). Affective and cognitive processes in moral internal moralization. In T. Higgins, D. Ruble, & W. Hartup (Eds.), Social cognition and social development. Cambridge, MA: Cambridge University Press.

Hoffman, M.L. (1984). Empathy: Its limitations and its role in a comprehensive moral theory. In W. Kurtines & J. Gewirtz (Eds.), Morality, moral behavior, and moral development. New York, NY: Wiley.

Hoover, K. (1980). College teaching today: A handbook for postsecondary instruction. Boston, MA: Allyn and Bacon.

Horn, J.L., & Donaldson, G. (1980). Cognitive development in adulthood. In O. Brim & J. Kagan (Eds.), Constancy and change in human development. Cambridge, MA: Harvard University Press.

Howe, H. (1983, November). Education moves center stage: An overview of recent studies. Phi Delta Kappan, 65.

Hudgins, B.B. (1977). Learning and thinking: A primer for teachers. Itasca, IL: F. E. Peacock.

Huessman, L.R., Lagarspetz, K., & Eron, L. (1984). Intervening variables in the TV violence-aggression relation: Evidence from two countries. Developmental Psychology, 20.

Hunt, J. (1981). Comments on "The modification of intelligence through early experience" by Ramey and Haskins. Intelligence, 5.

Hunt, J. MCV. (1961). Intelligence and experience. New York, NY: Ronald.

Hunter, M. (1982). Mastery teaching. El Segundo, CA: TIP Publications.

Hyde, J. (1981). How large are cognitive gender differences? American Psychologist, 36.

Hyman, R. T. (1970). Ways of teaching. New York, NY: Lippincott.

Iannuzzi, P., Strichart, S., & Mangrum, C. (1998). Teaching study skills and strategies in college. Boston, MA: Allyn and Bacon.

Innovation Abstracts. National Institute for Staff and Organizational Development, The University of Texas at Austin, Austin, TX.

Integrity in the college curriculum. (1985). Washington, D.C.: Association of American Colleges.

Irving, O., & Martin, J. (1982). Withitness: The confusing variable. American Educational Research Jouranl, 19.

Irwin, J.W. (1986). Teaching reading comprehension. Englewood Cliffs, NJ: Prentice Hall.

Jacobs, L., & Case, C. (1992). Developing and using tests effectively. San Francisco, CA: Jossey-Bass.

Janes, J., & Hauer, D. (1988). Now what? Reading on surviving (and even enjoying) your first experience at college teaching (2nd ed.). Littleton, MA: Copley Publishing.

Jarvis, D. (1991). Junior faculty development: A handbook. NY: Modern Language Association of America.

Jencks, C., Smith, M., Acland, H., Bane, M., Cohen, D., Gintis, H., Heyns, B., & Michelson, S. (1972). Inequality: A reassessment of the effect of family and schooling in America. New Basic Books.

Jensen, A.R. (1980). Bias in testing. New York, NY: Free Press.

Jensen, A.R. (1981). Raising the IQ: The Ramey and Haskins study. Intelligence, 5.

Jensen, W.R., Sloane, H.N., & Young, K.R. (1988). Applied behavior analysis in education: A structured teaching approach. Englewood Cliffs, NJ: Prentice Hall.

Johnson, D., & Johnson, R. (1975). Learning together and alone: Cooperation, competition, and individualization. Englewood Cliffs, NJ: Prentice Hall.

Johnson, D., & Johnson, R. (1985). Motivational processes in cooperative, competitive, and individualistic learning situations. In C. Ames & R. Ames (Eds.), Research on motivation in education. Vol. 2: The classroom milieu. New York, NY: Academic Press.

Johnson, D., Johnson, R., & Smith, K. (1991). Active learning: Cooperation in the college classroom. Edina, MN: Interaction Book Company.

Johnson, D.W. (1986). Reaching out: Interpersonal effectiveness and self-actualization. (3rd ed.). Englewood Cliffs, NJ: Prentice Hall.

Johnson, G. R. (1995). First steps to excellence in college teaching. Madison, WI: Magna Publishing.

Johnson, M., & Wertheimer, M. (Eds.) (1979). The psychology teacher's resource book: First course. Washington, DC: American Psychological Association.

Jones, E. (Ed.). (1996). Preparing competent college graduates: Setting new and higher expectations for student learning. San Francisco, CA: Jossey-Bass.

Jones, V.F., & Jones, L.S. (1986). Comprehensive classroom management: Creating positive learning environments (2nd ed.). Boston, MA: Allyn & Bacon.

Joshua, S., & Dupin, J.J. (1987). Taking into account student conceptions in instructional strategy: An example in physics. Cognition and Instruction, 4.

Joyce, B., & Weil, M. (1986). Models of teaching. Englewood Cliffs, NJ: Prentice Hall.

Kanfer, F.H., & Gaelick, L. (1986). Self-management methods. In F. Kanfer & A. Goldstein (Eds.): Helping people change: A textbook of methods (3rd ed.). New York, NY: Pergamon.

Kaplan, B. (1984). Development and growth. Hillsdale, NJ: Erlbaum.

Kaplan, M. (1998). To improve the academy: Resources for faculty, instructional, and organizational development. Stillwater, OK: New Forums Press.

Kaplin, W. & Lee, B. (1995). The Law of Higher Education, 3rd ed. San Francisco, CA: Jossey-Bass Publishers.

Karron, G. (1994). Teaching Large Classes (How to Do It Well and Remain Sane), in Handbook of College Teaching, Theory and Applications ed. Keith W. Prichard and R. McLaren Sawyer. Westport, CT.: Greenwood Press.

Kartje, J. (1996). 0 mentor! My mentor! Peabody Journal of Education, 71.

Karweit, N. (1981). Time in school. Research in Sociology of Education and Socialization, 2.

Karweit, N., & Slavin, R. (1981). Measurement and modeling choices in studies of time and learning. American Educational Research Journal, 18.

Kasten, K. (1984). Tenure and Merit Pay as Rewards for Research, Teaching, and Service at a Research University. Journal of Higher Education 55.

Kazdin, A.E. (1984). Behavior modification in applied settings. Homewood, IL: Dorsey Press.

Kearsley, G. (1984). Instructional design and authoring software. Journal of Instructional Development, 7.

Keeton, M., with associates. (1976). Experiential learning: Rationale, characteristics, and assessment. San Francisco, CA: Jossey-Bass.

Keith-Spiegel, P., Wittig, A., Perkins, D., Balogh, D., & Whitley, B. (1993). The ethics of teaching: A casebook. Muncie, IN: Ball State University.

Keller, F. (1982). Pedagogue's progress: Fred Simmons Keller. Lawrence, KS: TRI Publications.

Keller, F., & Sherman, J. (1974). The Keller plan handbook. Menlo Park, CA: W. A. Benjamin.

Keller, F.S. (1966). A personal course in psychology. In R. Urlich, T. Stachnik, & J. Mabry (Eds.), Control of human behavior (Vol. 1). Glenview, IL: Scott, Foresman.

Kellough, R. (1990). A resource guide for effective teaching in postsecondary education. Lanham, MD.: University Press of America.

Kennedy, J.L., Cruickshank, D.C., Bush, A.J., & Myers, B. (1978). Additional investigations into the nature of teacher clarity. Journal of Educational Research, 72.

Kiewra, K.A. (1988). Cognitive aspects of autonomous note taking: Control processes, learning strategies, and prior knowledge. Educational Psychologist, 23.

King, M. (1993). Academic Advising, Retention, and Transfer, New Directions for Community Colleges 82, San Francisco, CA: Jossey-Bass.

Kirby, B. (1984). Sexuality. An evaluation of programs and their effects: An executive summary. Santa Cruz, CA: Network Publications.

Klausmeier, H.J., & Sipple, T.S. (1982). Factor structure of the Piagetian stage of concrete operations. Contemporary Educational Psychology, 7.

Kneedler, P. (1985). California assesses critical thinking. In A. Costa (Ed.), Developing minds: A resource book for teaching thinking. Alexandria, VA: Association for Supervision and Curriculum Development.

Kneedler, R. (1984). Special education for today. Englewood Cliffs, NJ: Prentice Hall.

Knowles, M. (1986). Using learning contracts. San Francisco, CA: Jossey-Bass.

Knox, A. (Ed.) (1980). Teaching adults effectively. San Francisco, CA: Jossey-Bass.

Kohlberg, L. (1975). The cognitive-developmental approach to moral education. Phi Delta Kappan, 56.

Kohlberg, L. (1981). The philosophy of moral development. New York, NY: Harper and Row.

Kohn, A. (1988). Humanism's paradoxical champion. Psychology Today, 22(9).

Kolesnik, W.B. (1978). Motivation: Understanding and influencing human behavior. Boston, MA: Allyn & Bacon.

Kotter, J. and Heskett, J. (1992). Corporate Culture and Performance. New York, NY: The Free Press.

Kounin, J. (1970). Discipline and group management in classrooms. New York, NY: Holt, Rinehart & Winston.

Krathwohl, D.R., Bloom, B.S., & Masia, B.B. (1956). Taxonomy of educational objectives. Handbook II: Affective domain. New York, NY: David McKay.

Kuh, G. & Whitt, E. (1988). The Invisible Tapestry: Culture in American Colleges and Universities, Report No. 1. Washington, DC, ERIC-ASHE Higher Education Reports.

Kulik, J.A., Kulik, C.C., & Bangert, R.L. (1984, April). Effects of practice on aptitude and achievement test scores. American Educational Research Journal, 21.

Kulik, J.A., Kulik, C.C., & Cohen, P.A. (1979). A meta-analysis of outcome studies of Keller's Personalized System of Instruction. American Psychologist, 34.

Kulik, J.A., Kulik, C.C., & Cohen, P.A. (1980). Effectiveness of computer-based college teaching: A meta-analysis of findings. Review of Educational Research, 50.

Kurtz, J.J., & Swenson, E.J. (1951). Factors related to over-achievement and under-achievement in school. School Review, 59.

Lamb, D.R. (1984). Physiology of exercise: Response and adaptation (2nd ed.). New York, NY: Macmillan.

Land, M.L., & Smith, L.R. (1979). Effect of low inference teacher clarity inhibitors on student achievement. Journal of Teacher Education, 31.

Langer, P.C. (1972). What's the score on programmed instruction? Today's Education, 61.

Laosa, L. (1984). Ethnic, socioeconomic, and home language influences on early performance on measures of ability. Journal of Educational Psychology, 76.

Larrivee, B. (1985). Effective teaching behaviors for successful mainstreaming. New York, NY: Longman.

Lathrop, A., & Goodson, B. (1983). Courseware in the classroom: Selecting, organizing, and using educational software. Reading, MA: Addison-Wesley.

Lee, C. (1967). Improving college teaching. Washington, D.C.: American Council of Education.

Lefcourt, H. (1966). Internal versus external control of reinforcement: A review. Psychological Bulletin, 65.

Leinhardt, G. (1986). Expertise in mathematics teaching. Educational Leadership, 43.

Leinhardt, G., & Greeno, J.D. (1986). The cognitive skill of teaching. Journal of Educational Psychology, 78.

Leinhardt, G., & Smith, D. (1985). Expertise in mathematics instruction: Subject matter knowledge. Journal of Educational Psychology, 77.

Lepper, M.R., & Greene, D. (1978). The hidden costs of rewards: New perspectives on the psychology of human motivation. Hillsdale, NJ: Erlbaum.

Lerner, B. (1981). The minimum competency testing movement: Social, scientific, and legal implications. American Psychologist, 36.

Leslie, D., Kellams, S., & Gunne, M. (1982). Part-time faculty in American higher education. NY: Praeger.

Levin, J.R. (1985). Educational applications of mnemonic pictures: Possibilities beyond your wildest imagination. In A. A. Sheikh (Ed.), Imagery in the educational process. Farmingdale, NY: Baywood.

Levin, J.R., Dretzke, B.J., McCormick, C.B., Scruggs, T.E., McGivern, S., & Mastropieri, M. (1983). Learning via mnemonic pictures: Analysis of the presidential process. Educational Communication and Technology Journal, 31.

Levine, A. (1978). Handbook on undergraduate curriculum. San Francisco, CA: Jossey-Bass.

Lewis, J., Jr. (1981). Do you encourage teacher absenteeism? The American School Board Journal, 168.

Liebert, R.M., Wicks-Nelson, R., & Kail, R.V. (1986). Developmental psychology (4th ed.). Englewood Cliffs, NJ: Prentice Hall.

Light, Richard. Making the Most of College: Students Speak Their Minds. Cambridge, MA: Harvard University Press, 2001.

Lindsay, P.H., & Norman, D.A. (1977). Human information processing: An introduction to psychology (2nd ed.). New York, NY: Academic Press.

Linn, R., Klein, S., & Hart, F. (1972). The nature and correlates of law school essay grades. Educational and Psychological Measurement, 32.

Linn, R.L. (1986). Educational testing and assessment: Research needs and policy issues. American Psychologist, 41.

Loehlin, J.C., Lindzey, G., & Spuhler, J.N. (1979). Cross-group comparisons of intellectual abilities. In L. Willerman & R. Turner (Eds.), Readings about individuals and group differences. San Francisco, CA: W. H. Freeman

Lowman, J. (1995). Mastering the techniques of teaching. San Francisco, CA: Jossey-Bass.

Lowman, Joseph. Mastering the Techniques of Teaching. Paperback edition. San Francisco: Jossey-Bass, 2000.

Lubbers C. & Gorcyca, D. (1997). Using Active Learning in Public Relations Instruction: Demographic Predictors of Faculty Use, Public Relations Review 23.

Lucas, C. & Murry, J. (2002). New faculty: A practical guide for academic beginners. New York, NY: Palgrave.

Lucas, C. (1996). Crisis in the academy, rethinking higher education in America. New York, NY: St. Martin's Press.

Luehrmann, A.L. (1981). Computer literacy—what should it be? The Mathematics Teacher, 74(9).

Luehrmann, A.L. (1984). Computer literacy: The what, why, and how. In D. Peterson (Ed.), Intelligent schoolhouse: Readings on computers and learning. Reston, VA: Reston.

Luehrmann, A.L. (1986). Don't feel bad teaching BASIC. In T. R. Cannings & S. W. Brown (Eds.). The information-age classroom: Using the computer as a tool. Irvine, CA: Franklin, Beedle & Associates.

Luiten, J., Ames, W., & Ackerson, G. (1980). A meta-analysis of the effects of advance organizers on learning and retention. American Educational Research Journal, 17.

Luna, G. & Cullen, D. (1995). Empowering the Faculty: Mentoring Redirected and Renewed. ASHE-ERIC Higher Education Reports 3.

Lyman, H.B. (1986). Test scores and what they mean (4th ed.). Englewood Cliffs, NJ: Prentice Hall.

Lyons, R., Kysilka, M., & Pawlas, G. (1999). The adjunct professor's guide to success: Surviving and thriving in the college classroom. Boston, MA: Allyn and Bacon.

Maccoby, E.E., & Jacklin, C.N. (1974). The psychology of sex differences. Stanford, CA: Stanford University Press.

MacDonald-Ross, M. (1974). Behavioral objectives: A critical review. Instructional Science, 2.

Maehr, M.L. (1974). Sociocultural origins of achievement. Monterey, CA: Brooks/Cole.

Mager, R. (1975). Preparing instructional objectives (2nd ed.). Palo Alto, CA: Fearon.

Magnan, B. (1989). 147 practical tips for teaching professors. Madison, WI: Magna Publications.

Magolda, M. (1992) Knowing and reasoning in college: Gender-related patterns in students' intellectual development. San Francisco, CA: Jossey-Bass.

Mahoney, K.B., & Hopkins, B.L. (1973). The modification of sentence structure and its relationship to subjective judgments of creativity in writing. Journal of Applied Behavior Analysis, 6.

Mahoney, M.J., & Thoresen, C.E. (1974). Self-control: Power to the person. Monterey, CA: Brooks/Cole.

Maier, N.R.F. (1933). An aspect of human reasoning. British Journal of Psychology, 24.

Maier, P., Barnett, L., Warrne, A., & Drunner, D. (1998). Using technology in teaching and learning (2nd ed.). London: Kogan Page.

Maier, S.F., Seligman, M.E.P., & Solomon, R.L. (1969). Pavlovian fear conditioning and learned helplessness. In B. Campbell & R. Church (Eds.), Punishment and aversive control. New York, NY: Appleton-Century-Crofts.

Maker, C.J. (1987). Gifted and talented. In V. Richardson-Koehler (Ed.), Educators' handbook: A research perspective. New York, NY: Longman.

Makosky, U. P., Whittemore, L. G., & Rogers, A. J. (Eds.) (1987). Activities handbook for the teaching of psychology. Vols. 2. Washington, DC: American Psychological Association.

Makosky, U. P., Whittemore, L. G., & Skutley, M. L. (Eds.) (1990). Activities handbook for the teaching of psychology. Vols. 3. Washington, DC: American Psychological Association.

Mann, R., et al. (1970). The college classroom: Conflict, change, and learning. New York, NY: Wiley.

Marchese, J. (1988).The search committee handbook: A guide to recruiting administrators. Washington, DC: American Association for Higher Education.

Marcia, J. (1987). The identity status approach to the study ego identity development. In T. Honess & K. Yardley (Eds.). Self and identity: Perspectives across the life span. London: Routledge & Kagan Paul.

Market Data Retrieval. (1982). Annual report on school computer use. Shelton, CT: Market Data Retrieval.

Market Data Retrieval. (1984). Annual report on school computer use. Shelton, CT: Market Data Retrieval.

Markie, P. (1994). A professor's duties: Ethical issues in college teaching. Lanham, MD: Rowman & Littlefield.

Marsh, H.W. (1987). The big-fish-little-pond effect on academic self-concept. Journal of Educational Psychology, 79.

Marsh, H.W., & Shavelson, R. (1985). Self-concept: Its multifaceted, hierarchical structure. Educational Psychologist, 20.

Martin, G., & Pear, J. (1988). Behavior modification: What it is and how to do it (3rd ed.). Englewood Cliffs, NJ: Prentice Hall.

Martinson, R.A. (1961). Educational programs for gifted pupils. Sacramento: California Department of Education.

Marton, F., Hounsell, D., & Entwistle, N. (1997). The experience of learning: Implications for teaching and studying in higher education (2nd ed.). London: Routledge.

Marzano, R. (1992). A different kind of classroom: Teaching with dimensions of learning. Alexandria, VA: Association for Supervision and Curriculum Development.

Maslow, A.H. (1968). Toward a psychology of being (2nd ed.). Princeton, NJ: Van Nostrand.

Maslow, A.H. (1970). Motivation and personality (2nd ed.). New York, NY: Harper and Row.

Matarazzo, J.D. (1972). Wechsler's measurement and appraisal of adult intelligence (5th ed.). Fair Lawn, NJ: Oxford University Press.

Maxwell, M. (1980). Improving student learning skills. San Francisco, CA: Jossey-Bass.

Mayer, R.E. (1979). Can advance organizers influence meaningful learning? Review of Educational Research, 49.

Mayer, R.E. (1983). Can you repeat that? Qualitative and quantitative effects of repetition and advance organizers on learning from science prose. Journal of Educational Psychology, 75.

Mayer, R.E. (1983). Thinking, problem solving, cognition. San Francisco, CA: W. H. Freeman.

Mayer, R.E. (1984). Twenty-five years of research on advance organizers. Instructional Science, 8.

Mayer, R.E., & Bromage, B. (1980). Different recall protocols for technical texts due to advance organizers. Journal of Educational Psychology, 72.

Mazur, Eric. Peer Instruction: A User's Manual. Upper Saddle River, NJ: Prentice Hall, 1997.

McClelland, D. (1973). Testing for competence rather than for intelligence. American Psychologist, 28.

McClelland, D. (1985). Human motivation. Glenview, IL: Scott, Foresman.

McClelland, D., Atkinson, J.W., Clark, R.W., & Lowell, E.L. (1953). The achievement motive. New York, NY: Appleton-Century-Crofts.

McCormick, C.B., & Levin, J.R. (1987). Mnemonic prose-learning strategies. In M. Pressley & M. McDaniel (Eds.), Imaginery and related mnemonic processes. New York, NY: Springer-Verlag.

McDonald, F. (1976). Teachers do make a difference. Princeton, NJ: Eductional Testing Service.

McGinley, P., & McGinley, H. (1970). Reading groups as psychological groups. Journal of Experimental Education, 39.

McGovern, T. V. (Ed.). (1993). Handbook for enhancing undergraduate education in psychology. Washington, DC: American Psychological Association.

McKeachie, W. (Ed.) (1980). Learning, cognition, and college teaching. San Francisco, CA: Jossey-Bass.

McKeachie, W. J. (2002). McKeachie's teaching tips: Strategies, research, and theory for college and university teachers (11th ed.). Boston, MA: Houghton Mifflin.

McKeachie, W., Pintrich, P., Lin, Y., Smith, D. & Sharmo, R. (1990). Teaching and learning in the college classroom: A review of the research literature (2nd ed.). Ann Arbor: University of Michigan.

McKeachie,Wilbert J. Teaching Tips: Strategies, Research, and Theory for College and University Teachers. 12th edition. Boston: Houghton Mifflin, 2006.

McKenzie, S., & Cangemi, J. P. (1978). What new students in introduction to psychology really want to learn: A survey. Journal of Instructional Psychology, 5.

McKenzie, T.L., & Rushall, B.S. (1974). Effects of self-recording on attendance and performance in a competitive swimming training environment. Journal of Applied Behavior Analysis, 7.

McLeod, R. B. (1971). The teaching of psychology. American Psychologist, 26.

McNeill, D. (1966). Developmental psycholinguistics. In F. Smith & G. Miller (Eds.), The genesis of language: A psycholinguistic approach. Cambridge, MA, MA: MIT Press.

McNemar, Q. (1964). Lost: Our intelligence? Why? American Psychologist, 19.

Medley, D.M. (1979). The effectiveness of teachers. In P. Peterson & H. Walberg (Eds.), Research on teaching: Concepts, findings, and implications. Berkeley, CA: McCutchan.

Mehan, H. (1979). Learning lessons. Cambridge, MA, MA: Harvard University Press.

Meichenbaum, D. (1977). Cognitive behavior modification: An integrative approach. New York, NY: Plenum.

Meichenbaum, D. (1986). Cognitive behavior modification. In F. Kanfer & A. Goldstein (Eds.), Helping people change: A textbook of methods (3rd ed.). New York, NY: Pergamon.

Menges, J. (1999), Institutional Support. San Francisco, CA: Jossey-Bass Publishers.

Menges, R. (1999). Dilemmas of Newly Hired Faculty, in Faculty in New Jobs. San Francisco, CA: Jossey-Bass.

Menges, R. J. (1999). Faculty in new jobs: A guide to settling in, becoming established, and building institutional support. San Francisco, CA: Jossey-Bass.

Menges, R., & Mathis, B. (1988). Key resources on teaching, learning, curriculum, and faculty development. San Francisco, CA: Jossey-Bass.

Menges, R., Weiner, M., et. al. (1995). Teaching on solid ground. San Francisco, CA: Jossey-Bass.

Merrill, M.C., Schneider, E.W., & Fletcher, K.A. (1980). TICCIT. Englewood Cliffs, NJ: Educational Technology Publications.

Messer, S. (1970). Reflection-impulsivity: Stability and school failure. Journal of Educational Psychology, 61.

Metcalfe, B. (1981). Self-concept and attitude toward school. British Journal of Educational Psychology, 51.

Meyers C. & Jones T. (1993). Promoting Active Learning, Strategies for the College Classroom San Francisco, CA.: Jossey-Bass.

Milem J., et al., (2000). Faculty Time Allocation. Journal of Higher Education, 71.

Miller, G.A. (1956). The magical number seven, plus or minus two: Some limits on our capacity for processing information. Psychological Review, 63.

Miller, G.A., Galanter, E., & Pribram, K.H. (1960). Plans and the structure of behavior. New York, NY: Holt, Rinehart & Winston.

Miller, R.B. (1962). Analysis and specification of behavior for training. In R. Glaser (Ed.), Training research and education: Science edition. New York, NY: Wiley.

Millis, B., & Cottell, P. (1998). Cooperative learning for higher education faculty. Phoenix, AZ: American Council on Education and The Oryx Press.

Milton, O. (1972). Alternatives to the traditional. San Francisco, CA: Jossey-Bass.

Milton, O. (1978). On college teaching: A guide to contemporary practices. San Francisco, CA: Jossey-Bass.

Milton, O. (1982). What will be on the final? Springfield, IL: Thomas.

Milton, O., & Edgerly, J. (1977). The testing and grading of students. New Rochelle, NY: Change Magazine.

Milton, O., Pollio, H., & Eison, J. (1986). Making sense of college grades: Why the grading system does not work and what can be done about it. San Francisco, CA: Jossey-Bass.

Miner, L., Miner, J. & Griffith, L. (1998). Proposal Planning &Writing, 2nd ed. Phoenix, AZ: The Oryx Press.

Mitchell, B.M. (1984). An update on gifted and talented education in the U.S. Roeper Review, 6.

Moely, B.E., Hart, S.S., Santulli, K., Leal, L., Johnson, T., Rao, N., & Burney, L. (1986). How do teachers teach memory skills? In J. Levin & M. Pressley (Eds.), Educational Psychologist, 21 (Special issue on learning strategies).

Moffat, M. (1989). Coming of age in New Jersey. New Brunswick, NJ: Rutgers Univrsity Press.

Mooney, C. (1991). Professors feel conflict between roles in teaching and research. Chronicle of Higher Education, A15.

Morano, M. (1999). Challenges encountered by new advisers: Honest answers, practical solutions. The Mentor 1.

Morgan, M. (1984). Reward-induced decrements and increments in intrinsic motivation. Review of Educational Research, 54.

Morgan, M. (1985). Self-monitoring of attained subgoals in private study. Journal of Educational Psychology, 77.

Morris, C.G. (1988). Psychology: An introduction (6th ed.). Englewood Cliffs, NJ: Prentice Hall.

Morris, W. (1967). Effective college teaching. Washington, DC: American Council on Education.

Morrow, L. (1983). Home and school correlates of early interest in literature. Journal of Educational research, 76.

Morrow, L., & Weinstein, C. (1986). Encouraging voluntary reading: The impact of a literature. Reading Research Quarterly, 21.

Moshman, D., Glover, J.A., & Bruning, R.H. (1987). Developmental psychology. Boston, MA: Little, Brown.

Moskowitz, B.A. (1978). The acquisition of language. Scientific American, 239.

Moskowitz, G., & Hayman, M.L. (1976). Successful strategies of inner-city teachers: A year-long study. Journal of Educational Research, 69

Moxley, J. (1992). Publish, don't perish, The scholar's guide to academic writing and publishing. Westport, CT.: Greenwood Press.

Murray, H.G. (1983). Low inference classroom teaching behavior and student ratings of college teaching effectiveness. Journal of Educational Psychology, 75.

Murry, J. (2000). Avoiding legal pitfalls in recruiting and selecting new faculty: What every academic administrator should know. Academic Leadership 7(2).

Musgrave, G.R. (1975). Individualized instruction: Teaching strategies focusing on the learner. Boston, MA, MA: Allyn & Bacon.

Myers, C., & Jones, T. (1993). Promoting active learning: Strategies for the college classroom. San Francisco, CA: Jossey-Bass.

National Commission on Excellence in Education. (1983). A nation at risk: The imperative for educational reform. Washington, DC: U.S. Government Printing Office.

National Education Association. (1985). Estimates of school statistics, 1984-85. Washington, DC: Author.

National Education Association. (1984). Nationwide teacher opinion poll. Washington, DC: Author.

National Task Force on Educational Technology. (1986). Transforming American education: Reducing the risk to the nation. T. H. E. Journal, August.

Naveh-Benjamin, M., McKeachie, W.J., & Lin, Y. (1987). Two types of test-anxious students: Support for an information processing model. Journal of Educational Psychology, 79.

Neff, A., & Weimer, M. (Eds) (1989). Classroom communications: Collected readings for effective discussion and questioning. Madison, WI: Magna Publishing.

Neff, R., & Weimer, M. (Eds.). (1990). Teaching college: Collected readings for the new instructor. Madison: Magna.

Neill, S. D. (April 1989). No significant relationship between research and teaching. research reveals, University Affairs, 30.

Nelson, K. (1981). Individual differences in language development: Implications for development and language. Developmental Psychology, 17.

New Jersey Institute for Collegiate Teaching and Learning. (1990). The challenges of the college classroom. South Orange, NJ: Seton Hall University.

New, C. & Quick, J. (1999). Steering your way to a winning grant proposal. Technology & Learning 19(10).

Newble, D., & Cannon, R. (1995). A handbook for teachers in universities and colleges: A guide to improving teaching methods. England: Kogan Page Ltd.

Nicholls, J.G., & Miller, A. (1984). Conceptions of ability and achievement motivation. In R. Ames & C. Ames (Eds.), Research on motivation in education. Vol. 1: Student Motivation. New York, NY: Academic Press.

Nickerson, R., Perkins, D., & Smith, E. (1985). Teaching thinking. Hillsdale, NJ: Erlbaum.

Nilson, L. (1996). Teaching at its best: A research-based resource for the Vanderbilt teaching community. Nashville, TN: Center for Teaching, Vanderbilt University.

Nilson, L. (1998). Teaching at its best, a research-based resource for college instructors. Bolton, MA.: Anker Publishing Company.

Norman, D.P. (1982). Learning and memory. San Francisco, CA: W. H. Freeman.

Nungester, R.J., & Duchastel, P.C. (1982). Testing versus review: Effects on retention. Journal of Educational Psychology, 74.

Nyquist, J., Abbott, R., & Wulff, D. (Eds.) (1989). Teaching assistant training in the 1990s. New Directions for Teaching and Learning, 39. San Francisco, CA: Jossey-Bass.

Nyquist, J., Abbott, R., Wulff, D., & Sprague, J. (Eds.). (1991). Preparing the professoriate of tomorrow to teach: Selected readings in TA training. Dubuque, IA: Kendall/Hunt.

Nyquist, Jody D., and Donald H.Wulff. Working Effectively with Graduate Assistants. Thousand Oaks, CA: Sage Publications, 1996.

O'Banion, T. (1994). Teaching and learning in the community college. Washington: Community College Press.

O'Banion, T. (1997). A learning college for the 21st century. NY: (American Council on Education/Oryx Press Series on Higher Education).

O'Connor, R.D. (1969). Modification of social withdrawal through symbolic modeling. Journal of Applied Behavior Analysis, 2.

O'Day, E.F., Kulhavy, R.W., Anderson, W., & Malczynski, R.J. (1971). Programmed instruction: Techniques and trends. New York, NY: Appleton-Century-Crofts.

O'Leary, K.D., & O'Leary, S. (Eds.). (1977). Classroom management: The successful use of behavior modification (2nd ed.). Elmsford, NY: Pergamon.

O'Leary, K.D., & Wilson, G.T. (1987). Behavior therapy: Application and outcome. Englewood Cliffs, NJ: Prentice Hall.

O'Leary, S.G., & O'Leary, K.D. (1976). Behavior modification in the schools. In H. Leitenberg (Ed.), Handbook of behavior modification and behavior therapy. Englewood Cliffs, NJ: Prentice Hall.

O'Sullivan, J.T., & Pressley, M. (1984). Completeness of instruction and strategy transfer. Journal of Experimental Child Psychology, 38.

Ollendick, T.h., Dailey, D., & Shapiro, E.S. (1983). Vicarious reinforcement: Expected and unexpected effects. Journal of Applied Behavior analysis, 16.

Ollendick, T.H., Matson, J.L., Esveldt-Dawson, K., & Shapiro, E.S. (1980). Increasing spelling achievement: An analysis of treatment procedures utilizing an alternating treatments design. Journal of Applied Behavior Analysis, 13.

Olson, D.R. (1985). Computers as tools of the intellect. Educational Researcher, 14.

Orlansky, J., & String, J. (1981). Computer-based instruction for military training. Defense Management Journal, 2nd Quarter.

Orlich, D., et al. (1985). Teaching strategies: A guide to better instruction. Lexington, MA: Health.

Ornstein, A.C. (1980). Teacher salaries: Past, present, and future. Phi Delta Kappan, 61.

Ornstein, A.C., & Miller, H.L. (1980). Looking into education: An introduction to American education. Chicago, IL: Rand McNally.

Ory, J., & Ryan, K. (1993). Tips for improving testing and grading. Newbury Park, CA: Sage.

Orzechowski, R. (March 1995). Factors to Consider Before Introducing Active Learning into a Large, Lecture-Based Course. Journal of College Science Teaching 24.

Osborn, A.F. (1963). Applied imagination (3rd ed.). New York, NY: Scribner's.

Owen, L. (1985). None of the above: Behind the myth of scholastic aptitude. Boston, MA: Houghton Mifflin.

Page, E.B. (1958). Teacher comments and student performances: A 74-classroom experiment in school motivation. Journal of Educational Psychology, 49.

Palincsar, A.S. (1986). The role of dialogue in providing scaffolded instruction. In J. Levin & M. Pressley (Eds.), Educational Psychologist, 21 (Special issue on learning strategies).

Palincsar, A.S., & Brown, A.L. (1984). Reciprocal teaching of comprehension-fostering and monitoring activities. Cognition and Instruction, 1.

Pallas, A.M., & Alexander, K. (1983). Sex differences in quantitative SAT performance: New evidence on the differential coursework hypothesis. American Educational Research Journal, 20.

Palmer, P. (1998). The courage to teach: Exploring the inner landscape of a teacher's life. San Francisco, CA: Jossey-Bass.

Palmer, P. J. (1998). The courage to teach. San Francisco, CA: Jossey-Bass.

Papert, S. (1980). Mindstorms. New York, NY: Basic Books.

Park, O., & Tennyson, JR.D. (1980). Adaptive design strategies for selecting number and presentation order of examples in coordinate concept acquisition. Journal of Educational Psychology, 72.

Park, S. (1996). Research, Teaching, and Service, Why Shouldn't Women's Work Count? Journal of Higher Education 67.

Parnell, D. (1990). Dateline 2000: The new higher education agenda. Washington, D.C.: Community College Press.

Parrott, L. (1994) How to write psychology papers, New York, NY: Harper Collins.

Pascarella, E., & Terenzini, P. (1991). How college affects students: Findings and insights from twenty years of research. San Francisco, CA: Jossey-Bass.

Pattison, P., & Grieve, N. (1984). Do spatial skills contribute to sex differences in different types of mathematical problems? Journal of Educational Psychology, 76.

Pauk, W. (1984). How to study in college (3rd ed.). Boston, MA: Houghton Mifflin.

Paulman, R.G., & Kennelly, K.J. (1984). Test anxiety and ineffective test taking: Different names, same construct? Journal of Educational Psychology, 76.

Paulsen, M., & Feldman, K. (1995). Taking teaching seriously: Meeting the challenge of instructional improvement. Washington, DC: The George Washington University.

Pavio, A. (1971). Imagery and verbal processes. New York, NY: Holt, Rinehart & Winston.

Pearl, D., Routhlet, L., & Lazar, J. (Eds.). (1982). Television and behavior: Ten years of scientific progress and implications for the eighties (Vols. 1 & 2). Washington, DC: U.S. Government Printing Office.

Peeck, J., van den Bosch, A.B., & Kreupeling, W.J. (1982). Effect of mobilizing prior knowlege on learning from text. Journal of Educational Psychology, 74.

Pelham, W.E., & Murphy, H.A. (1986). Attention deficit and conduct disorders. In M. Hersen (Ed.), Pharmacological and behavioral treatment: An integrative approach. New York, NY: Wiley.

Pelikan, J. (1983). Scholarship and its survival: Questions on the idea of graduate education, Princeton. Carnegie Foundation for the Advancement of Teaching.

Peper, R.J., & Mayer, R.E. (1986). Generative effects of note taking during science lectures. Journal of Educational Psychology, 78.

Perkins, D.N. (1986). Thinking frames. Educational Leadership, 43.

Perlman, B., McCann, L. I., & McFadden, S. M. (Eds.). (1999). Lessons learned: Practical advice for the teaching of psychology. Washington, DC: American Psychological Society.

Perlman, B., McCann, L. I., & McFadden, S. M. (Eds.). (2004). Lessons learned: Practical advice for the teaching of psychology (Vol. 2). Washington, DC: American Psychological Society.

Perna, F., Learner, B.& Yura, M. (1995). Mentoring and career development among university faculty. Journal of Education, 177.

Perry, R. & Smart, J. (Eds.). (1997). Effective teaching in higher education: Research and practice. New York, NY: Agathon Press.

Perry, W. Jr. (1970). Forms of intellectual and ethical development in the college years. New York, NY: Holt, Rinehart and Winston.

Peterson, P. (1979). Direct instruction reconsidered. In P. Peterson & H. Walberg (Eds.), Research on teaching: Concepts, findings, and implications. Berkeley, CA: McCutchan.

Peterson, P., Janicki, T.C., & Swing, S.R. (1980). Aptitude-treatment interaction effects of three social studies teaching approaches. American Educational Research Journal, 17.

Peterson, P.L., & Comeaux, M.A. (1989). Assessing the teacher as a reflective professional: New perspectives on teacher evaluation. In A. Woolfolk (Ed.), Research perspectives on the graduate preparation of teachers. Englewood Cliffs, NJ: Prentice Hall.

Peterson, S.E., Degracie, J.S., & Ayabe, C.R. (1987). A longitudinal study of the effects of retention/promotion on academic achievement. American Educational Research Journal, 24.

Petkovich, M.D., & Tennyson, R.D. (1984). Clark's "learning from media": A critique. Educational Communication Technology Journal, 32.

Pettegrew, L.S., & Wolf, G.E. (1982). Validating measures of teacher stress. American Educational Research Journal, 19.

Pettijohn, T. (1994). Sources: Notable selections in psychology. Guilford, CT: Dushkin Publishing.

Pfeiffner, L.J., Rosen, L.A., & O'Leary, S.G. (1985). The efficacy of an all-positive approach to classroom management. Journal of Applied Behavior Analysis, 18.

Piaget, J. (1974). Understanding causality. New York, NY: Norton.

Pintrich, P., & Schunk, D. (Eds.). (1996). Motivation in education: Theory, research, and applications. Englewood Cliffs, NJ: Prentice-Hall.

Pintrich, P., Brown, D., & Weinstein, C. (1994). Student motivation, cognition, and learning: Essays in honor of Wilbert J. McKeachie. Hillsdale, NJ: Laurence Erlbaum & Associates.

Platt, W., & Baker, B.A. (1931). The relation of the scientific "hunch" to research. Journal of Chemical Evaluation, 8.

Pogrow, S. (1988). The computer movement cover-up. Electronic Learning, 7(7).

Popham, W.J. (1969). Objectives and instruction. In W. J. Popham, E. W. Eisner, H. J. Sullivan, & L. I. Tyler (Eds.), Instructional objectives (Monograph Series on Curriculum Evaluation, No. 3). Chicago, IL: Rand McNally.

Posner, M.I. (1973). Cognition: An introduction. Glenview, IL: Scott, Foresman.

Postman, N. (1995). The end of education: Refining the value of school. New York, NY: Alfred A. Knopf.

Pregent, R. (1994). Charting your course: How to prepare to teach more effectively. Madison, WI: Magna Publications.

Premack, D. (1965). Reinforcement theory. In D. Levine (Ed.), Nebraska symposium on motivation (Vol. 13). Lincoln, NE: University of Nebraska Press.

Prensky, M. (2001). Digital Natives, Digital Immigrants Part 1. On The Horizon, 9(5), 1-6.

Pressley, M. (1986). The relevance of the good strategy user model to the teaching of mathematics. In J. Levin & M. Pressley (Eds.), Educational Psychologist, 21 (Special issue on learning strategies).

Pressley, M., & McCormick, C. (1995). Cognition, teaching and assessment. New York, NY: HarperCollins.

Pressley, M., Levin, J., & Delaney, H.D. (1982). The mnemonic keyword method. Review of Research in Education, 52.

Prichard, K., & Sawyer, R. (Eds.). (1994). Handbook of college teaching. Westport, CT: Greenwood Press.

Pring, R. (1971). Bloom's taxonomy: A philosophical critique. Cambridge, MA Journal of Education, 1.

Pritchard, R. (Ed.). (1997). Helping teachers teach well: A new system for measuring and improving teaching effectiveness in higher education. San Francisco, CA: Jossey-Bass.

Purkey, W.W. (1970). Self-concept and school achievement. Englewood Cliffs, NJ: Prentice Hall.

Quality Education Data (1988). Microcomputer and VCR usage in schools, 1987-1988. Denver: Quality Education Data.

Quam, K. (1998). Ready, Set, Teach: Learn to Teach, Teach to Learn. Commack, NY: Kroshka Books.

Radford, J., & Rose, D. (Eds.) (1980). The teaching of psychology. New York, NY: John Wiley & Sons.

Ramaley, J. (2000). Embracing civic responsibility. AAHE Bulletin 52.

Ramsden, P. (1992). Learning to teach in higher education. London: Routledge.

Ramsden, P. (Ed.). (1988). Improving learning: New perspectives. NY: Nichols.

Raths, L. et al., (1986). Teaching for thinking, 2nd ed. New York, NY: Teachers College Press.

Raudsepp, E., & Haugh, G.P. (1977). Creative growth games. New York, NY: Harcourt Brace Jovanovich.

Ravitch, D. (1985). Scapegoating the teachers. In F. Schultz (Ed.), Annual editions: Education, 1985/1986. Guilford, CT: Duskin.

Redfield, D.L., & Rousseau, E.W. (1981). A meta-analysis of experimental research on teacher questioning behavior. Review of Educational Research, 51.

Reed, S.K. (1982). Cognition: Theory and applications. Monterey, CA: Brooks/Cole.

Reeve, E. & Ballard, D. (1993). A Faculty Guide to Writing Grant Proposals. AACC Journal, 30.

Reid, D.K., & Hresko, W.P. (1981). A cognitive approach to learning disabilities. New York, NY: McGraw-Hill.

Reimer, R.H., Paolitto, D.P., & Hersh, R.H. (1983). Promoting moral growth: From Piaget to Kohlberg (2nd ed.). New York, NY: Longman.

Reis, S.M. (1981). An analysis of the productivity of gifted students participating in programs using the revolving door identification model. Storrs, CT: University of Connecticut, Bureau of Educational Research.

Renzulli, J.S., & Smith, L.H. (1978). The learning styles inventory: A measure of student preferences for instructional techniques. Mansfield Center, CT: Creative Learning Press.

Resnick, L.B. (1981). Instructional psychology. Annual Review of Psychology, 32.

Reynolds, A. (1992). Charting the changes in junior faculty. Journal of Higher Education 63 (6).

Rhoads, R., & Valadez, J. (1996). Democracy, multiculturalism and the community college. New York ,NY: Garland Publishing.

Rhode, G., Morgan, D.P., & Young, K.R. (1983). Generalization and maintenance of treatment gains of behaviorally handicapped students from resource rooms to regular classrooms using self-evaluation procedures. Journal of Applied Behavior Analysis, 16.

Rice, M.I. (1984). Cognitive aspects of communicative development. In R.Schiefelbusch & J. Pickar (Eds.), The Acquisition of communicative competence. Baltimore, MD: University Park Press.

Richardson, V. (Ed.). (1999). Handbook of research on teaching. Washington, DC: American Educational Research Association.

Rickards, J., & August, G.J. (1975). Generative underlining strategies in prose recall. Journal of Educational Psychology, 67.

Rist, R. (1970). Student social class and teacher expectations: The self-fulfilling prophecy in ghetto education. Harvard Educational Review, 40.

Robbins, S. and Coulter, M. (1999). Management, 6th ed. Upper Saddle River, NJ: Prentice Hall.

Robinson, C.S., & Hayes, J.R. (1978). Making inferences about relevance in understanding problems. In R. Revlin & R. E. Mayer (Eds.), Human reasoning. Washington, DC: Winston.

Robinson, D.W. (1978). Beauty, monster, or something in between? 22 views of public schooling. The Review of Education, 4.

Robinson, F.P. (1961). Effective study. New York, NY: Harper and Row.

Roemer, R.E. (1978). The social conditions for schoolings. In A. B. Calvin (Ed.), Perspectives on education. Reading, MA: Addison-Wesley.

Roethlisberger, F.J., & Dickson, W.J. (1939). Management and the worker. Cambridge, MA, MA: Harvard University Press.

Rogers, C. (1969). Freedom to learn: A view of what education might become. Columbus, Ohio: Merrill.

Rogers, C. (1983). Freedom to learn for the 1980s. Columbus, Ohio: Charles E. Merrill.

Romano, C. (1999). On Collegiality, College Style. The Chronicle of Higher Education, May.

Romey, W. (1972). Risk-trust-love. Columbus, Ohio: Merrill.

Rosch, E.H. (1973). On the internal structure of perceptual and semantic categories. In T. Moore (Ed.), Cognitive development and the acquisition of language. New York, NY: Academic Press.

Rosch, E.H. (1975). Cognitive representations of semantic categories. Journal of Experimental Psychology, 104.

Rosch, T. and Reich, J. (1966). The enculturation of new faculty in higher education: A comparative investigation of three academic departments. Research in Higher Education 37(1).

Rosenshine, B. (1979). Content, time, and direct instruction. In P. Peterson & H. Walberg (Eds.), Research on teaching: Concepts, findings, and implications. Berkeley, CA: McCutchan.

Rosenshine, B. (1986). Synthesis of research on explicit teaching. Educational Leadership, 43(7).

Rosenshine, B. (1988). Explicit teaching. In D. Berliner & B. Rosenshine (eds.), Talks to teachers. New York, NY: Random House.

Rosenshine, B., & Furst, N. (1973). The use of direct observation to study teaching. In R. Travers (Ed.), Second handbook of research on teaching. Chicago, IL: Rand McNally.

Rosenshine, B., & Stevens, R. (1986). Teaching functions. In M. Wittrock (Ed.), Handbook of research on teaching (3rd ed.). New York, NY: Macmillan.

Rosenthal, R. (1973). The Pygmalion effect lives. Psychology Today.

Rosenthal, R. (1976). Experimenter effects in behavioral research (enlarged ed.). New York, NY: Halsted Press.

Rosovsky, H. (1990). The University, An Owner's Manual. New York, NY: WW Norton and Company.

Ross, S.M. (1984). Matching the lesson to the student: Alternative adaptive designs for individualized learning systems. Journal of Computer-Based Instruction, 11.

Ross, S.M., McCormick, D., Krisak, N., & Anand, P. (1985). Personalizing context in teaching mathematical concepts: Teacher-managed and computer-managed models. Educational Communication Technology Journal, 33.

Rothman, R. (1988, April 1). "Computer competence" still rare among students, assessment finds. Education Week.

Rothrock, D. (1982). The rise and decline of individualized instruction. Educational Leadership, 39.

Rotter, J. (1954). Social learning and clinical psychology. Englewood Cliffs, NJ: Prentice Hall.

Rouche, J. (1972). A modest proposal: Students can learn. San Francisco, CA: Jossey-Bass.

Rouche, J., Rouche, S., & Milliron, M. (1995). Strangers in their own land: Part-time faculty in American community colleges. Washington, DC: American Association of Community Colleges.

Rowe, M.B. (1974). Wait-time and rewards as instructional variables: Their influence on language, logic, and fate control. Part 1: Wait-time. Journal of Research in Science Teaching, 11.

Rumelhart, D. (1977). Understanding and summarizing brief stories. In D. LaBerge & S. J. Samuels (Eds.), Basic processes in reading. Hillsdale, NJ: Erlbaum.

Rumelhart, D., & Ortony, A. (1977). The representation of knowledge in memory. In R. Anderson, R. Spiro, & W. Montague (Eds.), Schooling and the acquisition of knowledge. Hillsdale, NJ: Erlbaum.

Runkel, P., Harrison, R., & Runkel, M. (Eds.). (1969). The changing college classroom. San Francisco, CA: Jossey-Bass.

Russo, R. (1998). Straight man. New York, NY: Vintage Books.

Rust, L.W. (1977). Interests. In S. Ball (Ed.), Motivation in education. New York, NY: Academic Press.

Ryan M. and. Martens, G. (1989). Planning a college course: A guidebook for the graduate teaching assistant. Ann Arbor, MI: National Center for Research to Improve Postsecondary Teaching and Learning.

Ryan, J. B. (1974). Keller's personalized system of instruction: An appraisal. Washington, DC: American Psychological Association.

Ryans, D.G. (1960). Characteristics of effective teachers, their descriptions, comparisons and appraisal: A research study. Washington, DC: American Council on Education.

Sacks, P. (1996). Generation X goes to college : An eye-opening account of teaching in postmodern America. Chicago, IL: Open Court.

Sadker, M., & Sadker, D. (1985). Sexism in the schoolroom of the '80s. Psychology Today.

Sadker, M., & Sadker, D. (1986). Questioning skills. In J. Cooper (Ed.), Classroom teaching skills (3rd ed.). Lexington, MA: D. C. Heath.

Salili, F., Maehr, M.L., Sorensen, R.L., & Fyans, L.J. (1976). A further consideration of the effect of evaluation on motivation. American Educational Research Journal, 13(2).

Sandefur, J.T. (1985). Competency assessment of teachers. Action in Teacher Education, 7.

Sandman L., et al., (2000). Critical Tensions, How to Strengthen the Scholarship Component of Outreach. Change 32.

Sanford, N. (1967). Where colleges fail. San Francisco, CA: Jossey-Bass.

Sarnacki, R.E. (1979). An examination of test-wiseness in the cognitive test domain. Review of Research in Education, 49.

Savage, T.V. (1983). The academic qualifications of women choosing education as a major. Journal of Teacher Education, 34.

Saving, K. & Keim, M. (1998). Student and advisor perceptions of academic advising in two midwestern colleges of business. College Student Journal 32.

Scarr, S., & Carter-Saltzman, L. (1982). Genetics and intelligence. In R. Sternberg (Ed.), Handbook of human intelligence. New York, NY: Cambridge, MA University Press.

Scarr, S., Weinberg, R.A., & Levine, A. (1986). Understanding development. New York, NY: Harcourt Brace Jovanovich.

Schein, E. (1988). Organizational culture and leadership. San Francisco, CA: Jossey-Bass.

Schiedel, D., & Marcia, J. (1985). Ego integrity, intimacy, sex role orientation, and gender. Developmental Psychology, 21.

Schmier, L. (1995). Random thoughts: The humanity of teaching. Madison, WI: Magna Publications.

Schmier, L. (1996). Random thoughts II: Teaching from the heart. Madison, WI: Magna Publications.

Schoenfeld A. & Robert Magnan, (1994). Mentor in a manual, climbing the academic ladder to tenure, 2nd ed. Madison, WI.: Magna Publications, Inc.

Schoenfeld, A., & Magnan, R. (1997). Mentor in a manual. Madison, WI: Atwood.

Schoenfeld, A.H. (1979). Explicit heuristic training as a variable in problem solving performance. Journal for Research in Mathematics Education, 10.

Schon, D. (1983). The reflective practitioner. New York, NY: Basic Books

Schon, D. (1987). Educating a reflective practitioner: Toward a new design for teaching and learning in the professions. San Francisco, CA: Jossey-Bass.

Schug, M. (1985). Teacher burnout and professionalism. In F. Schultz (Ed.), Annual Editions: Education, 85. Guilford, CT: Duskin.

Schuster, J. (1993). Preparing the next generation of faculty: The graduate school's opportunity, in preparing faculty for the new conception of scholarship. New Directions for Teaching and Learning 54.

Sears, J., & Marshall, J. (Eds.). (1989). Teaching and thinking about curriculum: Critical inquiries. NY: Teachers College Press.

Seiber, J.E., O'Neil, H.F., & Tobias, S. (1977). Anxiety, learning, and instruction. Hillsdale, NJ: Erlbaum.

Seidman, E. (1985). In the words of the faculty: Perspectives on improving teaching and educational quality in community colleges. San Francisco, CA: Jossey-Bass.

Selby J. & Calhoun, L. (1998). Mentoring Programs for New Faculty: Unintended Consequences? Teaching of Psychology 25.

Seldin, P. (1995). Improving college teaching. Jaffrey, NH: Anker.

Seldin, P. (1997). The teaching portfolio: A practice guide to improved performance, and promotion/tenure decisions (2nd ed.). Bolton, MA: Anker.

Seldin, P. (2004). The teaching portfolio: A practical guide to improved performance and promotion/tenure decisions (3rd ed.). Bolton, MA: Anker.

Self, J.A. (1974). Student models in computer-aided instruction. International Journal of Man-Machine Studies, 6.

Seligman, C., Tucker, G., & Lambert, W. (1972). The effects of speech style and other attributes on teachers' attitudes toward pupils. Language in Society, 1.

Serralde de Scholz, H.C., & McDougall, R. (1978). Comparison of potential reinforcer ratings between slow learners and regular students. Behavior Therapy, 9.

Shane, H.G. (1982). The silicon age and education. Phi Delta Kappan, 63.

Shavelson, R.J., & Bolus, R. (1982). Self-concept: The interplay of theory and methods. Psychology, 74.

Shavelson, R.J., Hubner, J.J., & Stanton, G.C. (1976). Self-concept: Validation of construct interpretations. Review of Educational Research, 46.

Shavelson, R.S., & Dempsey, N. (1975). Generalizability of measures of teacher effectiveness and teaching process (Beginning Teacher Evaluation Study, Tech. Rep. No. 3). San Francisco, CA: Far West Laboratory for Educational Research and Development.

Shea, M. & others. (1990). On teaching. Boulder, CO: University of Colorado.

Sheffield, E. (Ed.). (1974). Teaching in the universities: No one way. Montreal: Queen's University Press.

Sherman, J.G., Ruskin, R.S., & Semb, G.B. (Eds.) (1982). The Personalized System of Instruction: 48 seminal papers. Lawrence, KS: TRI Publications.

Shields, P., Gordon, J., & Dupree, D. (1983). Influence of parent practices upon the reading achievement of good and poor readers. Journal of Negro Education, 52.

Shostak, R. (1986). Lesson presentation skills. In J. Cooper (Ed.), Classroom teaching skills (3rd ed.). Lexington, MA: D. C. Heath.

Shuell, T.J. (1986). Cognitive conceptions of learning. Review of Educational Research, 56.

Shuell, T.J. (1981). Dimensions of individual differences. In F. H. Farley & N. J. Gordon (Eds.), Psychology and education: The state of the union. Berkeley, CA: McCutchan.

Shulman, L.S. (1987). Knowledge and teaching: Foundations of the new reform. Harvard Educational Review, 19(2).

Siegal, M.A., & Davis, D.M. (1986). Understanding computer-based education. New York, NY: Random House.

Silberman, M. (1996). Active learning, 101 strategies to teach any subject. Needham Heights, MA: Allyn and Bacon.

Silverstein, B. (1982). Teaching a large lecture course in psychology: Turning defeat into victory. Teaching of Psychology, 9.

Simon, D.P., & Chase, W.G. (1973). Skill in chess. American Scientist, 61.

Simon, W. (1969). Expectancy effect in the scoring of vocabulary items: A study of scorer bias. Journal of Educational Measurement, 6.

Simpson, R. & Jackson, W. (1990). A Multidimensional Approach to Faculty Vitality, in Enhancing Faculty Careers, Strategies for Development and Renewal, ed. Schuster, J., et al. San Francisco, CA: Jossey-Bass.

Skinner, B.F. (1954). The science of learning and the art of teaching. Harvard Educational Review, 24.

Skinner, B.F. (1953). Science and human behavior. New York, NY: Macmillan.

Skinner, B.F. (1968). The technology of teaching. Englewood Cliffs, NJ: Prentice-Hall.

Skinner, B.F. (1984). The shame of American education. American Psychologist, 39.

Slavin, R. (1978). Student teams and achievement divisions. Journal of Research and Development in Education.

Slavin, R. (1980). Effects of individual learning expectations on student achievement. Journal of Educational Psychology, 72.

Slavin, R. (1980). Using student team learning (rev. ed.). Baltimore, MD: The Johns Hopkins University, Center for Social Organization of Schools.

Slavin, R. (1983). Cooperative learning. New York, NY: Longman.

Slavin, R. (1986). Educational psychology: Theory into practice. Englewood Cliffs, NJ: Prentice Hall.

Slavin, R., & Karweit, N. (1984). Mathematics achievement effects of three levels of individualization: Whole class, ability grouped, and individualized (Report No. 349). Baltimore, MD: The Johns Hopkins University, Center for Social Organization in Schools.

Sleeter, C.E., & Grant, C.A. (1987). An analysis of multicultural education in the United States. Harvard Educational Review, 57.

Smelser, N. (1993). Effective Committee Service. Newbury Park, CA: Sage Publications.

Smith, F. (1975). Comprehension and learning: A conceptual framework for teachers. New York, NY: Holt, Rinehart & Winston.

Smith, P. (1990). Killing the Spirit, Higher Education in America. New York, NY: Viking.

Smith, R. A. (1995). Challenging your perceptions: Thinking critically about psychology. Pacific Grove, CA: Brooks/Cole.

Smith, S.M., Glenberg, A., & Bjork, R.A. (1978). Environmental context and human memory. Memory and Cognition, 6.

Snow, R.E. (1969). Unfinished pygmalion. Contemporary Psychology, 14.

Snow, R.E. (1977). Research on aptitude for learning: A progress report. In L. Shulman (Ed.), Review of research in education. Itasca, IL: F. E. Peacock.

Snowman, J. (1984). Learning tactics and strategies. In G. Phye & T. Andre (Eds.), Cognitive instructional psychology. Orlando, FL: Academic Press.

Snyderman, M., & Rothman, S. (1987). Survey of expert opinion of intelligence and aptitude testing. American Psychologist, 42.

Soar, R.S., & Soar, R.M. (1979). Emotional climate and management. In P. Peterson & H. Walberg (Eds.), Research on teaching: Concepts, findings, and implications. Berkeley, CA: McCutchan.

Solomon, G. (1986). Electronic research. Electronic Learning.

Solomon, R. & Solomon, J. (1993). Up the university, re-creating higher education in America. Needham Heights, MA: Addison-Wesley.

Soloway, E., Lockhead, J., & Clement, J. (1982). Does computer programming enhance problem solving ability? Some positive evidence on algebra word problems. In R. J. Seidel, R. E. Anderson, & S. B. Hunter (Eds.), Computer literacy. New York, NY: Academic Press.

Sorinelli, M., & Elbow, P. (Eds.). (1997). Writing to learn: Strategies for assigning and responding to writing across the disciplines. San Francisco, CA: Jossey-Bass.

Spearman, C. (1927). The abilities of man: Their nature and measurement. New York, NY: Macmillan.

Sprague, J. (1993). Retrieving the Research Agenda for Communication Education, Asking the Pedagogical Questions That Are Embarrassments to Theory. Communication Education 42.

Stallings, J. (1980). Allocated academic learning time revisited, or beyond time on task. Educational Researcher, 9.

Starch, D., & Elliot, E.C. (1913). Reliability of grading work in history. Scholastic Review, 21.

Starch, D., & Elliot, E.C. (1913). Reliability of grading work in mathematics. Scholastic Review, 21.

Stark, J., & Lattuca, L. (1997). Shaping the college curriculum: Academic plans in action. Needham Heights, MA: Allyn and Bacon.

Stark, J., Lowther, M., Bentley, R., Ryan, M.., Martens, G., Genthon, M., Wren, P., & Shaw, K. (1990). Planning introductory college courses: Influences on faculty. Ann Arbor, MI: National Center for Research to Improve Teaching and Learning.

Steams, S. (1994). Steps for active learning of complex concepts. College Teaching 42.

Stein, B.S., Littlefield, J., Bransford, J.D., & Persampieri, M. (1984). Elaboration and knowledge acquisition. Memory and Cognition, 12.

Sternberg, R. (1985). Beyond IQ: A triarchic theory of human intelligence. New York, NY: Cambridge, MA University Press.

Sternberg, R. (1986). Intelligence applied: Understanding and increasing your own intellectual skills. New York, NY: Harcourt Brace Jovanovich.

Sternberg, R., & Davidson, J. (1982). The mind of the puzzler. Psychology Today.

Stewart, J.R. (1980). Teachers who stimulate curiosity. Education, 101.

Stipek, D.J. (1988). Motivation to learn. Englewood Cliffs, NJ: Prentice Hall.

Stocking, S., & Bender, E. (1998). More quick hits: Successful strategies by award-winning teachers. Indiana: Indiana University Press.

Sublett, M. (1999). Turning Listeners Into Active Learners. College Teaching 47.

Sulzer-Azaroff, B., & Mayer, G.R. (1986). Achieving educational excellence using behavioral strategies. New York, NY: Holt, Rinehart & Winston.

Suppes, P. (1966). The uses of computers in education. Scientific American, 215(3).

Suppes, P. (1984). Observations about the application of artificial intelligence research to education. In D. F. Walker & R. D. Hess (Eds.), Instructional software: Principles and perspectives for design and use. Belmont, CA: Wadsworth.

Suppes, P., & Macken, E. (1978). The historical path from research and development to operational use of CAI. Educational Technology, 18.

Suppes, P., & Morningstar, M. (1972). Computer-assisted instruction at Stanford, 1966-1968: Data, models, and evaluation of the arithmetic programs. New York, NY: Academic Press.

Suppes, P., Jerman, M., & Brian, D. (1968). Computer-assisted instruction: The 1965-66 Stanford arithmetic program. New York, NY: Academic Press.

Sutherland, T., & Bonwell, C. (Eds.). (1996). Using active learning in college classes: A range of options for faculty. New Directions for Teaching and Learning, 67. San Francisco, CA: Jossey-Bass.

Svinicki, M. (Ed.). (1990). The changing face of college teaching. New Directions for Teaching and Learning, No. 42. San Francisco, CA: Jossey-Bass.

Swift, J., & Gooding, C. (1983). Interaction of wait-time, feedback, and questioning instruction in middle school science teaching. Journal of Research in Science Teaching, 20.

Taylor, J.B. (1983). Influence of speech variety on teachers' evaluations of reading comprehension. Journal of Educational Psychology, 75.

Taylor, R.P. (Ed.). (1980). The computer in the school: Tutor, tool, tutee. New York, NY: Teachers College Press.

Tenbrink, T.D. (1986). Writing instructional objectives. In J. Cooper (Ed.), Classroom teaching skills (3rd ed.). Lexington, MA: D.C. Heath.

Tennyson, R.D., & Cocchiarella, M.J. (1986). An empirically based instructional design theory for teaching concepts. Review of Educational Research, 56.

Tennyson, R.D., & Rothen, W. (1977). Pre-task and on-task adaptive design strategies for selecting number of instances in concept acquisition. Journal of Educational Psychology, 69.

Terman, L.M., & Oden, M.H. (1959). The gifted group in mid-life. In L. M. Terman (Ed.), Genetic studies of genius (Vol. 5). Stanford, CA: Stanford University Press.

Terwilliger, J.S. (1971). Assigning grades to students. Glenview, IL: Scott, Foresman.

The teaching professor. Madison, WI: Magna Publications. Monthly.

Theall, M., & Franklin, J. (Eds.). Effective practices for improving teaching. San Francisco, CA: Jossey-Bass.

Thomas, E.L., & Robinson, H.A. (1972). Improving reading in every class: A sourcebook for teachers. Boston, MA: Allyn & Bacon.

Thompson, T.J. (1979). An overview of microprocessor central processing units (CPUs). Educational Technology, 10.

Thorndike, E.L. (1913). Educational psychology. In The psychology of learning (Vol. 2). New York, NY: Teachers College, Columbia University.

Thorndike, R., Hagen, E., & Sattler, J. (1986). The Stanford-Binet Intelligence Scale (4th ed.). Chicago, IL: Riverside.

Thurstone, L.L. (1938). Primary mental abilities. Psychometric Monographs, No. 1.

Tiedt, P.L., & Tiedt, I.M. (1979). Multicultural education: A handbook of activities, information, and resources. Boston, MA: Allyn & Bacon.

Tierney W. and Bensimon, E. (1996). Promotion and tenure: community and socialization in academe. Albany, NY: State University of New York Press.

Tierney, W. (1997). Organizational socialization in higher education. Journal of Higher Education, 68.

Tierney, W. (1988). Organizational Culture in Higher Education: Defining the Essentials. Journal of Higher Education 59(1).

Timmer, S.G., Eccles, J., & O'Brien, K. (1988). How children use time. In F. Juster & F. Stafford (Eds.), Time, goods, and well-being. Ann Arbor, MI: Institute for Social Research, University of Michigan.

Timpson, W., & Bendel-Simso, P. (1996). Concepts and choices for teaching. Madison, WI: Atwood.

Timpson, W., Burgoyne, S., Jones, C., & Jones, W. (1997). Teaching and performing: Ideas for energizing your classes. Madison, WI: Atwood.

Tobias, S. (1979). Anxiety research in educational psychology. Journal of Educational Psychology, 71.

Tobias, S. (1981). Adaptation to individual differences. In F. Farley & N. Gordon (Eds.). Psychology and education: The state of the union. Berkeley, CA: McCutchan.

Tobias, S. (1982). When do instructional methods make a difference? Educational Researcher, 11(4).

Tobias, S. (1982, January). Sexist equations. Psychology Today.

Tobias, S., & Duchastel, P. (1974). Behavioral objectives, sequence, and anxiety in CAI. Instructional Science, 3.

Tobin, K. (1987). The role of wait time in higher cognitive learning. Review of Educational Research, 56.

Toma, D. (1997): Alternative inquiry paradigms, faculty cultures, and the definition of academic lives. Journal of Higher Education, 68.

Tompkins, J. (1996). A life in school. Reading, MA: Addison-Wesley.

Torrance, E.P. (1972). Predictive validity of the Torrance tests of creative thinking. Journal of Creative Behavior, 6.

Torrance, E.P. (1986). Teaching creative and gifted learners. In M. Wittrock (Ed.), Handbook of Research on Teaching (3rd ed.). New York, NY: Macmillan.

Torrance, E.P., & Hall, L.K. (1980). Assessing the future reaches of creative potential. Journal of Creative Behavior.

Travers, R. M. W. (1977). Essentials of learning (4th ed.). New York, NY: Macmillan.

Travers, R.M.W. (1982). Essentials of learning: The new cognitive learning for students of education (5th ed.). New York, NY: Macmillan.

Travis, J. (1996). Models for improving college teaching: A faculty resource. Washington, DC: George Washington University. (Ashe-Eric Higher Education Report Series)

Trillin, A. (1980). Teaching basic skills in college. San Francisco, CA: Jossey-Bass.

Tufte, Edward. The Cognitive Style of PowerPoint. Cheshire, CN: Graphics Press, 2003.

Tyler, L.E. (1974). Individual differences: Abilities and motivational directions. New York, NY: Appleton-Century-Crofts.

Van Houten, R., & Doleys, D.M. (1983). Are social reprimands effective? In S. Axelrod & J. Apsche (Eds.), The effects of punishment on human behavior. San Diego: Academic Press.

Van Mondrans, A.P., Black, H.G., Keysor, R.E., Olsen, J.B., Shelley, M.F., & Williams, D.D. (1977). Methods of inquiry in educational psychology. In D. Treffinger, J. Davis, & R. R. Ripple (Eds.), Handbook on teaching educational psychology. New York, NY: Academic Press.

Veenman, S. (1984). Perceived problems of beginning teachers. Review of Educational Research, 54.

Vella, J., Berardinelli, P., & Burrow, J. (1998). How do they know they know? Evaluating adult learning. San Francisco, CA: Jossey-Bass.

Vernon, P.E. (1979). Intelligence: Heredity and environment. San Francisco, CA: W. H. Freeman.

Vidler, D.C. (1977). Curiosity. In S. Ball (Ed.), Motivation in education. New York, NY: Academic Press.

Walberg, H.J., Pascal, R.A., & Weinstein, T. ((1985). Homework's powerful effects on learning. Educational Leadership, 42.

Walker, D.F., & Hess, R.D. (1984). Instructional software: Principles and perspectives for design and use. Belmont, CA: Wadsworth.

Walker, E. I., & McKeachie, W. J. (1967). Some thoughts about teaching the beginning course in psychology. Belmont, CA: Brooks/Cole.

Walvoord, B. E., & Anderson, V. J. (1998). Effective grading: A tool for learning and assessment. San Francisco, CA: Jossey-Bass.

Ward, B., & Tikunoff, W. (1976). The effective teacher education problem: Application of selected research results and methodology to teaching. Journal of Teacher Education, 27.

Waxman, H.C., & Walberg, H.J. (1982). The relation of teaching and learning: A review of reviews of process-product research. Contemporary Educational Review, 1.

Weaver, W.T. (1979). The need for new talent in teaching. Phi Delta Kappan, 61.

Webb, N. (1980). A process-outcome analysis of learners in group and individual settings. Educational Psychology, 15.

Webb, N. (1982). Student interaction and learning in small groups. Review of Educational Research, 52.

Webb, N. (1985). Verbal interaction and learning in peer-directed groups. Theory into Practice, 24.

Webster, D. (1985). Does Research Productivity Enhance Teaching? Educational Record, 66.

Wechsler, D. (1958). The measurement and appraisal of adult intelligence (4th ed.). Baltimore, MD: Williams & Wilkins.

Weimer M., & Neff R. A. (Eds.) (1990). Teaching college: Collected reading for the new instructor. Madison, WI: Magna Publishing.

Weimer M., Parrett, J., & Kerns, M. (1988). How am I teaching: Forms and activities for acquiring instructional input. Madison, WI: Magna Publishing.

Weimer, M. (1990). It's a myth: nobody knows what makes teaching good, in teaching college, collected readings for the new instructor, ed. Weimer and Neff, Madison, WI.: Magna Publications.

Weimer, M. (1990). Improving college teaching: Strategies for developing instructional effectiveness. San Francisco, CA: Jossey-Bass.

Weimer, M. (1990). Study your way to better teaching. New Directions for Teaching and Learning, 42.

Weimer, M. (1993). Improving your classroom teaching. Newbury Park, CA: Sage.

Weimer, M. (Ed.). (1987). Teaching large classes well. San Francisco, CA: Jossey-Bass.

Weimer, M., & Neff, R. (Eds.). (1990). Teaching college: Collected readings for the new instructor. Madison, WI: Magna Publications.

Weimer, M., Parrett, J., & Kearns, M. (1988). How am I teaching? Forms and activities for acquiring instructional input. Madison, WI: Magna.

Weiner, B. (1979). A theory of motivation for some classroom experiences. Journal of Educational Psychology, 71.

Weiner, B. (1980). The role of affect in rational (attributional) approaches to human motivation. Educational Researcher, 9.

Weiner, B. (1984). Principles for a theory of student motivation and their application within an attributional framework. In R. Ames & C. Ames (Eds.), Research on motivation in education (Vol. 1). Orlando, FL: Academic Press.

Weiner, B., Russell, D., & Lerman, D. (1978). Affective consequences of causal ascriptions. In J. H. Harvey, W. J. Ickes, & R. F. Kidd (Eds.). New directions in attribution research (Vol. 2). Hillsdale, NJ: Erlbaum.

Weinstein, C., & Hume, L. (1998). Study strategies for lifelong learning. Washington, DC: American Psychological Association.

Weinstein, C.E., & Mayer, R.E. (1985). The teaching of learning strategies. In M. C. Wittrock (Ed.), Handbook of research on teaching (3rd ed.). New York, NY: Macmillan.

Weinstein, C.S. (1977). Modifying student behavior in an open classroom through changes in the physical design. American Educational Research Journal, 14.

Weinstein, M., & Goodman, J. (1988). Play fair. San Luis Obispo, CA: Impact Publications.

Weinstein, M., McCombs, B. (1999). Strategic learning: The merging of skill, will and self-regulation in academic environments. Hillsdale, NJ: Lawrence Erlbaum.

Wessells, M.G. (1982). Cognitive psychology. New York, NY: Harper and Row.

West, C.K., Fish, J.A., & Stevens, R.J. (1980). General self-concept, self-concept of academic ability and school achievement: Implication for causes of self-concept. Australian Journal of Education, 24.

Wheeler, D. (1992). The Role of the Chairperson in Support of Junior Faculty, in Mary Deane Sorcinelli and Ann E. Austin, eds., Developing New and Junior Faculty. New Directions for Teaching and Learning 50.

White, E. (1994). Teaching and assessing writing. San Francisco, CA: Jossey-Bass.

White, K.R. (1982). The relation between socioeconomic status and academic achievement. Psychological Bulletin, 91(3).

White, R.W. (1959). Motivation reconsidered: The concept of competence. Psychological Review, 66.

Whitford, F. W. (2011). College Teaching tips,. 2nd Edition, Upper Saddle River, NJ: Pearson Publishing.

Whitford, F. W. (2008). College Teaching tips,. 1st Edition, Upper Saddle River, NJ: Prentice-Hall.

Whitford, F. W. (2006). Teaching psychology: A guide for the new instructor,. 4th Edition, Upper Saddle River, NJ: Prentice-Hall.

Whitford, F.W. (1992). Teaching psychology: A guide for the new instructor, 1st Edition, Englewood Cliffs, NJ: Prentice Hall.

Whitford, F.W. (1996). Teaching psychology: A guide for the new instructor, 2nd Edition, Englewood Cliffs, NJ: Prentice Hall.

Whitford, F.W. (1998). Quick guide to the internet for psychology 1998, Boston, MA: Allyn and Bacon.

Whitford, F.W. (2001). Teaching psychology: A guide for the new instructor, 3rd Edition, Upper Saddle River, NJ: Prentice-Hall.

Whitford, F.W. and Gotthoffer, D. (1999). Quick guide to the internet for psychology 1999, Boston, MA: Allyn and Bacon.

Whitford, F.W. and Gotthoffer, D. (2000). Quick guide to the internet for psychology 2000, Boston, MA: Allyn and Bacon.

Whitford, F.W. and Gotthoffer, D. (2001). Psychology on the net 2001, Boston, MA: Allyn and Bacon.

Whitman, N. (1986). Increasing students' learning: A faculty guide to reducing stress among students. Washington, DC: Association for the Study of Higher Education.

Why Teachers Fail. (1984). Newsweek.

Wilkerson, L., & Gijselaers, W. (Eds.). (1996). Bring problem-based learning to higher education: Theory and practice. San Francisco, CA: Jossey-Bass.

Wilkins, W.E., & Glock, lM.D. (1973). Teacher expectations and student achievement: A replication and extension. Ithaca, NY: Cornell University Press.

Willerman, L. (1979). The psychology of individual and group differences. San Francisco, CA: W. H. Freeman.

Wilson, R., et al. (1975). College professors and their impact on students. New York, NY: Wiley.

Wilson, S.M., Shulman, L.S., & Richert, A.R. (1987). 150 different ways of knowing: Representations of knowledge in teaching. In J. Calderhead (Ed.), Exploring teacher thinking. London, UK: Cassell.

Winett, R.A., & Winkler, R.C. (1972). Current behavior modification in the classroom: Be still, be quiet, be docile. Journal of Applied Behavior Analysis, 15.

Winograd, P., & Johnston, P. (1982). Comprehension monitoring and the error-detection paradigm. Journal of Reading Behavior.

Winter, D., McClelland, D., & Stewart, A. (1982). A new case for the liberal arts. San Francisco, CA: Jossey-Bass.

Witherall, C., & Noddings, N. (Eds.). (1991). Stories lives tell: Narrative and dialogue in education. NY: Teachers College Press.

Witkin, H.A., Moore, C.A., Goodenough, D.R., & Cos, R.W. (1977). Field-dependent and field-independent cognitive styles and their educational implications. Review of Educational Research, 47.

Wittrock, M. (Ed.) (1986). The handbook of research on teaching. New York, NY: Macmillan.

Wittrock, M.C. (1978). The cognitive movement in instruction. Educational Psychologist, 13.

Wlodkowski, R., & Ginsberg, M. (1995). Diversity and motivation: Culturally responsive teaching. San Francisco, CA: Jossey-Bass.

Wlodkowski, R.J. (1981). Making sense out of motivation: A systematic model to consolidate motivational constructs across theories. Educational Psychologist, 16.

Woolfolk, A.E., & Brooks, D. (1983). Nonverbal communication in teaching. In E. Gordon (Ed.), Review of research in education (Vol. 10). Washington, DC: American Educational Research Association.

Woolfolk, A.E., & Woolfolk, R.L. (1974). A contingency management technique for increasing student attention in a small group. Journal of School Psychology, 12.

Wright, W. (1995). Teaching improvement practices. Bolton, MA: Anker Publishing.

Yerkes, R.M., & Dodson, J.D. (1908). The relation of strength of stimulus to rapidity of habit formation. Journal of Comparative Neurology, 18.

Young, T. (1980). Teacher stress: One school district's approach. Action in Teacher Education, 2.

Zan Manen, M. (1991). The tact of teaching: The meaning of pedagogical thoughtfulness. Albany, NY: SUNY Press.

Zimmerman, D.W. (1981). On the perennial argument about grading "on the curve" in college courses. Educational Psychologist, 16.